JAPAN:
THE STORY
OF A NATION

FORMERLY ENTITLED

Japan Past and Present

JAPAN:
THE STORY
OF A NATION

EDWIN O. REISCHAUER

Alfred A. Knopf, Publisher

NEW YORK

THIS IS A BORZOI BOOK
PUBLISHED BY ALFRED A. KNOPF, INC.

Copyright © 1970 by Edwin O. Reischauer

Published in the United States by Alfred A. Knopf, Inc., New York,
and simultaneously in Canada
by Random House of Canada Limited, Toronto.
Distributed by Random House, Inc., New York.

Library of Congress Catalog Card Number: 77–10895

Manufactured in the United States of America

Based on Japan Past and Present. Copyright 1946, 1952
© 1964 by Alfred A. Knopf, Inc. Originally published 1946,
reprinted three times; Second Edition, revised and enlarged,
published January 1953, reprinted seven times; Third Edition,
revised, published February 1964, reprinted four times.

First Edition

To My Brother Bob

the first American casualty in World War II

Shanghai, August 14, 1937

PREFACE

This book is a successor volume to my *Japan: Past and Present*, which was first published in 1946 and was expanded and brought up to date in two revised editions, in 1953 and again in 1964. In these later rewritings, I added new sections on postwar Japan, but made only minimal changes in the story up to Japan's surrender in 1945. The time, however, has now come for a more thorough revision. My account of prewar Japan was jotted down hastily during the first two months after the end of the war. Since then popular perceptions of Japan and the Japanese have changed greatly, requiring modifications in wording, detail, and emphasis. I too in the meantime have learned a great deal about Japan's prewar history and have developed new insights and interpretations. The lengthening perspective on postwar Japan also calls for even more substantial changes in the last few chapters.

The net result is a book so thoroughly changed from beginning to end as to deserve a new title. Some sections of the first third of the original book, covering the period up to the early nineteenth century, have been carried on into this edition with only minor changes, but the greater part of the next third, covering the period from Japan's transformation in the middle of the nineteenth century until World War II, has been entirely rewritten, and virtually all of the last third of the book, covering the two and a half decades since the end of the war, is new.

I hope, however, that despite these extensive changes, the spirit and style of the original book have been preserved. It was my intention in 1945 to write a comprehensive, informative, and sound account of Japan's historical development in as brief and simple form as possible, with a minimum of confusing names and unessential facts. In the Preface to the two revised editions I gave the following explanation of how I came to write in this particular way:

During the war and early postwar period I spent four years in Washington, at which time I forgot much of the detailed information about Japanese history I had once known, but to my surprise I discovered that the fading of unessential detail had helped to clarify for me the main outlines of Japanese history as a whole. On two or three occasions while in Washington, I was requested to give four or five hours of lectures covering the whole historical development of Japan. These requests seemed unreasonable to one accustomed to the more leisurely pace of university lectures, but again to my surprise I found that a meaningful account of this vastly complex story could be made in a few hours' time, if confined to essentials and presented in general and broadly interpretive terms. This experience suggested the possibility of a similar presentation of Japanese history in print.

The late George Sansom, the distinguished British diplomat turned historian, kindly contributed a Foreword to the original edition of *Japan: Past and Present*, in which he generously suggested that I had succeeded in my aim. It would be unfair to him to continue using his Foreword for a book so greatly changed from the original edition he saw. But my deep respect for him and pride in his kind words persuade me that it would not be amiss to quote them in my own Preface to this volume.

FOREWORD

Few countries have been more copiously described than Japan, and perhaps few have been less thoroughly understood. In the last century there were a number of works dealing with the picturesque or the exotic aspects of that country, most of which, though sometimes a trifle deceptive, were passable books of travel. During the same period there were written a few important studies of Japanese political and social history which are still standard works, though they are used only by a few specialists. But it is a remarkable fact, which I think will be accepted by any teacher who has been responsible for instruction in schools or colleges, that before the outbreak of the war in the Far East there was no single short book which gave a lucid and tolerably complete picture of Japan's early history and her development in modern times. There were plenty of learned treatises on this or that, but nothing to give the average educated reader what he needed.

After the outbreak of war, there appeared in profusion a flood, or at least a considerable stream, of books about Japan, chiefly of topical interest. Some of these were interesting and useful. Others, however, were of a different type. Understandably, but regrettably, they belonged to that class of historical work, all too common in the last few decades, of which the purpose is not to discover or expound truth but to promote one of those perversions of systematic thought which are known by the suitably ill-sounding name of "ideologies." Now that the war is over, the average reader has a right to expect something more rational, more readable and more reliable.

I think that Dr. Reischauer's book fulfils these requirements. He has excellent qualifications for his task—familiarity with the country he describes, a first-class linguistic equipment, a good training as an historian, and most important of all an approach to his subject which is neither prejudiced nor sentimental. He narrates the leading facts of Japanese history from early times, with just and interesting comment. He explains easily and competently the evolution of modern Japan to the conditions described in his concluding chapters. I can truthfully say that I do not know of any short book on Japanese history which gives so much useful information in so brief and simple a form.

G. B. Sansom

In the three editions of *Japan: Past and Present*, my brief prefatory remarks were largely devoted to acknowledging my debt to those who had helped me in the task. Since this book has been so largely rewritten, it would no longer be fair to mention them in this Preface, implying that they had read and approved the present text. I do wish, however, to express my thanks to two colleagues at Harvard, Professors Donald H. Shively and Albert M. Craig, who have been good enough to read through the manuscript and give me many valuable suggestions and corrections.

I should also like to take this opportunity to express once again my gratitude to the two men whom I regard as my chief mentors in the field of Japanese history. One, of course, is Sir George Sansom, whose beautifully written and deeply perceptive books on Japan's premodern history have been an inspiration to everyone interested in the subject. The other is Serge Elisséeff, the distinguished French scholar of Russian birth. I owe Professor Elisséeff a great personal debt as the man who, with great wisdom and kindness, initiated me into the field of Japanese history and for many years guided my scholarly development. I join with all others in the field also in being in his debt for his unparalleled contributions to the development of Japanese studies in the United States, through his inspiring teaching at Harvard University between 1932 and 1957 and his strong leadership in the field of East Asian Studies as the Director of the Harvard-Yenching Institute from 1934 to 1956. No one deserves as much credit as does Professor Elisséeff for the present healthy state of the study of Japan in this country.

EDWIN O. REISCHAUER

Belmont, Massachusetts

Contents

List of Maps

JAPAN:
THE STORY
OF A NATION

1 ❀ LAND AND PEOPLE

In the islands of Japan nature fashioned a favored spot where civilization could prosper and a people could develop into a strong and great nation. A happy combination of temperate climate, plentiful rainfall, fairly fertile soil, and reasonable proximity to other great homes of civilized man predestined the ultimate rise of the inhabitants of these islands to a place among the leading peoples of the world.

The four main islands of Japan, strung out in a great arc along the coast of East Asia, cover the same spread of latitude and the same general range of climate as the east coast of the United States. The northern island of Hokkaido parallels New England; the heart of the country from Tokyo west to the Inland Sea corresponds to North Carolina; and the southern island of Kyushu parallels Georgia. The seasons, temperature, and rainfall are comparable to those of the American east coast, except that Japan, located some hundreds of miles out in the ocean, experiences somewhat less extreme temperatures in both winter and summer and receives considerably more precipitation.

Americans have often tended to overemphasize the smallness of Japan, contrasting it with the vast stretches of our own country or other geographic giants like China. A more reasonable comparison would be with the countries of Western Europe. Japan is smaller than France or Spain, but it is slightly larger than the British Isles or Italy, the homes of the two greatest empires the Western world has ever seen. Like Italy, Japan is a mountainous country. Throughout all four of the main islands are great stretches of towering mountains and jumbled hills. The combination of rugged coastlines, precipitous mountains, and lush vegetation makes of the whole country one of the beauty spots of the world. Perhaps this is one reason why the Japanese throughout history have shown a high degree of artistic appreciation and creativity. Such terrain, however, leaves little for the Japanese farmer, who finds less than 20 percent of the land area level enough for cultivation. The mountains of Japan have pushed the Japanese out upon the seas, making them the greatest seafaring people of Asia. Sea lanes have been the great highways within Japan; sea routes have beckoned the Japanese abroad; and the cold and warm currents which bathe the shores of the islands have always provided rich fishing grounds for Japanese fishermen.

Nature has been rather niggardly with Japan in mineral resources. The islands have coal in some abundance, but few other subsoil riches in significant quantities. Plentiful water is Japan's only great natural resource. It nourishes a dense forest cover over most mountain areas; through thousands of small irrigation channels, laboriously constructed over the past two millennia, it provides a con-

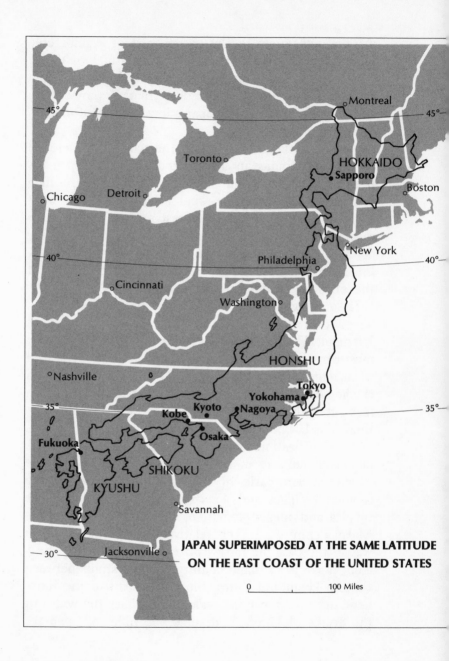

Montreal

45° 45°

Toronto○

HOKKAIDO
●Sapporo
Boston

Chicago○ Detroit○

○New York

40° Philadelphia○ 40°

○Cincinnati

Washington○

HONSHU

○Nashville

35° Tokyo● 35°
Yokohama●
Kobe● Kyoto● ●Nagoya
●Osaka

Fukuoka●

SHIKOKU

KYUSHU

○Savannah

30° JAPAN SUPERIMPOSED AT THE SAME LATITUDE
Jacksonville○ ON THE EAST COAST OF THE UNITED STATES

0   100 Miles

stant water supply to the greater part of Japan's crop land, making possible the highest agricultural yields per acre in the world; fully exploited for hydroelectricity, it adds an important power resource; and it provides adequate water supplies for Japan's huge cities and modern industrial enterprises.

Next to its favorable climate, the geographic factor of greatest importance in shaping the history of Japan has been its isolation. Of all the lands which enjoyed a high civilization in premodern times, Japan was the most isolated, and even today, when distances no longer are so meaningful and Japan has become a great global trading country, the Japanese remain relatively more isolated by linguistic and cultural barriers than are the peoples of the other industrialized nations.

Japan is part of the East Asian zone of civilization, which centers around China and includes Korea and Vietnam. This is the part of the world that has derived most of its basic culture from the civilization developed in ancient times on the plains of North China. Although the home throughout history of a large part of the human race—roughly a quarter to a third—the East Asian cultural zone has been the most isolated of the great spheres of early civilization. It was cut off from the other centers of ancient culture in India, the Middle East, and the Mediterranean Basin by the great land barrier of the mountain ranges and deserts of Central Asia and the jungles and rugged terrain of Southeast Asia and the Malay Peninsula. In this relatively isolated zone, Japan was in the past the most isolated area of all. Like England, Japan is an island country, but the straits between western Japan and Korea, the nearest part of the continent, are over 100 miles wide, many times the width of the Straits of Dover; and some 500 miles of open sea stretch between Japan and China. In the days of primitive navigation, these water barriers were very broad indeed.

Culturally, Japan is a daughter of Chinese civilization, much as the countries of Northern Europe are daughters of Mediterranean culture. The story of the spread of Chinese civilization to the alien peoples of Japan during the first millennium after Christ is much like the story of the spread of Mediterranean civilization to the alien peoples of Northern Europe during the same period. But the greater isolation of the Japanese from the home of their civilization and from all other peoples meant that in Japan the borrowed culture had more chance to develop along new and often unique lines. One popular concept is that the Japanese have never been anything more than a race of borrowers and imitators. The truth is quite the contrary. Although geographic isolation has made them conscious of learning from abroad, it has also allowed them to develop one of the most distinctive cultures to be found in any civilized area of comparable size. Take, for example, things as basic as their traditional clothing, their cuisine, or their domestic architecture and the manner in which they live at home. The thick straw floor mats, the sliding paper panels in place of interior walls, the open, airy structure of the whole house, the recess for art objects, the charcoal heating braziers, the peculiar wooden or iron bathtubs, and the place of bathing in daily life as a means of relaxation at the end of a day's work and, in winter, as a way of restoring a sense of warmth and well-being—all these and many other simple but fundamental features of home and daily life are unique to Japan and attest to a unique culture rather than one of simple imitation.

Japan's cultural distinctiveness has perhaps been accentuated by her linguistic separateness. Although the Japanese writing system has been derived from that of China and innumerable Chinese words have been incorporated into Japanese in much the same way that English has borrowed thousands of Latin and Greek words, Japanese basically is as different from Chinese as it is from English. Its structure is strikingly like Korean, but even then it appears to be no more closely related to Korean than English is to the Sanskrit-derived languages of India. Possessing a writing system more complex than any other in common use in the modern world and a language with no close relatives, the Japanese probably face a bigger language barrier between themselves and the rest of the world than does any other major national group.

Geographic isolation and cultural and linguistic distinctiveness have made the Japanese highly self-conscious and acutely aware of their differences from others. In a way, this has been a great asset to them in the modern age of nation-states, for they have faced no problem of national identity. Indeed, Japan constitutes what may be the world's most perfect nation-state: a clear-cut geographic unit containing almost all of the people of a distinctive culture and language and virtually no one else. On the other hand, extreme self-consciousness bred of isolation has been a handicap in other ways. It has made the Japanese somewhat tense in their contacts with others. They have shown relatively little sensitivity to the feelings or reactions of other peoples. At times they have seemed obsessed with a sense either of superiority or of inferiority toward the outside world. Japan's isolation may help to explain some of the extremes in her international relations and also, perhaps, the uneasiness Japanese feel today about their place in the world.

The Japanese are basically Mongoloid in race, closely related to their neighbors in Korea and China, but like all modern peoples, they are the product of extensive racial mixture. Many different groups found their way to Japan, a few as early as paleolithic times, and since this was the geographic end of the line, they could not move on but stayed and mixed with later comers.

One interesting racial ingredient was provided by the Ainu. These are a proto-Caucasoid people, that is, a group that split off from the white race so early that not all the characteristics of this race had as yet developed. At one time the Ainu may have occupied most of Japan, or they may have been only relatively late intruders from the north. In any case, some twelve centuries ago their ancestors lived in the northern island of Hokkaido and the northern third of the main island of Honshu. Since then they have been slowly pushed north and culturally and racially absorbed by the Japanese. Today they are on the point of vanishing, but they have left behind a strong genetic legacy that accounts for the relative abundance of facial and body hair of some Japanese as compared with other Mongoloids, and possibly helps to explain the great variety of facial types among Japanese.

There is a popular theory that some early immigrants to Japan were carried there by the Japan Current from Southeast Asia past Taiwan and the Ryukyu Islands, and strong similarities in mythology, social customs, and early architecture between Japan and Southeast Asia are cited in support of this concept. There is, however, no archeological evidence to back it up. A better explanation of these similarities is that they resulted from very early waves of cultural influence and possibly peoples moving outward from South China, some to Southeast Asia and others to Japan, perhaps by way of Korea.

The archeological record shows clearly that a large number, if not most, of the early inhabitants of Japan came to the islands from Korea and areas further afield in northeast Asia, and there is indisputable historical evidence that a considerable flow of people continued from the peninsula into Japan until the eighth century A.D. By then, however, the mixing was almost complete, and the Japanese had already become the homogeneous people we know today. They also already occupied most of what we now call Japan. Only in the extreme north were the culturally alien Ainu still to be absorbed, and in southern Kyushu there were still some groups which may have been culturally as well as politically distinct, but were in any case on the verge of complete assimilation.

Paralleling the flow of people and probably carried in part by it, a series of cultural influences also spread from the Asian continent to Japan. From about the fifth millennium B.C. on, a primitive hunting and gathering society flourished throughout the islands. It is called *Jomon* for its mat-patterned pottery, which shows tremendous artistic vigor in the great variety and boldness of its designs. The Ainu of the north continued this Jomon tradition into historic times.

Meanwhile, a new culture had started to spread from Korea to the islands. It appeared first in northern Kyushu about the third century B.C. and then moved progressively up the Inland Sea to central Japan, along the Pacific coast to the Kanto Plain in eastern Japan, and on into the mountains to the north by the first century A.D., mixing with and absorbing the older Jomon culture as it went. This new culture, called *Yayoi*, was based on an agricultural economy using irrigation techniques for rice

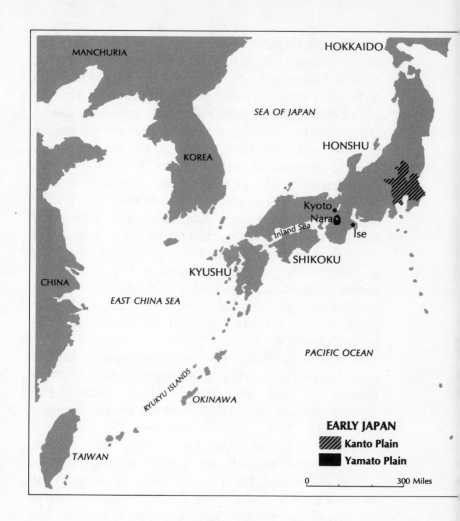

MANCHURIA

HOKKAIDO

SEA OF JAPAN

HONSHU

KOREA

Kyoto
Nara
Ise

Inland Sea

CHINA

KYUSHU

SHIKOKU

EAST CHINA SEA

PACIFIC OCEAN

RYUKYU ISLANDS

OKINAWA

TAIWAN

EARLY JAPAN
▨ Kanto Plain
■ Yamato Plain

0   300 Miles

growing much like those of today. It was also characterized by a rather simple wheel-turned pottery and the use
of both bronze and iron. Much of this agricultural and
metal technology was derived from China. In fact, the
spread of this great cultural wave may have been caused
in part by the founding of the first great unified empire
in China in the late third century B.C. and the subsequent
Chinese conquest of northern Korea in 108 B.C. One is
reminded of the almost contemporary Roman conquests
of Gaul and Britain, which sent cultural waves further
afield in Northern Europe. Chinese records of the third
century A.D. tell of an agricultural society in Japan with
sharp class distinctions, ruled over by semireligious leaders, some men and others women, who served as me-
diums, or shamans. The land was divided into a large
number of separate tribal units, several of which were
under the loose control of what the records call the
"queen's country."

Starting in the late third century, the Japanese learned
from Korea the practice of erecting *tumuli* (earthen
mounds) to house their noble dead. The growing size
of these mounds gives evidence of the increasing power
and wealth of the political units and the aristocratic
nature of their leadership. By the early fifth century,
broad political control and a great concentration of
wealth are evident, for these tumuli—commonly in the
shape of a fat keyhole, round in the rear and square in
front—had become extremely imposing structures. The
largest tumulus, with its surrounding moats, is a half
mile long. Around the tumuli were placed numerous
cylindrical pieces of pottery called *haniwa*, many of which
were topped by esthetically delightful and archeologi-
cally informative figures of armored warriors, houses,
horses, and other animals. These and numerous horse

trappings and other objects found in the tumuli suggest a mounted warrior aristocracy ruling over an agricultural population.

Since some of the larger tumuli in the vicinity of the modern cities of Nara and Osaka are traditionally identified as the tombs of early Japanese emperors, and since these rulers were quite possibly the descendants of the "queen" mentioned in the Chinese records, the archeological evidence, the Chinese accounts, and the native tradition all begin to merge quite convincingly in the fifth century. Japanese tradition mirrors a plausible history of conquest by one tribal group from Kyushu up the Inland Sea to the small Yamato Plain near its eastern end, and the extension of this group's control over great numbers of similar tribal units.

The priest-chief rulers of Yamato claimed descent from the Sun Goddess, and made her worship the supreme cult of the land. This cult became centered at the Grand Shrine in Ise, still the most holy spot in Japan and representative of the simple but esthetically pleasing architecture of this remote age. The feminine progenitress of the ruling line as well as the Chinese record of women rulers suggest an original matriarchal society, which only slowly and under continental influence became the strongly male-dominated family system of historic times. The symbols of authority of the priest-chiefs of Yamato, which are still the "Three Imperial Regalia" of Japan, are all objects frequently found in Japanese archeological sites and are also common on the nearby continent. These are a bronze mirror, clearly derived from China but symbolic of the Sun Goddess, a long iron sword, and a so-called "curved jewel" (magatama), a small comma-shaped stone which originally may have represented a bear claw.

The Japanese state that emerges into the light of history in the fifth and sixth centuries was clearly a further development of the tribally divided country described in the earlier Chinese records. Society was organized into a number of hereditary units called *uji*, often translated as "clans." The members of these units, while not necessarily related, formed a sort of extended pseudofamily under a hereditary head and worshipping a common deity at the *uji* shrine. Within the *uji* were hereditary subunits (called *be*), which performed specialized functions, such as weaving, pottery making, or the cultivation of particular tracts of land. The *uji* were grouped in hierarchic order under the supreme authority of the Yamato rulers. Some served them directly as specialized subunits of the Yamato group; others formed semi-autonomous regional units.

The authority of the Yamato rulers by this time extended over most of modern Japan, except for the northland, which was still inhabited by Ainu. The Yamato court also exercised a certain suzerainty over parts of southern Korea. The native tradition ascribes this fact to a semimiraculous conquest by a warrior empress, but it more probably was connected with the movement of people from Korea to Japan, illustrated by the continental origin claimed by at least a third of the Yamato aristocracy as late as the eighth century. One is reminded of the somewhat similar English hold over Normandy in the Middle Ages. In any case, Japanese power in southern Korea was apparently at its height in the late fourth century and gradually waned thereafter, coming to an end in 562.

Many characteristics of *uji* society were to remain typical of Japan in her later history. This was certainly true of the strong emphasis on hereditary authority and hierarchy. The aristocratic mounted warrior of the tumulus period was to emerge again as a dominant figure in feudal times. The early Yamato rulers, of course, developed into the imperial line, which served throughout Japanese history as the ultimate source of political authority, and is today by far the oldest reigning family in the world.

The religious beliefs and practices of *uji* times have also continued as one of the main religious streams of Japanese history. While nameless at first, these beliefs were subsequently called *Shinto*, "the way of the gods," to distinguish them from Buddhism. The worship of the Sun Goddess and other *uji* ancestors and deities was part of a much broader worship of the wonders and mysteries of nature. A waterfall, a mountain crag, a mysterious cave, a large tree, a peculiarly shaped stone, an unusual person, or even some lowly thing like an insect, notable only for its capacity for irritation, might inspire a sense of awe. Such objects of worship were called *kami*, a term somewhat misleadingly translated as "god," but obviously not comparable to the Judeo-Christian concept of God. This simple Shinto notion of deity should be borne in mind in trying to understand the "deification" in modern times of emperors and of soldiers who died for their country.

Early Shinto had almost no ethical content, except for an emphasis on ritual purity, which may have contributed to the Japanese love of bathing. On the other hand, it had numberless places of worship and countless festivals and ceremonials. Places where people felt a sense of awe became cult spots and eventually shrines. Today tens of thousands of such shrines dot the landscape of Japan, each with its characteristic *torii* gateway. Some are great institutions dating back to antiquity, thousands are village shrines still identified as the abode of the local *uji* deity, and others are merely miniature edifices of stone or wood recently erected in front of a gnarled old tree or on a mountain top.

The underlying stream of Shinto today remains little changed since prehistoric times. Much has been done during the past 1,300 years to make it into a more organized religion. During the past century, it was consciously used, through an emphasis on the early mythology connected with it, as an inspiration for national solidarity and fanatical patriotism. But despite these later additions, Shinto remains basically unchanged. It centers around the worship of nature, reverence for ancestral deities, and a sense of communion with them and the spirits of nature.

2 ❀ THE ADOPTION OF THE CHINESE PATTERN

The peoples of Northern Europe have always been conscious of their double heritage—their primitive Teutonic roots and the cultural legacy of ancient Greece and Rome. Similarly, the Japanese have a double heritage—the native culture of early Japan and the higher civilization of China. As in Northern Europe, true history started for Japan only when the broad stream of a highly developed civilization reached her shores and, in a new geographic setting, combined with the simpler traditions of the local people to form a new culture, derived directly from the old civilization but differentiated from it by new geographic and cultural ingredients.

The Japanese had long had some contact with Chinese civilization. Envoys and traders had gone back and forth between the two countries since at least the first century A.D. Immigrants from Korea had for centuries brought to Japan some of the arts and sciences of the continental civilization. Knowledge of Chinese writing, for example, had become well established in Japan by the fifth century. These early borrowings from China, however, were made only very slowly and almost unconsciously, as has been the usual pattern in the spread of civilization throughout the world. But an abrupt acceleration in the rate of learning from the continent started in the second half of the sixth century, when the Japanese suddenly became conscious of the advantages of the superior continental civilization and the desirability of learning more about it.

Why this spurt in the process of learning from China should have come at just this moment in Japanese history is not certain. The Japanese may have reached a level of cultural attainment and political organization which for the first time permitted more rapid and more conscious learning from abroad. And the renewed vigor displayed by Chinese culture at that time may have facilitated the process.

China's history as a highly civilized part of the world reaches back to the second millennium before Christ. Her first great period as a colossal military empire came during the time of Rome's greatness, roughly from about 220 B.C. to A.D. 220. The era of political disruption which followed came to an end only in the second half of the sixth century, when a new and greater Chinese empire emerged from the chaos of three centuries of civil wars and barbarian invasions. This new empire was far richer and stronger than the first. In fact, during the seventh and eighth centuries China was, with little doubt, the richest, most powerful, and technologically most advanced country in the world. This period, which was known by the dynastic name of T'ang, was a time of unprecedented grandeur, might, and brilliant cultural attainment.

It is small wonder that the primitive Japanese in their isolated island country felt the reflected glory of the new

Chinese empire and awoke to a new awareness of Chinese civilization. The result was a cultural surge forward in Japan that stands in sharp contrast to the slow, fumbling progress of Northern Europe at this same time. The difference lay not so much in the somewhat similar tribal peoples of Japan and Northern Europe, as in the attractiveness of their respective models. While Rome was falling completely to pieces, China was rising to new heights of grandeur.

The start of the heavy flow of Chinese influences to Japan is usually dated 552, the year the Buddhist religion is said to have been officially introduced to the Yamato court from a kingdom in southern Korea. Actually, Buddhism had probably entered Japan even earlier, but this incident affords a convenient date to mark the time when the Japanese first started consciously to learn from the Chinese. During the next few centuries Buddhism served as an important vehicle for the transmission of Chinese culture to Japan, just as Christianity served as a vehicle for the transmission of Mediterranean civilization to Northern Europe. Buddhism is by origin an Indian religion, but it had slowly spread to China and had won a place of importance in Chinese culture during the troubled era between the two great empires. It was a vigorous proselytizing religion at that time, and missionary zeal carried it beyond China to Korea and from there to Japan. From the sixth to the eighth centuries, Korean, Chinese, and even occasional Indian priests came to Japan. In turn, scores of Japanese converts went to China to learn more about the new faith. Returning from the continent, these Japanese student priests, even more than foreign missionary teachers, took the lead in transmitting to Japan the new religion and many other aspects of

Chinese civilization. They were the true pioneers in planting and nurturing in Japan the arts, institutions, and ideas of China.

In the second half of the sixth century, Buddhism and other new influences from abroad so affected the Yamato court that clashes broke out between a faction favoring the acceptance of Buddhism and other continental ideas and an opposition group which resisted the new religion and all change. The victory of the pro-Buddhist faction in about 587 cleared the way for a more rapid acceptance of Chinese ideas and knowledge, and under the able leadership of the crown prince and regent, Shotoku, many startling reforms were undertaken. Among Prince Shotoku's innovations was the issuing in 604 of a so-called Seventeen-article Constitution, which was a set of precepts based on Buddhism and Chinese Confucian political and ethical concepts. Another innovation was the sending of a large official embassy to China in the year 607. This embassy, and many others that followed it during the next two and a half centuries, played a vital role in the great period of learning from China. Their immediate political significance was slight, and the economic importance of the exchange of goods carried on under their auspices was limited, but the cultural influence of the embassies was immense.

The Japanese leaders, showing extraordinary wisdom for a people only just emerging into the light of civilization, carefully chose promising young men to accompany the embassies so that they could study at the sources of knowledge in China. The result was, in a sense, the first organized program of foreign study in the world. These men, selected for their knowledge of Chinese literature, philosophy, history or Buddhist theology and ritual, or for their skill in the arts of painting, poetry or music, studied in China during the year of the embassy's stay, and some remained in China for a decade or two between embassies. Upon their return to Japan, they became leaders in their respective fields, the men most responsible for the successful transmission to this isolated land of the science, arts, and ideals of the great continental civilization.

Students who had returned from China formed an important element in a clique at the Yamato court which seized power in 645 through a carefully engineered coup d'état. The incident and its aftermath of rapid innovations are known as the Taika Reform. From that time on, the Yamato state was definitely committed to a policy of trying to create in Japan a small replica of China, a miniature T'ang in the forested islands on the eastern fringes of the civilized world. With the glory of China before their eyes, it is not surprising that the Japanese made this attempt. Other petty states in Korea, Manchuria, and on the southwestern borders of China, dazzled by the grandeur and might of T'ang, were doing the same. A millennium or more later, the borrowing of political, social, and economic institutions from more advanced countries was to become commonplace throughout the world; but it is surprising that the Japanese at this early date were able to go about transplanting the superior continental institutions and techniques in such a systematic way and could throw themselves into the task with such zeal.

Under the influence of Chinese ideas, the Japanese for the first time thought of the Yamato state as an empire, and at that, an empire on an equal footing with China. Prince Shotoku even dared to phrase a letter to the

Chinese as coming from the Emperor of the Rising Sun to the Emperor of the Setting Sun. With the new imperial concept, the ruler of the Yamato state for the first time assumed the dignity and majesty of an emperor. The priest-chief of the clan became in theory an all-powerful, autocratic monarch in the Chinese tradition. But he did not lose his original role as high priest; he retained a dual position. Even in modern times, the Japanese emperor remained in theory the Shinto high priest of the ancient Yamato tradition, and at the same time the all-powerful secular ruler of the Chinese system.

Possibly under the influence of Chinese social concepts and of the Chinese prejudice against ruling empresses, the custom of occasional rule by women came to an end in Japan in the second half of the eighth century, after a Buddhist priest had threatened to usurp the throne through his influence over a reigning empress. Only a millennium later, long after the imperial line had become politically powerless, did a woman again appear on the throne. Japanese women, who in the earliest times seem to have enjoyed a position of social and political dominance over men, gradually sank to a status of subservience. Their rights and influence in early feudal society were still considerable, but in time even these were lost, as they were turned into mere handmaidens to the dominant male population.

Below the emperor, the Japanese created an elaborate central government, patterned after that of T'ang China, the most highly developed and complex governmental structure the world had as yet seen. Under a Supreme Council of State, with its Prime Minister and Ministers of the Left and Right, were eight ministries, in concept not unlike the ministries of a modern government. Under the ministries in turn were scores of bureaus and other offices. The ministries, bureaus, and offices were staffed by a bureaucracy meticulously divided into twenty-six ranks. This organization was fantastically overdeveloped for the needs of a small and loosely organized state, still close to a primitive tribal society. Much of the central government remained little more than a paper organization which functioned, if at all, far differently from the Chinese prototype. But the wonder is not that the Japanese fell short of complete success: the surprising thing is that they had the ambition and energy to undertake such a grandiose task, and that they already had sufficient understanding of the principles and mastery of the mechanisms of Chinese government to create a fair semblance of its complex central administration.

One gains some idea of the scope of the undertaking and the degree of success by considering the capital cities founded by the Japanese as part of their attempt to transform Japan into a little T'ang. In earlier ages there had been no cities or towns, nor even any semipermanent buildings. Now the Japanese attempted to build a capital city comparable to Ch'ang-an, the great capital of T'ang. Located in northwest China and now known as Hsian, Ch'ang-an at that time was a metropolis of close to a million people and was probably the largest city in the world. It was a great rectangle in shape, some 5 by 6 miles, surrounded by massive walls. A magnificent palace stood at the northern end of the city and broad straight thoroughfares divided it neatly in checkerboard fashion.

The first Japanese imitation of Ch'ang-an was undertaken in the year 710 near the modern town of Nara in the Yamato Plain. The Japanese naturally reduced the scale, allowing the new capital an area of some 2 1/2 by 3 miles. They failed to build the customary Chinese city wall, and the population of the capital was so far short of the goal that the western half of the city was never built up at all; but broad thoroughfares were laid out, and stately tile-roofed Buddhist temples and probably imposing palaces and residences were constructed. Even today, several of these Buddhist temples still stand. Together with an earlier temple, the Horyuji, dating from the seventh century, they are the oldest wooden buildings in the world and the finest remaining examples of East Asian architecture of the T'ang epoch.

Toward the end of the eighth century, the Japanese court, possibly with a view to escaping the increasing influence of the great Buddhist temples which ringed the Nara capital, decided to abandon this first city and built a new capital. In 794 this second city, called Heian, was laid out 30 miles north of Nara. Again the scale was grandiose, a rectangle some 3 by 3 1/2 miles, and again the Chinese city wall and the western half of the city never materialized. But this second capital did not disappear. Remaining the imperial capital of Japan until 1868, it grew into the modern city of Kyoto. The checkerboard pattern of the principal streets of Kyoto still reflects accurately the Chinese-style city laid out over a thousand years ago.

The development of a central government in Japan based on Chinese models was an easier task than the creation of the Chinese type of provincial administration. Communications were still too imperfect and the spirit of local autonomy too strong to permit direct rule of all parts of the land by a bureaucracy dispatched to the provinces from the court. But the Japanese created at least the outward forms of the Chinese system. The land was divided into provinces and counties, and over these were placed officials with high-sounding titles. All too soon, however, the chief provincial officials, loath to leave the pleasures and power of the court, began to delegate their authority to their subordinates, and since these tended to be local aristocrats, control by the central government was probably never very strong.

Nonetheless, the Japanese government did attempt to adopt the extraordinarily complex and ambitious Chinese system of land ownership and taxation. In early T'ang China, agricultural land was in theory nationalized and distributed equally among the peasants, so that each adult tax-paying male could carry an equal share of the tax load. This he paid partly in produce and partly in labor, or in military service, which was considered a form of labor for the state. Even in China, however, despite the long tradition of centralized bureaucratic rule, this cumbersome system worked imperfectly and tended to break down completely every few decades. The Japanese wrote the system into elaborate law codes drawn up on Chinese models; to put it into practice in clan-ridden Japan was a different matter. For a century or so, the system seems to have operated after a fashion in the capital area and in localities held directly by the Yamato clan, but in more remote parts of the country it was probably a dead letter from the start.

Closely connected with the Chinese tax system was the huge peasant conscript army it provided. China, with her long frontiers and warlike nomad neighbors to the north and northwest, needed such large levies, but they were quite meaningless in isolated Japan. A so-called army was created from peasant conscripts of the capital area where the tax system was in force, but these peasant soldiers never constituted anything more than labor gangs. Despite the creation on paper of a foot soldier army, the aristocrat on horseback seems to have remained the true Japanese fighting man.

The process of learning and borrowing from China was, of course, not limited to the political field. In fact, what the Japanese were learning at this time in cultural and intellectual areas was to have a deeper and more lasting influence than the borrowed political institutions. The latter for the most part decayed within a century or so and eventually disappeared in all but name, but many of the religious concepts, artistic skills, and literary forms learned during these centuries, far from losing their original vigor, continued to develop and helped form the basic cultural patterns of later ages.

After the triumph of the pro-Buddhist faction at the Yamato court in the second half of the sixth century, the continental religion enjoyed the uninterrupted favor of the central government. Splendid temples were erected at government expense, and impressive Buddhist ceremonies were sponsored by the court and the noble families. Many a Japanese emperor retired from the heavy burdens of his dual secular and religious role to the more peaceful life of a Buddhist monk. As was the case with so much else in the newly imported culture, the influence of Buddhism was still weak in the provinces, but in the capital district the new religion was supreme, and enjoyed official favor far greater than that afforded the native cults of Shinto.

With Buddhism came many of the arts and crafts of China. The Buddhist temples were themselves great architectural masterpieces, and they housed beautiful and deeply spiritual bronze, lacquer or wooden statues of Buddhist divinities, exquisite religious paintings, and other magnificent works of art. Some had been brought from the continent. Others of equal beauty and artistic merit were produced in Japan. The Horyuji and other Buddhist temples in the Nara area, as well as a large storehouse called the Shosoin, are crammed with the artistic achievements of that age. They attest to the amazing success with which the Japanese transplanted much of the best in the Chinese artistic tradition and indicate the early development of a happy combination of artistic taste and superb craftsmanship which ever since has characterized the Japanese.

In art, the Japanese could have had no better teachers than the Chinese, but in the field of writing, Chinese influence was less fortuitous. Japanese is a language of simple phonetic structure, but polysyllabic, highly inflected words. It can be written easily by phonetic symbols, but the Chinese writing system is not adapted to phonetic transcription or the representation of inflections. The Chinese language itself lacks inflections, and in ancient times the words were mostly monosyllabic. As a consequence, the Chinese found it possible to develop and hold to a writing system in which all the individual words were represented by separate symbols, originally of pictographic origin, which we usually call characters. These characters range from a simple line — to represent "one," to more complex characters such as the architectonic wonder in twenty-five strokes 灣 representing the word "bay."

The Chinese student has always been faced with the grim necessity of mastering several thousand of these characters before he could be considered literate. The ancient Japanese were faced with this problem and the added difficulty that the Chinese writing system was not suited to the writing of their own language. Had Japan been the neighbor of some Western or South Asian country using a phonetic script such as our own alphabet, the Japanese would have quickly learned to write their native tongue with efficiency and ease. Unfortunately, geographic accident decreed otherwise, and the Japanese were burdened with the most cumbersome of writing systems. Like the youth of China, the youth of Japan was sentenced generation after generation to years of mentally numbing memory work simply to learn the rudiments of writing.

Because of the tremendous prestige of all things Chinese and the difficulty of adapting Chinese characters to the writing of Japanese, the early Japanese made little effort to write their own language. Proper names and brief poems in Japanese were spelled out laboriously with one Chinese character used phonetically for each syllable, but little else was attempted. Instead, the Japanese wrote in straight and often reasonably good classical Chinese. Using Chinese much as medieval Europeans used Latin, they wrote their histories, geographies, law books, and official documents of all sorts. They even attempted to imitate Chinese literary forms, and men of education prided themselves on their ability to compose poems in Chinese.

The most interesting and significant form of literary endeavor at this time was history writing. This was to be expected in a cultural daughter of China, for the Chinese have always been prone to take the historical approach to any subject or situation. The writing of history was an important function of government in China, and as a result, the Chinese were inveterate and extremely good historians. Since the Japanese leaders regarded their country as an empire on the Chinese model, they felt that Japan too needed an official written history. Several early efforts to write one resulted in two extant works, the *Nihon shoki* (or *Nihongi*), compiled in Chinese in 720, and a smaller work called the *Kojiki*, in mixed Japanese and Chinese and said to date from 712. Both are fairly reliable historical accounts for the period after about A.D. 400, and they also contain much native mythology and historical tradition from earlier eras which throw a great deal of light on primitive Japanese beliefs and social institutions before they were submerged under the flood of more advanced ideas and institutions from China.

However, the statesmen and historians of the time were not satisfied with a simple, uncolored presentation of the mythology and historical traditions of the Yamato clan as transmitted orally by professional court reciters. They were determined to prove by their work that the rulers of Yamato were and always had been true emperors, the unique rulers of Japan, and that Japan was a great and old country, a worthy equal of China. Supplementing their mythology and scanty historic tradition with elements from Chinese philosophy and history, they wove the whole into an impressive pseudohistory that describes the descent of the grandson of the Sun Goddess from heaven to Japan and the founding of the Japanese empire in 660 B.C. by the latter's great-grandson, Jimmu. This date, like so much else in these accounts, is of course pure fantasy, possibly arrived at in the early seventh century simply by counting back 1,260 years, a major time cycle according to Chinese reckoning.

The place of the *Nihon shoki* and *Kojiki* in the historiography of Japan is fundamental, but unfortunately that is not their only claim to fame. They were to be lifted from comparative obscurity many centuries later by patriots seeking in the primitive pre-Chinese period of Japanese history native virtues which would justify their own belief in the superiority of Japan. Despite the naiveté of the early mythology preserved in the *Kojiki* and *Nihon shoki*, later Japanese in a sense made these two books into bibles of ultranationalism; and at times official policy even forced upon the Japanese people the acceptance of these myths as sober historical fact.

3 ✤ THE GROWTH OF A
NATIVE CULTURE

The period of greatest learning from the continent
lasted from the late sixth century until the middle of the
ninth century, but then a subtle change began to take
place in the Japanese attitude toward China. The prestige of all things Chinese remained great, but the Japanese were no longer so anxious to learn from China or
so ready to admit the superiority of all facets of Chinese
civilization over their own. The period from 710 to 794,
when the capital was in the vicinity of Nara, was the
time of the height of the political and cultural pattern
borrowed from China. Even after the move of the capital
in 794 to Heian, or Kyoto, the prestige of Chinese ways
of doing things remained great, but by the early tenth
century a profound shift in cultural emphasis had become apparent. As a consequence, the spirit of the Heian
period, as the age from the ninth to the early twelfth
century is called, came in time to be sharply different
from that of the so-called Nara period. The emphasis
was no longer on borrowing new elements of culture
from China but on assimilating and transforming those

that had already been borrowed to make them more congenial to Japanese tastes and better fitted to Japanese realities.

One reason for the lessened interest in learning from China was the political decay of T'ang, which became marked as the ninth century progressed. Perhaps even more fundamental was the intellectual growth of the Japanese themselves, for it resulted in a gradual reassertion of a spirit of cultural independence. Three centuries of assiduous learning from the Chinese had created, at least in the capital district, a cultured society with its own political and social institutions, patterned of course after Chinese models, but changed and adapted to fit Japanese needs by conscious experimentation and slow unconscious modification. The Japanese were no longer a primitive people, overawed by the vastly superior continental civilization and eager to imitate blindly anything Chinese. Japan was reaching a state of intellectual maturity and was ready to develop along her own lines.

One sign of the changing attitude was the ending of official contacts with China. The last of the great embassies left Japan for T'ang in 838 and returned the next year. Later embassies were proposed but were argued down by courtiers who felt their value no longer warranted the tremendous risks of the trip across the East China Sea. Some private traders and student monks continued to travel between the two lands, but for the most part Japan lapsed into her earlier state of virtual isolation from the continent. This isolation in turn made the Japanizing of the imported Chinese civilization all the more inevitable and rapid.

The cultural change is perhaps best illustrated by the development of an adequate means of writing the native tongue. This writing system was developed slowly during the ninth and tenth centuries by the process of using certain Chinese characters in greatly abbreviated form as simple phonetic symbols devoid of any specific meaning in themselves. Since the Chinese characters each represented one monosyllabic word, the phonetic symbols derived from them stood for a whole syllable, such as *ka*, *se*, or *mo*. The result was a syllabary rather than an alphabet. Japanese syllables normally end in vowels, and these are limited to the five basic vowels, *a*, *e*, *i*, *o*, and *u*, as in Italian.

The Japanese syllabary, or *kana* as it is called, was at first a confused affair. For one thing, the Chinese characters used were abbreviated in two different ways. In one system, called *hiragana*, the whole character was written in a very stylized or cursive form. Thus, the Chinese character 奴 meaning "slave" became the *hiragana* symbol ぬ standing for the sound *nu*. In the other system, called *katakana*, some element of the character was chosen to represent the phonetic value of the whole. Thus, this same Chinese character for "slave" became the *katakana* symbol ヌ also standing for *nu*. Another complexity was that the choice of characters for abbreviation as *kana* was at first quite haphazard, and usually several were used for any one syllable. In fact, both *hiragana* and *katakana* became standardized only within the past century, and variant *kana* forms are still commonly used in everyday correspondence.

The Japanese syllabaries formed more clumsy writing systems than alphabets, but they were, nevertheless, reasonably efficient for writing Japanese, and with their development appeared a growing literature in the native tongue. As noted before, even at the height of the Chinese period, poems had been composed in Japanese and laboriously written down by the use of unabbreviated

Chinese characters to represent each syllable phonetically. In this way were recorded the 4,516 poems collected around the year 760 in a great anthology known as the *Manyoshu* (*Collection of Myriad Leaves*). The simple phonetic systems of writing, however, made even the writing down of poems much easier than before. This fact may have contributed to what became a virtual craze among Japanese courtiers and their ladies to jot down poems on almost every conceivable occasion and exchange them profusely in their frequent love letters. The best of these poems were collected on imperial command in the *Kokinshu* (*Ancient and Modern Collection*) of 905, and in twenty later anthologies over the next five centuries.

Most of these poems, following a strict pattern of thirty-one syllables called the *tanka* ("short poem"), were quite brief. The *tanka* was too slight to do more than suggest a natural scene and, by some deft turn of phrase, evoke an emotion or some sudden insight, but within its narrow limits it could be both delicate and moving.

The *kana* syllabaries also made possible more extensive literary works in Japanese. In the tenth century, stories, travel diaries, and essays appeared, written in a Japanese which sometimes achieved considerable literary distinction. For the most part, educated men, much like their counterparts in medieval Europe, scorned the use of their own tongue for any serious literary purpose and continued to write histories, essays, and official documents in Chinese; but the women of the imperial court, who usually had insufficient education to write in Chinese, had no medium for literary expression other than their own language. As a result, while the men of the period were pompously writing bad Chinese, their ladies consoled themselves for their lack of education by writing good Japanese, and created, incidentally, Japan's first great prose literature.

The golden age of the first flowering of Japanese prose was the late tenth and early eleventh centuries. Most of the writers were court ladies living in ease and indolence, and their commonest form of literary expression was the diary, liberally sprinkled with "short poems" to commemorate moments of deep emotional feeling. Some of the diaries told of travels, but more often they concerned the luxuries, ceremonials, and constant flirtation and love-making which characterized court life at this time. The outstanding work of the period, however, was not a diary but an extremely lengthy novel, *The Tale of Genji*, written by Lady Murasaki early in the eleventh century. This is an account of the love adventures and psychological development of an imaginary Prince Genji. It is not only the earliest forerunner of a major genre of world literature, but both in itself and in Arthur Waley's magnificent English translation constitutes one of the great literary achievements of mankind. The diaries and novels by court ladies were clear evidence of the existence of a true native Japanese culture. They had no exact prototypes in Chinese literature: everything about them was distinctly Japanese. The transplanted Chinese civilization had flowered into a new culture, and the Japanese, a people but recently introduced to the art of writing, had produced a great literature of their own.

One may wonder why Japanese writing is still burdened with Chinese characters, if a thousand years ago the Japanese had already developed a phonetic script which was well suited to their language. The only explanation is the continued prestige of Chinese. Most learned men continued to write in Chinese, but as their knowledge of the foreign tongue declined during the period of lessened contact with China, *kana* additions crept increasingly into their bastard Chinese texts. Others inserted into Japanese *kana* texts Chinese words written in characters. The result of both tendencies was the development of a hybrid writing system that has become the standard written Japanese of modern times. In it, nouns and other uninflected words and the roots of verbs and adjectives are represented by characters insofar as possible, leaving for *kana* the inflections and whatever else cannot be conveniently written in characters.

The inevitable complexities of such a system of writing have been compounded by other factors. Chinese characters, having come to Japan over a prolonged period of time and from different dialectical areas in China, often are pronounced in more than one way in Japan, none of them very close to the original Chinese pronunciations. In addition, they are used not just for borrowed Chinese words, but also for Japanese words of corresponding meaning. It is as if the Chinese character for "water," 水, were to be used in English to represent the word "water" in "water wheel" and also to represent the element "aqua" in "aquatic." Many characters also represented Chinese words which corresponded in meaning to several different Japanese words. For example, the Chinese word *shang*, written by the character 上, has Japanese equivalents variously read as *ue*, *kami*, *agaru*, *ageru*, and *noboru*, to list the commonest, just as it has such English equivalents as "on," "above," "upper," "to mount," and "to present."

The coexistence of both Japanese and Chinese readings for most characters and the multiplicity of Japanese readings for many of them means that every line of modern Japanese presents a series of little problems in reading and interpretation. The result is a writing system of almost unparalleled difficulty and cumbersomeness that has stood as a serious impediment to the intellectual and technical development of Japan.

The obvious cure for this situation would be to abandon Chinese characters and return to the pure phonetic writing as it existed around the year 1000—or, still better, to adopt the Latin alphabet. But this would be no easy task. In modern times tens of thousands of technical and scientific words have been borrowed from Chinese or coined in Japan by joining two or more Chinese characters and pronouncing the resulting compound in the Chinese way. Unfortunately, Chinese-type words in the Japanese vocabulary run very strongly to homophones. A standard dictionary lists no less than twenty distinct words of Chinese type pronounced *kōkō*, and an exhaustive list of more specialized scientific terminology would probably add several dozen more. Because of these homophones, many, if not most, modern scientific terms, to be understood, must be seen as they are written in characters. Consequently, the dropping of Chinese characters from modern written Japanese would entail a wholesale modification of the technical and scientific vocabulary. Thousands of Chinese-type words would have to be abandoned, and new ones based on native Japanese roots or on words from Western languages would have to be substituted for them. It would be a tremendous undertaking, but in the long run probably well worth the attempt.

Although the appearance by the tenth and eleventh centuries of a new and distinctive Japanese culture is perhaps best seen in the literature of the time, it is evident in other fields also. The arts of painting, sculpture, and architecture all showed definite and sometimes marked Japanese characteristics quite distinct from the original Chinese patterns, and political and social institutions changed so radically as to bear little resemblance to the Chinese prototypes.

The key figure of the Chinese political system was the bureaucrat, the scholar–civil servant who operated the complicated central government and went out to the provinces to collect taxes and maintain order. Thousands of these bureaucrats were required, and the recruiting of wise and capable men for the higher posts was a matter of crucial importance to the whole state. For this purpose, the Chinese had developed a system of civil service examinations. It centered around the great central university of Ch'ang-an, where periodic examinations were given on classical subjects. Candidates who succeeded best in the examinations went directly to high government posts. In this way, men of scholarly talents from all walks of life could reach positions of responsibility, and among the educated classes a vital tradition of public service was built up.

The Japanese borrowed only the outward forms of this system. With their strong traditions of family loyalty and hereditary rights, they could not bring themselves to accept its spirit. They created a central university where the Chinese classics were studied and examinations were held, but only in rare cases did scholars with little family backing attain positions of much responsibility. In the provinces, political authority remained in the hands of local aristocrats masquerading as civil servants appointed by the central administration, while at the capital courtiers of noble lineage held most posts of importance, leaving to the scholar-bureaucrats the humbler clerical jobs.

In China, the central government was constantly kept busy fighting the natural tendency for the tax-paying peasants and their lands to gravitate into the hands of powerful families with sufficient influence at court to protect their holdings from the encroachments of tax collectors. In Japan, this tendency was even stronger, for there was no powerful civil servant class to protect the interests of the state, and local aristocrats, in key positions as provincial officers, joined with court nobles in despoiling the public domain. The nationalized land system had probably never really been applied to more remote parts of the country, and during the late eighth and ninth centuries it decayed rapidly even in the capital district. Local men of influence built up tax-free estates, often by illegal means, and court aristocrats acquired in their own names large tracts of land as rewards for their services or through political manipulations of a less honorable nature.

On the one hand, the local gentry needed protection for their holdings from the tax collectors of the central government. On the other hand, powerful court families and great monasteries were acquiring large tax-free estates, and needed local men to represent their interests on these lands. From these reciprocal needs a pattern of land-holding gradually developed in which provincial manors and estates were controlled and operated by local aristocrats, but were owned, at least in theory, by influential court families or powerful religious institutions in the capital district. The peasant, who came to have rights to the cultivation of his own little tract of land, gave to the local aristocrat, acting as estate manager, a generous portion of his produce; and the estate manager, in turn, passed on to the noble court family or great monastery a share of his income in payment for protection from the central government.

Tax-free manors grew and expanded during the eighth and ninth centuries, until by the tenth century, the national domain had virtually disappeared. With its disappearance, the income of the state from taxes, the economic basis for the Chinese form of centralized government, dwindled to almost nothing. As a result, provincial governmental agencies, which had never been strong, withered away almost completely, and left behind little except imposing administrative titles, such as governor or vice-governor. Even the central administration became largely an empty shell, a great paper organization with few working personnel, scanty funds, and pathetically reduced functions. The court nobles continued to sport high titles, and they were punctilious in maintaining the pomp and ceremony of court life. However, the complex system of actual rule through the eight ministries was for all practical purposes abandoned, and new and simplified organs of government were developed to handle what few political duties the central government still had.

The net result of all this was that centralized government ceased to exist for most parts of Japan. Each estate, freed from encroachment by tax collectors and other state agents, became a small autonomous domain, a semi-independent economic and political unit. The contacts it had with the outside world were not with any government agency, but with the great court family or religious institution to which it supplied a part of its produce and from which it received a loose sort of control. The noble court families and monasteries thus became multiple successors to the old centralized state. They had become, in a sense, states within the hollow framework of the old imperial government, each supported by the income from its own estates and, through family government or monastery administration, exercising many of the functions of government in its widely scattered manors throughout the land.

The imperial family, though retaining great prestige because of its past political role and its continuing position as leader in the Shinto cults, became in fact simply one among these central economic and political units. It exercised a theoretical rule over a shadow government, but in reality it controlled only its own estates and lived on the income from them, not from government taxes. In time, even control over its own private affairs was lost, as one of the court families, the Fujiwara, gradually won mastery over the court and the imperial family by intrigue and skillful political manipulations.

The Fujiwara were a prolific family of many branches, descended from a courtier who had taken the lead in the pro-Chinese coup d'état of 645. The family had come to control many estates throughout the land and thus enjoyed an income probably greater than that of any other family, not excluding the imperial family itself. Its method of winning unchallenged dominance at the capital was to gain direct control over the imperial family through intermarriage. A daughter of the head of the family would be married to a young emperor, and the emperor, bored with the endless ceremonies required by his double role as secular and religious leader, would easily be persuaded to abdicate and retire to a simpler, freer life as soon as the son the Fujiwara girl had borne him was old enough to sit through these ceremonies in his place. This would leave a Fujiwara girl as empress dowager, and her father, the powerful head of a large and rich court family, as the grandfather of the new child emperor.

By such tactics the Fujiwara gained complete control over the imperial family during the middle decades of the ninth century. From that time on, it became customary for the head of the Fujiwara family, instead of an imperial prince, to act as regent for a child emperor or to occupy the new post of chancellor (kampaku) when an adult was on the throne. During the course of the ninth and tenth centuries, appointment to these two alternating posts, as well as to that of prime minister and to most of the other high offices in the central administration, became the hereditary right of members of the Fujiwara family. In fact, the family had become so dominant at court by the tenth century that the latter two-thirds of the Heian period is commonly called the Fujiwara period. The successive heads of the Fujiwara family completely overshadowed the emperors not only as the real holders of the reins of government, but also as the openly recognized arbiters of taste and fashion at court. The greatest figure of the whole Heian period was not an emperor or prince, but Fujiwara Michinaga, who dominated the court between 995 and 1027, just at the time when Lady Murasaki was writing The Tale of Genji.

In the late eleventh century, an energetic retired emperor temporarily won back control over the court from the Fujiwara, and from time to time other retired emperors repeated this feat. Of course, control over the empty shell of the Chinese-type government was in any case becoming progressively less significant as power slipped away from the imperial court. But the Fujiwara, despite occasional challenges by the imperial family, maintained their domination over the court for exactly a millennium. Divided into a number of separate lines, each with its own family name, they retained their virtual monopoly of all high court posts almost without interruption until the great political transformation of the second half of the nineteenth century.

In another country such a long and almost complete dominance exercised by one family over the reigning family would probably have resulted in a usurpation of the throne. Not so in Japan. Hereditary authority and the emperors' role in Shinto ritual were such strong forces that outright usurpation was not to be contemplated. Instead, the Fujiwara set a lasting Japanese pattern of control from behind the scenes through a figurehead. For most of Japanese history, it has probably been the rule rather than the exception for the man or group in nominal control to be in reality the pawn of some other man or group. This fact has often helped to conceal the realities of Japanese life and confuse the casual observer.

4 ❋ THE DEVELOPMENT OF A FEUDAL SOCIETY

During the tenth and eleventh centuries, the Fujiwara held the spotlight, but behind the brilliance of the literary and artistic accomplishments of the court they dominated, others off stage were preparing the next acts in the drama. The capital aristocrats had transformed the borrowed civilization of China into a native culture, but they had lost control over the political and economic life of the country. While they were going through the forms and ceremonies of little more than a sham government and devoting their energies more to the arts of poetry-writing and love-making than to governing, the provincial aristocrats were gaining practical experience, managing their estates and controlling the peasants on them with little direction from the capital. The decadent, effeminate courtiers at Kyoto were producing a literature and an art that future generations would look back to with pride, but their less sophisticated and hardier country cousins were laying the foundations for an entirely new Japan.

The decline of Chinese political institutions at this

time and the weakening of the central government's control over the provinces have made the period of Fujiwara supremacy appear to be one of unmitigated political decline. In reality, the political decay at court was more than offset by the rapid growth of the once-backward provincials in political experience and in general sophistication. During the height of the Chinese period they had participated but little in the brilliant culture transplanted from T'ang to the capital district, and they had been completely overshadowed by the noble families at court. But little by little they absorbed much of the basic knowledge and many of the essential skills of the continental civilization, and by the tenth and eleventh centuries they had reached a stage of cultural development which permitted them to start laying the broad foundations for a new society and a new political structure only indirectly related to the old patterns established by the court. The central figure in this new society, as in the *uji* society that had preceded the period of borrowing from China, was the aristocratic fighting man on horseback. In ancient times he had been the warrior leader of the clan. Now he was the manager of a tax-free estate, defending his lands from marauders by his skill as a horseman and his prowess with bow and sword. Dressed in loose-fitting but efficient armor made up of small strips of steel held together by brightly colored thongs, he had become a close counterpart of the knight of early feudal Europe.

These Japanese knights usually owed allegiance to court families or central monasteries that were the nominal owners of their estates, but this relationship, which had been the outgrowth of an earlier need for protection from the tax collectors of the central government, afforded them no protection from their local enemies. For this, they required the aid of other fighting men, the knights on other estates. Quite naturally these warrior aristocrats began to form small local cliques for their mutual protection. The cliques were held together by common interests, ties of marriage, old friendships, and sometimes the qualities of leadership or the prestige of a local warrior hero. Such associations of knights flourished in particular in eastern Japan, probably because the greatest concentration of estates in the whole land was to be found on the Kanto Plain around the modern city of Tokyo, and also perhaps because the continuing campaigns against the retreating Ainu in northern Honshu made the value of such associations all the more evident.

In the tenth and eleventh centuries there were many clashes and small wars between different groups of knights in the provinces. These contests are often described in histories as revolts against imperial authority, for one faction or the other would win the nominal backing of the central government. The provincial knights, however, for the most part showed little desire to assume the governmental prerogatives of the Kyoto court. They were content to leave the central government undisturbed as long as they themselves could continue to control the peasants on their estates and organize their cliques for local defense without interference from the capital.

The court aristocrats, rather than the knights themselves, eventually brought the provincial warriors onto the capital stage. The courtiers, whose own military skills were limited, would from time to time bring knights from their provincial estates to the capital to help protect their interests or to overawe their rivals at court. Sometimes these warriors were used to defend the court from the great local monasteries, which often attempted to force their will upon the effete courtiers by a joint display of Buddhist relics and armed might drawn from the fighting men of their own estates. At other times, the knights were brought in to settle, by a show of force or by actual combat, factional disputes over the imperial succession or the headship of the Fujiwara family. In the middle of the twelfth century, succession disputes of this type led to fairly large-scale clashes between the two strongest warrior cliques of the time in support of two quarreling court factions. These warrior cliques centered around two great provincial families, the Minamoto, based largely in the Kanto area in eastern Japan, and the Taira, whose center of power was the Inland Sea region. Both families claimed descent from cadet branches of the imperial family which, because of declining income, had been forced to seek their fortunes in the provinces. There they had merged with the local aristocrats and had risen to leadership among them because of their prestige as descendants of emperors.

As a result of two small wars in 1156 and the winter of 1159–1160, one of the court factions won out over the other. A far more significant outcome was the sudden realization on the part of Taira Kiyomori, leader of the victorious Taira clique of warriors, that he and his band now formed the paramount military force in the land and that the emperor and his court were powerless in their hands. To the consternation of the courtiers, Kiyomori and his leading knights settled down in Kyoto and took over control of the court, Kiyomori taking for himself the title of prime minister and adopting the old Fujiwara trick of marrying his own daughter to the emperor and putting her son on the throne.

By settling in Kyoto and becoming in effect a new group of courtiers, Kiyomori and his henchmen weak-ened their hold over the knights of their clique who, remaining on their estates in the provinces, tended to resent the position and pretensions of the court aristocracy. Meanwhile, the estate managers of eastern Japan formed themselves into a new warrior clique centering around Minamoto Yoritomo, a survivor of the old Minamoto clique, and challenged Taira supremacy. In a bitterly fought war between 1180 and 1185, they swept from the Kanto region into the capital region and then pushed the Taira down the Inland Sea, finally crushing them in a naval battle at its western end. The Taira leaders either were killed or committed suicide, and the new boy emperor, who was the grandson of Kiyomori, perished with his Taira relatives.

Minamoto Yoritomo, profiting from the mistakes of the Taira, left Kyoto and the court alone and settled down at the small seaside town of Kamakura, near the estates of his relatives and partisans in the Kanto region of eastern Japan. In typically Japanese fashion, he decided to permit the emperors and the Fujiwara to continue their sham civil government unmolested. He rewarded his men not with government posts, but with the more lucrative positions of estate managers in manors formerly controlled by members of the Taira faction, and in 1192 he took for himself only the title of *shogun*, a term perhaps best translated as "generalissimo." Thus, although Yoritomo personally commanded the only strong military force in all Japan, he was content to permit the continuation of the fiction that an emperor and his civil government ruled the land and that he himself was merely the commander of the emperor's army. Yoritomo and his men, however, constituted the only effective central government Japan possessed, and Kamakura be-

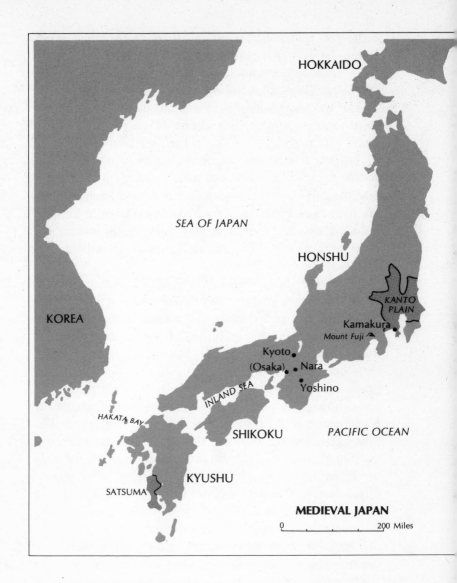

HOKKAIDO

SEA OF JAPAN

HONSHU

KOREA

KANTO
PLAIN

Kamakura
Mount Fuji

Kyoto
(Osaka) Nara
Yoshino

INLAND SEA

HAKATA BAY

SHIKOKU

PACIFIC OCEAN

SATSUMA

KYUSHU

MEDIEVAL JAPAN

0   200 Miles

came the true political capital. They had in fact established Japan's first military dictatorship, or *shogunate*. The Japanese term for this form of military rule is very revealing. They call it *bakufu* or "tent government."

The Kamakura shogunate was not in theory or in outward form a national government. It was merely a simple organization designed to control the relatively small band of knights who owed personal allegiance to the Minamoto. It was, in fact, nothing more than a "family government"—not of a single clan as had been customary in ancient times, but of a loose association of knights, held together in some cases by family bonds, but for the most part only by long-standing ties of friendship and loyalty.

Under the shogun, three small offices were created as the chief organs of this "family government"—an office to watch over and control the affairs of the individual knight members of the clique, an administrative board, and a final court of appeal. This court handed down legal decisions based upon the customary law which had gradually developed among the provincial warrior aristocrats during the preceding two centuries and which the Kamakura administration issued in codified form. The provincial organization of this government was even simpler than its central administration. It consisted only of the individual knights themselves, who as "stewards" (*jito*) freely managed their individual estates as each saw best, but who were organized for defense purposes under a "constable" (*shugo*) in each province.

The Minamoto government was designed merely to control the private affairs of the clique, but by controlling the members of this group, who had now been spread throughout the land as the key class of estate managers and local knights, the Kamakura shogunate effectively controlled all classes of society and therefore the whole nation. Its member knights ruled the peasants, who were serfs on their estates, and they also controlled the purse strings of the court aristocracy, which derived its income from these same estates. Although the Kamakura regime maintained the fiction of being a private organization, it had become the most effective central government Japan had yet known; and people of all classes, realizing that Kamakura alone had the power to enforce its decisions, looked there rather than to the emperor's court for leadership.

An ambitious retired emperor in 1221 dared challenge this indirect and unannounced control of national life by Kamakura, but found himself overwhelmed by the Minamoto cohorts. The incident revealed conclusively that imperial rule was at an end. The imperial family and the noble families around it continued to receive their income from the estates they nominally owned, but as far as political realities were concerned, the emperor and his court had become anachronistic survivals of an earlier age, with no administrative role in the new political order. Hereditary authority, however, continued to be so important in Japan that the emperors remained the unquestioned source of all political legitimacy, and the Kamakura shoguns never claimed to have any authority other than the military powers theoretically delegated to them by the emperors. This role as the fountainhead of legitimacy, together with the continuing religious functions of the emperors, kept alive the fiction of imperial rule during the next six centuries until new conditions brought the imperial family back to the center of the political stage in the nineteenth century.

The Kamakura shogunate naturally centered around the shogun, the leader of the clique, and in theory the only unifying force was the personal loyalty of each individual knight to him. In practice, however, the person of the shogun soon became unimportant, and the system proved to have amazing strength of itself. Yoritomo, the first shogun, jealously rid himself of a younger brother, who had been the chief general in the defeat of the Taira, and also did away with other leading members of his family. After Yoritomo's death in 1199, factional strife among his descendants, fostered by his wife's relatives, the Hojo family, which happened to be of Taira descent, soon led to the elimination of his heirs. In 1219 an assassination ended the main Minamoto line, and thereafter the Hojo, contenting themselves in typical Japanese fashion with the title of "regent," ruled through puppet shoguns, first chosen from the Fujiwara family and then from the imperial family.

Thus, one finds in thirteenth-century Japan an emperor who was a mere puppet in the hands of a retired emperor and of a great court family, the Fujiwara, who together controlled a government which was in fact merely a sham government, completely dominated by the private government of the shogun—who in turn was a puppet in the hands of a Hojo regent. The man behind the throne had become a series of men, each one in turn controlled by the man behind him.

The successive triumphs of the Taira and Minamoto marked the commencement of eight centuries of unbroken rule by warrior aristocrats. During this long period, Japanese political institutions, social organization, and value systems went through an evolution closely parallel to the whole feudal and early postfeudal experience of Western Europe. In both cases, feudalism seems to have resulted from a special blend between concepts of centralized imperial rule and native traditions of tribal organization and personalized bonds of loyalty. In Europe, these two ingredients came from the Roman Empire and the Germanic tribal background of the peoples of Northern Europe; in Japan, they came from T'ang China and the *uji* form of organization of primitive Japan. Apparently this blend is an unusual one in world history, because Japan affords the only close and fully developed parallel to Western feudalism.

Two basic differences in the feudal experiences of Europe and Japan, however, should be noted. Perhaps because of Japan's isolation and the consequent lack of sustained military pressure from abroad, the rate of evolution in Japanese feudal institutions seems to have been slower than in the West. The Kamakura system was at most only protofeudal, existing as it were within the shell of the older imperial system and tolerating the continuance of a pattern of estate ownership that derived from the old centralized state. It was not until the late fifteenth century that the shell was entirely destroyed and Japanese political institutions and land ownership came to approximate closely those of the period of high feudalism of twelfth-century Europe. High feudalism proved as unstable in Japan as in Europe, but a basically feudal framework was maintained in Japan until the midnineteenth century, long after it had been abandoned in the more internationally competitive society of Europe.

The other difference is that European feudalism, derived from the legal concepts of Rome, stressed legal rights and obligations, that is, a contractual relationship between those bound together by personalized feudal ties. Such legal ideas were not entirely absent in feudal Japan, but they were overshadowed by the Chinese emphasis on ethics over law. In imperial China, good government was considered to be basically a moral problem, and the ethical uprightness of the scholar-bureaucrat was valued over the mechanical rule of law. This may be why personal feudal obligations in Japan were conceived in moral rather than legal terms, and both authority and loyalty became absolute. There was thus no room for the development of the concepts of inalienable rights, shared authority, and representative bodies, which grew in postfeudal times in the West into the institutions of democracy.

Because of the long duration of feudal rule in Japan, it is small wonder that the impress of feudalism lies heavily upon modern Japan. It can be seen in the strong military traditions of the Japanese in the late nineteenth century, in their unconscious assumption as late as the 1930s that military men were somehow less selfish and more honest than civilians and therefore had a right to political authority, and even today in the pervasive patterns of boss-client or master-disciple relationships throughout Japanese society.

The rise of the provincial warrior class to a position of dominance in twelfth-century Japan produced a new culture as well as a new political system. The literature and art of the tenth and eleventh centuries had been an expression of the culture of a narrow court society. The new culture naturally inherited much from this glorious period, but the most significant and, in time, dominant elements in it came from the warrior class of the provinces. The knight brought with him his own attitudes and values. In contrast to the effete courtier at Kyoto, he gloried in a life of warfare, in the Spartan virtues, and in the ascetic practices of self-discipline and physical and mental toughening. He made a cult of his sword, a cult still kept alive as late as World War II by Japanese officers who proudly lugged long, cumbersome curved swords into the jungles of Southeast Asia. The warrior reemphasized personal loyalties and the importance of family ties. His two outstanding virtues, Spartan indifference to suffering or even death and a great capacity for unswerving personal loyalty, became widespread characteristics among the Japanese people as a whole.

The warrior's taste in literature produced a whole new type of prose writing—the heroic tale of warfare, quite different from the diaries and novels of the court ladies. These martial accounts, such as the *Heike monogatari* (*The Tale of the Taira Family*), usually centered around the conflicts between the Taira and Minamoto bands, which became the central themes of much of later Japanese literature. Warrior tastes may also have contributed to the development during the eleventh to thirteenth centuries of a marvelous technique of scroll painting. These picture scrolls portray, with a magnificent sweep of motion but also with great accuracy of detail, the famous battles of the period, the lives of Buddhist saints, the histories of monasteries, and even amusing Disney-like fantasies about animals, attributed to a Buddhist monk called Toba Sojo. The finest of all the battle scrolls, "The Burning of the Sanjo Palace," illustrating an incident in the winter war of 1159–1160, happens to be in the Museum of Fine Arts in Boston. The thirteenth century was also notable for a great renaissance in the field of Buddhist sculpture that makes it, together with the seventh and eighth centuries, the twin high points in the history of Japanese sculpture.

A great transformation of Buddhism also took place at this time, and the new currents became the mainstream of Buddhism as it has existed in Japan ever since. This religious development was unquestionably connected with the increasing spread of culture and knowledge to classes outside the old court aristocracy—to the provincial gentry, the townspeople, and even to the peasantry; and the rapid triumph of the new Buddhism over older forms of the religion was certainly in part the result of the rise of new classes to prominence in national life. The Buddhist awakening of early feudal times was also partly the outgrowth of new influences from China, as contacts with the continent, fostered by a growing international trade in East Asian waters, became more frequent. Buddhist monasteries themselves led in sponsoring trading ventures to China with a view to obtaining funds for the erection of new buildings. Many fine thirteenth- and fourteenth-century temples were to some extent paid for by such commercial activities, as was the beautiful *Daibutsu*, or "Great Buddha," at Kamakura, erected in the second half of the thirteenth century and said to be still the largest bronze statue in the world.

Buddhism had come to China as a highly intellectualized philosophy with rich and colorful religious ceremonials that appealed to the upper classes, but during the T'ang and post-T'ang periods, a growing emphasis on the less austere concepts of Buddhism led to a general philosophic reorientation and popularization that made it increasingly a religion of the people. Early Indian Buddhism stressed the evil and vanity of human existence. It held out little hope for improving man's lot in this world, but centered its interest primarily on "release from the cycle of rebirth." The Buddhists accepted the common Indian belief that the individual is born again and again into this world. He may be born into a better state or a worse one, depending on the sort of life he lives in each successive rebirth. This process goes on endlessly unless the individual realizes that his own desire for things that cannot really satisfy him brings about his repeated rebirths into a painful existence; the only way to escape "the cycle of rebirth" is to overcome all desire. One who has done this has attained *nirvana*, a state of mind in which he is above life's trials and his individual ego has lost its identity in the cosmos, much as a single drop of water loses its identity in the vastness of the ocean.

Such an attitude toward the normal course of human life seemed pessimistic to the Chinese and other East Asian peoples, who have tended to focus their chief interest on the perfection of the family, society, and the state. When Buddhism first came to China, the beautiful art, impressive literature, colorful ceremonies, broad learning, and peaceful monastic life, which had by that time become integral parts of the religion, recommended it to the Chinese as much, if not more, than the type of philosophy embodied in original Buddhism. In fact, Buddhism could have had no broad philosophic appeal to the masses in China and Japan until a great reorientation of its ideas had taken place.

Perhaps the most startling development in this reorientation was the change in the concept of *nirvana* itself. For the common believer, it became a Paradise where the individual soul went for an afterlife of bliss, while innumerable hells, rivaling Dante's creations, became the deserts of the wicked. Arguing that the degenerate age in which they lived made enlightenment and salvation by one's own efforts impossible, popular preachers of the time put forth the doctrine that salvation now was possible only by the grace of another—that is, through the intervention of one of the host of gods and demigods with which the Buddhist pantheon had become peopled. Belief, not philosophic enlightenment or exemplary conduct, was the way to salvation, and calling on the name of Buddha became the most meaningful act of faith.

These doctrines found vigorous expression in Japan in the tenth and eleventh centuries and eventually resulted in the development of new sects of Japanese Buddhism. These were quite different from the sects established in Japan in the eighth and ninth centuries, which had emphasized for the most part fine points of theology and metaphysics. In particular, the two great sects introduced shortly after the founding of the capital at Kyoto had come to typify an empty formalism. These were the *Shingon* ("True Word") sect, and the *Tendai* sect, named after a Buddhist center in China, Mt. T'ien-t'ai, and itself centered at a great monastery on Mt. Hiei overlooking the capital. These two sects stressed magical incantations, elaborate pictorial representations of Buddhist theology, and magnificent ceremonies. All this was dear to the hearts of the court aristocrats, but it had little appeal to the simple folk in the provinces.

The new Japanese sects grew out of Tendai, which had an all-embracing philosophy, including the popular concept of salvation through faith. The first was founded by the monk Honen in 1175. It quite understandably took the name of Pure Land sect (*Jodoshu*), for the Pure Land was a term for Paradise. In true reforming fashion, Shinran, one of the disciples of Honen, split away from his teacher, and in 1224 founded the True Pure Land sect, or more simply the True sect (*Shinshu*). This sect in time outstripped in popularity all other

Japanese Buddhist churches. Even today it is the largest traditional Buddhist group within Japan and one of the few with a significant missionary movement abroad. Both these Pure Land sects were definitely expressions of the religious feelings of the lower classes, which were for the first time assuming importance in the intellectual life of the nation. They taught a simpler way to salvation for less sophisticated minds, and from the start they won much of their strength by direct street-corner preaching to the poor.

Shinran showed his opposition to the intellectual aristocracy of the earlier monastic sects by at first forbidding the founding of monasteries, and he preached the "equality of all in Buddhism." In an effort to bring the clergy closer to the people and nearer everyday life, he permitted his priests to marry, a custom which gradually spread to most types of clergy in all sects. One of Shinran's successors started a movement to translate into the Japanese language some of the Buddhist scriptures, which had been transmitted to Japan in classical and often very difficult Chinese. This same priest also founded discussion groups among lay believers which evolved into large and powerful lay congregations.

These congregations were perhaps the chief organs of intellectual life for the lower classes during the early feudal period. In time some even became the agencies through which the people asserted themselves politically. Congregations of the True Pure Land sect killed their feudal leaders in two west coast provinces in 1488 and thereafter controlled this area themselves. During the sixteenth century the great temple-castle of the sect, located in the rising commercial city of Osaka, was able to defy siege by the strongest feudal lord in Japan for a period of ten years.

Side by side with the two Pure Land sects there soon developed a third popular sect, founded in 1253 by the priest Nichiren and usually known by his name. Basically much like the other two, it relied even more on street-corner preaching, but differed radically from them in its religious fanaticism, which was the legacy of its dynamic but bellicose founder. Nichiren, in sharp contrast to the tolerant and pacifistic spirit which Buddhism had normally shown, was an intolerant fighting man of religion who openly attacked other Buddhist sects as leading men only to damnation. His sect became a fighting church that often engaged in open warfare with the members of other sects during the turbulent feudal period. Nichiren, again in contrast to the dominant international spirit of Buddhism, was himself a nationalist, a forerunner of the nationalists of modern times. To him, Japan was the land of the gods and the center of the universe, and Japanese Buddhism was the only true Buddhism. It is significant that the most dynamic new religious movement in contemporary Japan, the Soka Gakkai, is theologically an offshoot of the Nichiren sect.

One cannot fail to be struck by the many parallels between medieval Japanese Buddhism and European Christianity in medieval and early modern times. In fact, in many ways Japanese Buddhism had come to resemble Christianity more than original Buddhism. In contrast to the earlier emphasis on the extinction of personal identity through individual effort, it stressed a personal afterlife in Paradise achieved through faith in another's grace. The early feudal religious reformers also resembled to a surprising degree the Protestant reformers of Europe in their translations of the scriptures, their creation of lay congregations, their marriage of the clergy, their militant sectarianism, and their nascent nationalism.

While the lower classes were turning to the popular Buddhist sects for religious and intellectual expression, the warrior class found a different answer to its religious and philosophic needs in still another Buddhist sect brought to Japan in the late twelfth and early thirteenth centuries by Japanese monks returning to their homeland from study in China. This sect was known as Zen, a word meaning "meditation," and it derived from a long tradition in both India and China. In China it had also drawn from a native form of nature mysticism known as Taoism. In fact, Zen was in many ways as much a Taoist reaction to Buddhism as it was an authentic offshoot of the original Indian religion.

In Zen, the emphasis was on being in harmony with the cosmos—on achieving oneness with nature. Zen was antischolastic and antirational. Its adherents sought sudden intuitive insight as a result of extreme physical discipline and mental concentration, rather than wisdom through book learning or through logical thought. As a means of training in Zen, the master would pose a seemingly trivial or irrational problem, such as the nature of the sound caused by a clapping motion made with only one hand instead of with two. The student would meditate upon this problem for days, but any answer describing the nature of sound or the reasons for the absence of sound would not be tolerated by the master. The train of meditation started by this problem was intended to result in a flash of sudden enlightenment regarding the nature of the Buddha, the oneness of the universe, or other problems equally profound.

The antischolasticism, the mental discipline, still more the strict physical discipline of the adherents of Zen, which kept their lives very close to nature, all appealed to the warrior class, with its predilection for the Spartan life. Zen gave the military men of feudal Japan a philosophical foundation on which to base their lives. And with their support, its tenets and outlook came to have wide influence and great prestige. Zen contributed much to the development of a strength of character which typified the warrior of feudal Japan; and it is at least one of the sources of the strong sense of discipline and inner toughness which is widely characteristic of the Japanese today.

5 ❋ GROWTH AND CHANGE IN THE FEUDAL SYSTEM

The Kamakura system, however well it worked at first, was peculiarly susceptible to the ravages of time and change. It was effective as long as its member knights remained a small and well-knit group, loyal to each other, but as the generations passed, loyalties based on family friendships and comradeship in half-forgotten campaigns wore thin. Scattered as they now were throughout the estates of the whole land, the descendants of the old band of knights from the Kanto region who had won control over Japan in 1185 felt less and less the oneness of spirit of the original clique or the old sense of personal loyalty to Kamakura. Another factor in the dissolution of the clique was its growth in numbers. With each generation, the members increased, but the number of positions as estate managers could not grow correspondingly. The natural tendency was for each knight to divide his income from the estate he managed among all his sons. As a result of this process, many a knight in the latter part of the thirteenth century received so small an income that he had difficulty in maintaining his status

as a mounted warrior, able to answer the call of Kamakura equipped with horse, armor, and weapons.

Despite these weaknesses, the system lasted a century
and a half. During this time it withstood the most
serious threat of aggression from abroad that Japan was
to experience before the twentieth century: the attempted Mongol invasions of 1274 and 1281. The Mongols, a nomadic people of the steppe lands north of
China, conquered in the first half of the thirteenth
century all of Central Asia, southern Russia, and much
of the Near East, and their armies penetrated to Silesia
and through Hungary to the Adriatic Sea. At the eastern
end of this vast empire, they completed the subjugation
of Korea in 1259 and crushed the last organized resistance in China itself in 1276. In the East, only Japan
remained free of their rule, and the Mongol emperor
Kublai Khan, probably looking for more worlds to conquer, sent emissaries to Japan demanding the capitula-
tion of the island kingdom. The terrified courtiers in
Kyoto were ready to accede, but the warriors of Kamakura refused, and made their stand unmistakably clear
by beheading some of the emissaries.

Such a direct affront could not go unpunished, and in
1274 a strong Mongol force set out on Korean ships to
subdue Japan. Certain small islands were seized and a
landing was made at Hakata Bay near the modern city of
Fukuoka in northern Kyushu. Before any decisive en-
gagement had been fought, however, the Mongols decided to withdraw their fleet to the continent because
of the threat of inclement weather. That they would
return was a foregone conclusion. For the next several
years Kamakura kept many of its knights from the western part of the country on guard in northern Kyushu
and busy constructing a wall around Hakata Bay to con-

tain the vaunted Mongol cavalry in the event of a second landing.

The Mongols came again in 1281, this time with a great joint armada of Korean and Chinese ships, and again a landing was made at Hakata Bay. The invading forces numbered some 150,000 men, the greatest overseas expedition the world had as yet seen. The Mongols were accustomed to large-scale cavalry tactics, which had met no match anywhere in the world, and they had superior weapons at their disposal, such as the gunpowder bomb hurled by a catapult. Against this overwhelming force, the Japanese had a mere handful of knights, accustomed only to single combat. But the Mongols were slowed by the wall the Japanese had built and by the attacks of smaller, more mobile Japanese boats in the narrow waters of the bay. Before they could deploy their full forces ashore, a typhoon descended upon the fleet and destroyed it, bringing the invasion to a disastrous conclusion. To the Japanese, the typhoon was the *kamikaze*, the "divine wind," protecting the land of the gods from foreign invaders. The incident has of course loomed large in Japanese historical tradition, and it contributed to an irrational conviction on the part of many Japanese that their land was sacred and inviolable.

The danger was past, but dissatisfaction and unrest on the part of the warrior class of western Japan remained as an aftermath of the invasions. Many knights had become impoverished during the long months and years away from home in the service of Kamakura, and there were no spoils to divide among the victors. The wavering loyalty of the knights had suffered a serious blow; yet the Kamakura system was strong enough to survive another half century.

The final blow came from a new and surprising source,

an emperor who is known by his posthumous name of Go-Daigo (or Daigo II). This emperor was a historical misfit who had the antiquated idea that the imperial line should really rule. Gathering a force of discontented warriors from the capital region and local monastery estates, he led a revolt against Kamakura in the year 1331. The revolt in itself would have meant little if the whole Kamakura system had not been ripe for dissolution. The warriors of western Japan for the most part declared for the imperial cause, and Ashikaga Takauji, the general sent from eastern Japan to subdue the uprising, suddenly switched sides in 1333. A second force was raised in the Kanto region, but this time the general in command did not even march on Kyoto. Instead he seized Kamakura itself, destroyed the Hojo family, and thus brought to an end a century and a half of centralized rule.

Go-Daigo, who naively assumed that the way was now open for the resumption of imperial rule as it had existed five or six centuries earlier, was in for a rude awakening. Ashikaga Takauji was a realist who knew where power lay, and he soon deserted the emperor, driving him from Kyoto in 1336 and placing a member of a collateral line of the imperial family on the throne. Go-Daigo and his followers withdrew to the mountain fastnesses south of Nara and set up a rival imperial court at a place called Yoshino. From this vantage point they and their successors continued the struggle against the Ashikaga family for almost sixty years, but in 1392 they were finally induced to give up and were lured back to Kyoto by the promise that Go-Daigo's line would alternate on the throne with the line set up by Takauji. In view of the Ashikaga family's earlier record of treachery, it is not surprising that it did not live up to this agreement. No member of Go-Daigo's line ever sat on the throne again, and it faded into obscurity.

Go-Daigo had failed completely in his fantastic attempt to restore imperial rule in feudal Japan, but Ashikaga Takauji was little more successful in his attempt to re-create the unity of Kamakura. He had himself appointed shogun in 1338, and his descendants retained this title until 1573, but the Ashikaga shogunate never exercised effective rule over the whole land, as Kamakura had. After the third shogun, Yoshimitsu, forced the surrender of Go-Daigo's successors in 1392, there was a brief period of relative peace and national unity, but Ashikaga power soon declined, and by 1467 warfare had become endemic throughout the country. During the latter half of the Ashikaga shogunate (which is usually called the Muromachi period after the place of residence of the shogun in Kyoto), the Ashikaga, like the emperors and the Fujiwara before them, lost all semblance of political power and became mere symbols of authority.

The fourteenth and fifteenth centuries present a picture of increasing political disruption and confusion, as all central control slowly disintegrated. The basic cause for this growing political disunity was the size of the warrior class, which had become so numerous that a united government based simply on ties of personal loyalty was no longer possible. New forms of political organization had to develop before unity could be restored, but the process was slow. The first step actually was the creation of new feudal units smaller than the old nationwide warrior clique. Certain provincial "constables," or other warriors who for one reason or another had won a strong local following, gradually assumed the role of incipient feudal lords in the late Kamakura period. In the wars that marked the end of the Kamakura regime, it became evident that the individual knights felt a greater sense of loyalty to local leaders of this type than to the Hojo or their puppet shogun.

Through the fourteenth and fifteenth centuries, these local lords became increasingly dominant. They had started with a sort of *primus inter pares* status as merely the appointed or popularly recognized captains over their fellow knights, but gradually they established themselves as true territorial lords, in full control of clearly defined areas and demanding absolute loyalty from the lesser military families within their domains. By the sixteenth century they had fully transformed themselves into the territorial lords called *daimyo* who proved to be the central figures of later Japanese feudalism. As these feudal lords rose to power, the individual knights sank in status. One reason for this basic change was that the old estates gradually lost their identity in the domains of the daimyo, and the position of estate manager became a thing of the past. Then too, large bodies of foot soldiers began to replace the individual knight as the backbone of the fighting forces of Japan. Thus the knight lost his special place both as a military man and as a key figure in the political and economic order.

Some descendants of the old warrior families themselves became daimyo. Others became part of a new petty aristocracy of military and administrative officials serving in the domains of the daimyo and supported by tracts of land held as subfiefs under the daimyo or, as increasingly became the case, by fixed salaries assigned from the daimyo's treasury. But there was no longer a clear-cut line between these knights as fighting men and the peasantry, who were as capable of serving as foot soldiers as the best of the warrior class. For this reason, the congregations of the True Pure Land sect could challenge the supremacy of the feudal leaders. Peasants in time of war were now soldiers, and in the fifteenth and sixteenth centuries many men of humble origin pushed their way into the upper ranks of the new feudal aristocracy, while many members of the old warrior class sank to the status of peasants.

The gradual disappearance of the estates into the domains of the daimyo was an unfortunate development for the imperial family and the old court aristocracy in Kyoto, who for centuries had derived their income from these estates. Revenues from this source had long been dwindling, and by the late fifteenth century they ceased altogether. During the next century the imperial line, the various branches of the Fujiwara, and the other old court families eked out a miserable and precarious existence; they managed to survive, earning their living by serving as patrons of trade and manufacturing guilds in Kyoto and by exploiting the few arts and skills permitted them by aristocratic tradition. One emperor was even reduced to selling his calligraphy, writing out in his beautiful hand a poem or motto requested by some patron and receiving in exchange a small gift. Lack of funds to pay for proper funeral services or coronation ceremonies forced the imperial family to get along without a properly invested emperor during three different periods in the sixteenth century. The fortunes of the imperial line had indeed sunk low; only the strong Japanese sense of hereditary authority kept it and its satellite court aristocracy from disappearing entirely.

The transformation of political institutions and society that took place during the Ashikaga period was not achieved without great turmoil. It was a time of almost incessant warfare, as the descendants of the Kamakura knights struggled with one another for local leadership and then for broader territorial supremacy. Great families rose and fell in a bewildering pattern reminiscent of the endless warfare of feudal Europe. The political chaos and the sad state of the imperial court have left behind a traditional picture of these two and a half centuries as a dark age in Japanese history. But this is far from correct, for the political confusion was but a sign of institutional and social growth, and despite the turmoil, the Japanese as a whole were making great strides forward culturally and economically.

With the financial eclipse of the court aristocracy, cultural leadership in the capital city of Kyoto naturally passed to the shogun's court. In fact, some of the Ashikaga shoguns are far better known to history as patrons of the arts than as political leaders. Gathering about them some of the finest artists and literary men of the day, they at times presided over a culturally brilliant if politically powerless court. As was to be expected in this turbulent age, the major monasteries became more than ever the chief havens of learning and the centers of creative art, and many of the greatest artists and men of letters were Buddhist monks. Zen monks in particular dominated the cultural life of the time not only because they received official patronage, but because they were in closer contact with China than any other group and were consequently the first to learn of new cultural trends on the continent. Actually, the predominantly Zen culture of the Ashikaga period was a rich blending of the native culture with many new elements from the continent.

Buddhist monks played an important role in the development at this time of Japan's first true dramatic form, the so-called Nō drama. A major purpose of Nō was to teach Buddhist concepts. Since it had evolved originally from religious dances, symbolic dances were one of its most important features. But perhaps the greatest merit of the Nō was the fine poetic recitations chanted by the actors and an accompanying chorus. The texts of the Nō drama still remain one of the great literary expressions of the Japanese people, and a small band of devotees even today keeps the Nō alive as a highly stylized dramatic form.

Zen monks, despite their antischolastic traditions, led in making pure literary Chinese once again into an important literary medium. They also played a part in the introduction from China of fresh architectural influences, which resulted in significant new styles. The Zen culture of the Ashikaga period, however, found its fullest expression in painting. Zen monks, living simple lives close to nature, took with enthusiasm to the Chinese style of monochrome landscape painting, which had reached an apogee of artistic excellence in the Sung period (960–1279). The work of Japanese painter-monks, such as Sesshu (1420–1506), often rivaled the skill and depth of feeling of the Chinese masters.

The medieval Zen monks also brought from China three other arts which in time became so characteristic of Japanese culture that they are now considered to be typically Japanese. One was flower arrangement, which started with the placing of floral offerings before representations of Buddhist deities, but eventually became a fine art which is now part of the training of every well-bred Japanese girl. The second was landscape gardening, in which, in contrast to the formal, geometric gardens of the West, the Ashikaga masters tried to create in a restricted space a small replica of the mountains, forests, and waters of nature itself, sometimes in close verisimilitude but sometimes only symbolically, as in the rock garden of the Ryoanji in Kyoto, which is composed only of rocks and sand. (The works of these Ashikaga masters and their successors in the seventeenth century have made Kyoto the world Mecca of landscape gardening.) The third was the tea ceremony, a rite in which a beautiful but simple setting; a few fine pieces of old pottery; a slow, formalized, extremely graceful ritual for preparing and serving the tea; and a spirit of complete tranquillity all combined to express the love of beauty, the devotion to simplicity, and the search for spiritual calm which characterized the best of Zen.

All three of these arts, as well as monochrome landscape painting, shared a common esthetic idiom. They were close to nature and rejected artificial, man-made patterns of regularity; they showed a deep love of simplicity; and they displayed a disciplined cultivation of the essence—the handful of blossoms or branches in a flower arrangement, the simple instruments and spare movements of the tea ceremony, the restricted space and sometimes austere design of the gardens, the few but bold lines of paintings that suggested sweeping landscapes and vast cosmic powers. It was an esthetics which well complemented the emphasis on discipline and self-cultivation that the feudal Japanese had derived from Zen and the warrior ethos. It was also an esthetics peculiarly suited to the relative simplicity and poverty of medieval Japan. It is interesting that it has proved in recent years to have worldwide appeal in our own more complex and affluent age.

Increased trade contacts with the continent, which had

brought many new cultural impulses from China, also served as an impetus to an unprecedented and rapid expansion of the Japanese economy. Another stimulus may have been the decline and disappearance of the estates. As long as these had existed, they tended to be self-contained economic units, but their going allowed a wider exchange of goods and therefore a greater specialization in production by localities or by groups within each locality. The multiple political authorities of a feudal society, each ready to impose restrictions and fees on trade, remained a problem. To get around this obstacle, merchants dealing in certain commodities and artisans producing certain manufactured goods tended to form guilds which could collectively bargain with the feudal authorities for fixed fees and monopoly rights that would permit their economic endeavors to prosper.

Under these conditions, trade and manufacture expanded steadily, and centers of paper-making, metalworking, weaving, and the like grew up all over the country. Small marketplaces developed into little trading towns. Kyoto remained the largest city of Japan, but gradually a rival city of purely commercial and industrial origin grew up at the eastern end of the Inland Sea. This town, later to be called Osaka, was until the late sixteenth century a type of free city outside the domains of the feudal lords and dominated only by the local merchants and the great temple-castle of the True Pure Land sect.

The real measure of the economic growth of Japan during the feudal period is perhaps best seen in foreign trade. There had been some trade with the continent ever since Prince Shotoku sent the first official embassy to China, but overseas trade began to assume significant proportions only in the late twelfth century. From that time on, it grew steadily until by the fifteenth and sixteenth centuries it was a large factor in the economic life of Japan. The Japanese imported from the continent tropical products, which had originally come from Southeast Asia or even from India, and manufactured goods from China, such as silks, porcelains, books, manuscripts, paintings, and copper cash. The last loomed largest in bulk and value, because from the thirteenth century on, money increasingly replaced rice and cloth as the chief medium for exchange in Japan, and the Japanese depended almost entirely on China as the source for their currency. This was because an effort in the eighth century to mint Chinese-type coins in Japan had proved economically premature and had soon been abandoned, and there was now no strong central authority able to produce a national coinage.

In the early feudal period, Japanese exports were limited for the most part to raw materials, such as sulphur, lumber, pearls, gold, mercury, and mother of pearl. However, by the fifteenth and sixteenth centuries Japan herself was exporting large quantities of manufactured goods to China and other countries. Chief among these were swords and painted folding fans and screens. Folding fans and screens apparently were inventions of either the Koreans or the Japanese and were highly prized in China. The curved swords of medieval Japan, made of the finest laminated steel and superior even to the famous blades of Damascus or Toledo, were in great demand throughout East Asia and were exported by the thousands.

In the early days, the Koreans were the chief mariners and traders in the waters between Japan and the continent, but slowly the Japanese themselves took to the sea. In the late eleventh century, Japanese traders were crossing to Korea; in the twelfth, some were venturing as far as China; and by the fourteenth and fifteenth centuries, they were beginning to dominate the shipping and commerce of the whole East China Sea. Various groups in Japan participated in this lucrative trade with the continent. As mentioned above, many Buddhist monasteries sponsored trading ventures in order to raise funds, as did some of the feudal lords, including the Ashikaga themselves. In fact, the Ashikaga, in order to secure some of the profits of this trade for their shaky regime, accepted the Chinese theory that international trade was simply the bringing of tribute to the Chinese court by barbarian peoples and the beneficent bestowal of gifts upon the barbarians by the court in return. To fit this pattern, some of the Ashikaga shoguns, with complete disregard for the theory of imperial rule, permitted themselves to be invested as "Kings of Japan" by the emperors of the Ming dynasty of China, and then sold credentials to private Japanese traders to give them legal and official status in their trading ventures in China.

Despite the interest in foreign trade on the part of the monasteries and the shogun in central Japan, the leadership in overseas ventures in time fell to the feudal lords, warriors, and merchants of western Japan, who merged to form a class of adventurous and hardy mariners. Like their counterparts in Europe, these men of the sea were primarily traders, but they were not averse to piracy when opportunity offered. Credentials from the Ashikaga or trading permits from the Chinese court meant little to them. Already in the thirteenth century, piratical acts by Japanese warrior-merchants had become frequent in Korean waters, and during the fourteenth century, Japanese pirates became a menace to the very existence of the kingdom of Korea. Emboldened by their successes in Korean waters, they shifted their activities more and more to the coast of China. As the Ming dynasty declined in the sixteenth and early seventeenth centuries, the Japanese pirates who ravaged the great coastal cities of China almost at will contributed greatly to the final collapse of the dynasty after 1644.

The so-called Japanese pirates of the sixteenth century were not always pirates, however, nor were they always Japanese. Many Chinese joined them in preying on the coastal trade and cities of China. One of the most important elements in this mixed group of Chinese and Japanese was furnished by the natives of Okinawa and the other Ryukyu Islands. Closely related to the Japanese and speaking a variant form of the language, they owed a dual allegiance in the seventeenth century to China and to the great Shimazu domain of Satsuma in southern Kyushu.

When European merchant-adventurers rounded the Malay Peninsula and entered East Asian waters early in the sixteenth century, they found the seas dominated more by Japanese than by Chinese. In the course of the century, thousands of Japanese established themselves as traders and adventurers in the towns and colonies of Southeast Asia; and the Spanish and Portuguese, recognizing the martial traditions and fine fighting qualities of the Japanese, frequently employed them as mercenaries in their battles. In a typical colonial city like Manila, the Japanese community grew large and strong, and in the early seventeenth century, Japanese adventurers were influential enough at the Siamese capital to engineer a successful revolution which put a friendly faction in power.

During the "dark ages" of political confusion in Japan, the people had developed industrially to a point where they equaled or even excelled their Chinese teachers in many fields of manufacturing. Despite the feudal political framework, they had built up a far stronger commercial system than they had achieved in previous ages; and in a burst of new physical power and vitality, their warrior-traders had come to dominate the waters of East Asia. Japan had entered into feudalism in the twelfth century a small, weak, and economically backward land on the fringes of the civilized world. It emerged in the sixteenth century from a prolonged period of feudal anarchy an economically advanced nation, able in many ways to compete on terms of equality with the newly encountered peoples of Europe and even with the Chinese.

6 ✤ THE REESTABLISHMENT OF
NATIONAL UNITY

The vigorous Japan of the early sixteenth century still showed no signs of re-creating an effective central government, but the foundation for a new form of political unity had been laid. This foundation consisted of the daimyo domains, into which almost all of Japan was now divided. Since each domain was an effective political unit in itself, national unity could be achieved simply by establishing some form of association or accepted leadership among the daimyo.

The realms of the daimyo varied greatly in size, but they tended to be compact, well-defined political units, perhaps subordinate to some other domain, but in any case entirely independent of the emperor or shogun. The daimyo himself was a paternalistic but absolute ruler within his own realm. Aiding him was a class of officials and military officers, who formed the little court at the central castle of the daimyo and lived on the hereditary lands or salaries he assigned them. Because of their military heritage and the conditions of the age, most of the daimyo were intent upon developing the military strength of their domains. Some of the more powerful, who ruled over several provinces, built up efficient fighting machines, with the peasantry as the backbone of the economic life of the realm and the reservoir for military manpower, with the warrior aristocracy furnishing administrators for the government and officers for the army, and with the merchants providing a transport corps in time of war.

The natural tendency was for the larger and stronger domains to swallow up or win dominance over weaker neighbors. This process was probably hastened in the second half of the sixteenth century by the introduction of firearms from Europe and their widespread use in battle. The result was the creation before the end of the century of a single paramount power in Japan. The first great figure in the reunification of the country was Oda Nobunaga, a daimyo who ruled over three provinces around the modern city of Nagoya east of Kyoto. In 1568 he seized control over Kyoto and its vestigial imperial and shogunal courts, and then proceeded to consolidate his power over the central part of Japan by breaking the military might of the Tendai stronghold on Mt. Hiei and of the other powerful central monasteries, and by capturing the great temple-castle of the True Pure Land sect in Osaka after a ten-year siege. But Nobunaga never achieved his goal of winning hegemony over all Japan. His career was cut short when a treacherous vassal murdered him in 1582.

Nobunaga's place as undisputed ruler over central Japan was soon assumed by his ablest general, Hideyoshi, a man of lowly birth who had risen to power by sheer ability. He quickly established his own supremacy over Nobunaga's remaining vassals, and he reconstructed the great castle at Osaka as the seat of his military government. He also gave evidence of a reviving interest in the imperial court by taking the old Fujiwara post of chancellor (*kampaku*) and building for himself a palace and castle in the environs of Kyoto. In 1587 Hideyoshi forced the submission of the great Shimazu domain of Satsuma in southern Kyushu and thereby won control over all western Japan. Three years later, all of eastern and northern Japan submitted to him after he had eliminated the chief daimyo realm in the Kanto area. The restoration of political unity in Japan had at last been completed, and peace came to the land suddenly after more than a hundred years of incessant civil war.

Hideyoshi found himself in control of a superabundance of professional soldiers who knew nothing but warfare. Possibly in order to drain off some of their excess fighting spirit, and probably because he himself, like many successful generals before him, fell victim to the world conqueror complex, Hideyoshi decided to embark on a program of conquest, which for him meant the subjugation of China. To do this he needed passage through Korea, and when the Koreans refused, he invaded the peninsula in 1592 with a force of 160,000 men. The Japanese armies rapidly overran almost all of Korea, but were eventually checked when they overextended their lines of communication and met the armies of China, which had come to the aid of her Korean satellite. The Japanese were forced back to southern Korea, where they held on for several years despite a gradually deteriorating situation and difficulties in maintaining their communications by sea because of the Korean "turtle ships," which may have been the world's first ironclads. The effort to conquer Korea was renewed in 1597, but the death of Hideyoshi the next year gave the Japanese a welcome excuse for abandoning the whole venture, and their armies streamed home. Japan's first organized attempt at overseas conquest had ended in complete failure.

The political vacuum created by the death of Hideyoshi was soon filled by his foremost vassal, Tokugawa Ieyasu, who had been Hideyoshi's deputy in eastern Japan, where he had built himself a castle headquarters at the small village of Edo, the future Tokyo. In 1600, Ieyasu decisively defeated a coalition of rivals, and fifteen years later he destroyed the remnants of Hideyoshi's family when he captured the great Osaka castle, as much by trickery as by the huge forces he had mustered for the siege. Ieyasu, warned by the fate of the heirs of Nobunaga and Hideyoshi, was obsessed with the idea of building a political system strong enough to survive his death. Political stability became his primary goal, and it was equally sought by his successors. In this they were eminently successful. During the first half of the seventeenth century they created a political system which was to endure almost unchanged for two and a half centuries. In fact, they established a state of absolute peace, internal and external, that has never been matched over a comparable period of time by any other nation. Unfortunately, they secured peace and stability by a series of rigid controls over society, by ruthless suppression of many of the most creative tendencies in the Japan of that day, by isolating Japan from the rest of the world, and by preserving in unchanging form many feudal institutions and attitudes of the late sixteenth century, which became increasingly anachronistic during the next two centuries. In short, the Tokugawa system was extremely conservative even by the standards of early seventeenth-century Japanese society and became increasingly more so as time passed.

Ieyasu, like Yoritomo before him, rejected the idea of

rule from the old central district around Kyoto. Taking in 1603 the old Minamoto and Ashikaga title of shogun, he established his Tokugawa shogunate in eastern Japan, centering it around his Edo castle, which he and his successors expanded into one of the greatest fortresses ever created. It was protected by wide moats, high embankments, and massive walls, arranged in a series of concentric circles with an overall diameter of more than 2 miles. Today, the inner circles of the great castle form the beautiful imperial palace grounds in the heart of Tokyo.

The Tokugawa, in their search for stability, froze the political system as it had evolved by the late sixteenth century. They left the bulk of the country divided among a large number of autonomous daimyo, and sought merely to control these daimyo through preponderant military power and a system of careful supervision. The daimyo domains, called *han*, were of varying sizes and fluctuated in number, as some were abolished and new ones created. Toward the end of the Tokugawa period, they numbered around 265. The smallest by definition had to have a rice yield of at least 10,000 *koku*, (the *koku* being a unit of approximately 5 bushels). The largest had more than 1 million *koku*. The shoguns reserved for themselves a personal domain of about 7 million *koku* (out of a total estimated national yield of 26 million), and also controlled directly all major cities, ports, and mines.

The country was in a sense divided into two halves: the Tokugawa group and the outsiders. On the one side was the shogun, the "related" (*shimpan*) daimyo, who were branches of the Tokugawa family, and the "hereditary" (*fudai*) daimyo, who had been vassals of Ieyasu even before his victory in 1600. These together provided both the military defense and the administration of the Tokugawa shogunate. On the other side were the "outer" (*tozama*) daimyo. These were the survivors of the allies, neutrals, and enemies of Ieyasu in the great battle of 1600 who had recognized him as their overlord only after his victory. Some of the larger daimyo had their own enfeoffed rear vassals governing parts of their domains, and all had their own hereditary military and administrative retainers, most of whom received hereditary salaries rather than owning their own land. In the case of the shogun, these retainers were divided into two main categories. The "standard bearers" (*hatamoto*) were those with the larger incomes, and the rest were "honorable house men" (*gokenin*).

The holdings of the shogun and daimyo were not scattered haphazardly about Japan. Almost all the central part of the country, including the Kanto Plain in the east and the old capital district in the west, was held by the Tokugawa group. This central area was not only the strategic heart of the country, but contained most of the larger plains, the bulk of the urban population, and was the economically most advanced region. Three major related daimyo, from whom the shogun was to be chosen if the main line failed, were ensconced for defense purposes at three key points in this central region: the town of Mito east of Edo, Nagoya near the geographic center of the Tokugawa domains, and Wakayama south of Osaka in the west. The outer daimyo, some of whom nursed old hostilities toward the Tokugawa, were relegated largely to the northern and western peripheries of the nation, in north and west Honshu and the islands of Shikoku and Kyushu, where they were sometimes interlarded with related or hereditary daimyo assigned to keep watch over them.

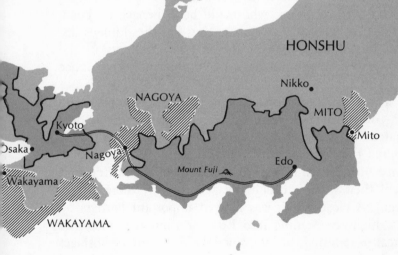

HOKKAIDO

TOKUGAWA JAPAN

Main Areas of Preponderant Direct Shogunal Rule
Some Major Daimyo Domains
Tokaido Road

0   100 Miles

SEA OF JAPAN

HONSHU

Nikko

NAGOYA

MITO

Kyoto

Mito

Osaka

Nagoya

Wakayama

Mount Fuji

Edo

WAKAYAMA

PACIFIC OCEAN

While the daimyo were all in theory autonomous, the Tokugawa actually worked out a careful system of checks and controls to prevent any of them or any combination of them from becoming a military challenge to the shogunate. The bulk of Japan's fighting men remained divided among the daimyo, but the size of their respective forces and the extent of their fortifications were strictly controlled by Edo. Intermarriage and other contracts between the daimyo families were carefully supervised. Though the daimyo domains paid no taxes to the central government, the Tokugawa called on them freely for construction work at Edo or other national services, and so kept them from amassing excessive wealth. The Edo government also developed a category of officials known as *metsuke*, who acted on the one hand as censors in ferreting out cases of maladministration by Tokugawa officials, and on the other hand as secret police spying on all men or groups who could be a menace to Tokugawa rule. The Edo shogunate thus has the dubious distinction of being one of the first governments in the world to develop an extensive and efficient secret police system and to make of it a major organ of state.

The most important measure taken by Edo to ensure its control over the daimyo was the development of a system of hostages and service at the shogunal court. Under the name of *sankin kotai* ("alternating in attendance"), most daimyo spent every other year in Edo, but kept their wives and children permanently there as hostages. A close watch was kept at important barriers on the highways leading into Edo for women leaving and firearms entering the city, since the departure of hostages or the smuggling in of weapons might have foreshadowed a revolt. Naturally, each daimyo had to maintain a large establishment in Edo, and sometimes several in the case of the bigger domains. These were serious economic drains on daimyo resources and an enrichment of the shogun's capital city. The annual comings and goings of the daimyo to Edo, accompanied by long trains of retainers, also constituted a great expense, but at the same time these daimyo processions, particularly on the Tokaido road from Kyoto to Edo, provided one of the more spectacular aspects of life during the Tokugawa period.

To perpetuate their rule, the Tokugawa needed not only to control the daimyo but to guarantee their own solidarity and ensure that the stupidity or ineptness of some future shogun would not destroy the regime. While they left the age-old fiction of imperial rule undisturbed, contenting themselves with the status of shogun, that is, the "generalissimo" of the emperor's military forces, they in fact established close surveillance and strict control over the imperial court, while giving it fairly generous economic treatment as the ultimate source of their own legitimacy. Aware that the deaths of Nobunaga and Hideyoshi had led almost at once to the downfall of their families, Ieyasu passed on the title of shogun to one of his less gifted but more stable sons in 1605, with the result that his own death in 1616 produced no political repercussions. He and his early successors also developed a complicated but strong central administration, quite capable of ruling the land with or without the shoguns, most of whom proved to be little more than figureheads.

The central administration was headed by two councils, a "council of elders" (roju), on occasions under a "great elder" (tairo), and a "council of junior elders" (wakadishiyori), both staffed by men chosen from among the hereditary daimyo. Under these there was an extensive bureaucracy drawn from among the standard bearers and honorable house men. There were various "commissioners" (bugyo), usually assigned in pairs, to supervise such matters as finances, shrines and temples, and the major cities of the country, and also a host of other officials and offices. There were, for example, law courts, the many military units into which the bulk of the shogun's retainers were divided, and intendants in charge of the extensive shogunal domains.

Two things should be noted about this governmental system. It was highly bureaucratic, despite its feudal social background. Eligibility for positions was determined primarily by hereditary status, but within this limitation, actual appointments, particularly to the higher posts, depended largely on talent. When Japan had in theory adopted the Chinese bureaucratic form of government in the seventh and eighth centuries, no true bureaucracy had developed. Now, even though the outward forms of government remained feudal, a true bureaucracy started to emerge, and with the passing of the years developed the typical strengths and weaknesses of that form of government. The other point worth mentioning is the strong tendency toward collective responsibility rather than personalized leadership. The figureheads remained individuals, but actual leadership was assumed by councils or officials working in pairs. Japan's genius for anonymous, bureaucratic, group leadership had already become well established.

The governments of the individual daimyo domains tended to mirror in miniature that of Edo. Most daimyo became figureheads, and their domain governments, small bureaucracies. They patterned their laws largely on those of the shogunate. The capitals of the larger domains also became, in a sense, small Edos centered around the daimyo's castle. Except for Kyoto and a few port cities, almost all the major cities of modern Japan started as the castle-town capitals of important daimyo. The castles themselves, which still dot the country, are quite unlike their European counterparts. The buildings which crown them, being essentially of wood, are relatively flimsy, but the real castle defenses are broad moats and massive earth-backed walls. The castles are largely the work of the late sixteenth century and were designed quite effectively to resist the cannon of that period.

The central administration of the Tokugawa was in many ways a political step forward, but they buttressed their policy of political stability with one of social stability that proved to be a long step backward. Nobunaga, by crushing the military power of the True Pure Land sect and by taking control of the commercial city of Osaka, had struck a severe blow at the rising political power of the middle and lower classes. Hideyoshi, the common foot soldier lacking even a family name who had risen to become the actual ruler of all Japan, had typified in himself the breakdown of the class cleavages of early feudalism, but it was he who struck the second great blow against the political aspirations of the lower classes. Wishing to reduce the overly large military establishments which were unnecessary in a unified land, he drew a sharp line between the peasants and the aristocratic warrior class of officers: all peasants were forced to surrender their swords and other weapons to the government and to forsake their role as peasant-soldiers.

The Tokugawa simply followed and elaborated this policy. Adopting the social theories of Confucianism, which had developed some 2,000 years earlier in China, they created a hierarchy of four social classes—the warrior-administrator, the peasant, the artisan, and the merchant. The top class of warrior-administrators was to a large degree an artificial creation in imitation of the true warrior class of early feudalism. The members of this new fixed aristocracy, which we call *samurai* (the usual Japanese term is *bushi*), held themselves aloof from the other classes and wore as a badge of distinction a long and a short sword. The merchants, in complete disregard of their relatively high economic and cultural position, were placed last in the social order because, according to Confucian theory and the natural prejudices of a political regime of agrarian, feudal origin, they were judged unproductive. This unnatural stratification of social classes was reactionary even in seventeenth-century Japan, but the Tokugawa and the favored samurai class rigidly insisted for two and a half centuries on the theory of the four classes and strictly enforced the separation of the samurai class from the others.

The early Tokugawa not only borrowed the antiquated social theories of early Confucianism; they encouraged the study of the whole Confucian philosophy, in the hope that it would be a stabilizing factor in the intellectual life of the land. Confucianism, with its emphasis on proper relationships between the ruler and the ruled, seemed admirably fitted to be a state philosophy that would foster a deep sense of loyalty to the regime. It had also served for a millennium as the underlying philosophy of an essentially bureaucratic state in China, and therefore was not ill suited to the type of bureaucratic political system Japan was developing.

As early as 1608 Ieyasu appointed a prominent Confucian philosopher to be "attendant scholar" at his court. From this small beginning grew a strong school of Confucianism at Edo that taught the orthodox interpretation as it had been formulated in China in the twelfth century by Chu Hsi (Shushi in Japanese). Soon groups of thinkers, representing various other schools of Confucianism, grew up in opposition to the orthodox school. One of the results of this scholarly interest in Confucianism in Tokugawa Japan was the development within the samurai class of a body of trained scholars and thinkers who, as statesmen, contributed to the efficient administration of the government and, as philosophers and teachers, helped keep Japan intellectually alive despite the oppressive limitations of the political and social system.

The long period of interest in Confucianism also served to imbue the people as a whole with many of the high ethical and moral standards of the Chinese, particularly their ideal of selfless and just public service and their passion for education. Buddhism remained the dominant religion of the masses and enjoyed official patronage, but Confucianism became the strongest intellectual and ethical force in Japan. As Buddhism began to show signs of inner decay, which has in modern times robbed it of much of the vigor it possessed in the Ashikaga period, Confucianism grew in influence and strength. In combination with the traditional warrior ethos, it became a major source for the unwritten ethical code of the samurai, which modern scholars have described in romantic terms as *bushido*, the "way of the warrior."

Perhaps the most drastic measures taken by the Edo government to ensure political stability were in the field of foreign relations, which, with the coming of Europeans to East Asian waters, assumed a new significance for the Japanese. The first Europeans to reach Japan were Portuguese mariners who landed on an island off the southern tip of Kyushu around 1543. Trade relations sprang up between the Portuguese and the feudal lords of western Kyushu. The Japanese showed immediate interest in the firearms of the Europeans and their use spread rapidly throughout Japan, greatly changing the nature of warfare.

Contacts with the Portuguese took on a new aspect when St. Francis Xavier, the famous Jesuit missionary, introduced Christianity to Japan during a two-year stay from 1549 to 1551. He and the Jesuits who followed him met with considerable success in their proselytizing. The Buddhist sects soon recognized Christianity as a dangerous rival and opposed it bitterly, but several of the lords of Kyushu favored the missionaries, for Portuguese traders tended to bring their ships to ports where the Jesuits had been made welcome. A minor daimyo, who himself had earlier embraced Christianity, managed with the aid of the Portuguese to build the fishing village of Nagasaki in western Kyushu into the chief port for foreign trade in all Japan. Many small lords had already become Christians when in 1578 one of the great daimyo of Kyushu was converted. Japanese of all classes in western Japan and particularly in Kyushu and Kyoto were beginning to embrace the new faith. It is estimated that there were some 150,000 Christians in Japan around the year 1580 and twice that number in the early seventeenth century, which was a larger percentage of the total population than is Christian today.

Hideyoshi and the Tokugawa who followed him had no particular objections to Christianity on religious grounds, but they looked upon it with deep suspicion as a political menace to their rule. The Christians, as a sizable group of Japanese owing some sort of allegiance to a remote European "ruler," the pope, were in their eyes a group which could not be trusted and might prove a threat to the reestablished unity of Japan. Hideyoshi and the early Tokugawa were also aware of the colonial expansion of the European powers in Southeast Asia, where Christian missionaries appeared to serve as forerunners of military penetration and conquest. The Japanese leaders were desirous of retaining profitable trade relations with the Europeans, but they gradually came to the conclusion that, for reasons of national safety and political stability, Christianity must go.

In 1587, the very year Hideyoshi completed the subjugation of western Japan, he issued a decree ordering all Christian missionaries banned from Japan. However, he made little effort to enforce this decree until ten years later, when irritated by the bickering between Portuguese Jesuits and Spanish Franciscans, who had started missionary activities in Japan in 1593, he executed nine European priests and seventeen native Christians. Ieyasu at first reversed this stern policy and befriended Spanish missionaries in an unsuccessful attempt to persuade Spanish merchants to establish direct trade contacts in the Edo region. But the arrival at this time of Protestant Dutch and English traders, who had no interest in proselytizing, convinced Ieyasu that it was not necessary to tolerate Christianity in order to have trade relations with European countries. In 1609 the Dutch established a trading post at Hirado, an island off the northwest coast of Kyushu, and the English, too, set up a trading post there in 1613. At about the same time Ieyasu reverted to Hideyoshi's policy of persecution, and his successor in 1617 reinstated the extreme measure of executing missionaries and native believers. In the next few years all the missionaries were either killed or forced to leave Japan, and thousands of Japanese Christians either apostatized or suffered the death of martyrs. A common practice of the time was to order people suspected of being Christians to tread upon a cross or some other sacred symbol, and to kill those who refused to comply.

The persecution of Christianity came to a dramatic conclusion in 1637 and 1638, when the long-Christianized peasantry of a region near Nagasaki rebelled in desperation over economic and religious oppression. Some 37,000 people, basing themselves in an old dilapidated castle, withstood for almost three months the assault of the assembled might of the central government, supported by the firepower of Dutch ships. The Christian rebels were eventually slaughtered almost to a man, and with this final catastrophe Christianity ceased to exist as an organized religion in Japan.

Meanwhile, the successors of Ieyasu, increasingly suspicious of all foreigners and determined to preserve the *status quo*, had started to close Japan to virtually all foreign intercourse. The English had already given up their trading post at Hirado as an unprofitable venture, and the Spaniards were expelled from Japan in 1624. The Portuguese in turn were expelled in 1638 for suspected complicity in the Christian rebellion, and when they sent an embassy to Japan two years later to seek the reopening of trade relations, the Japanese answered emphatically in the negative by executing the envoys.

The Tokugawa treatment of its own overseas traders and adventurers was just as severe as its treatment of the foreign traders and missionaries. Fearing that overseas Japanese and traders traveling to foreign ports might bring back the Christian religion or dangerous foreign ideas, Edo decreed in 1636 that henceforth no Japanese was to go abroad and no Japanese resident abroad was to return to Japan. Two years later this decree was followed by another prohibiting the construction of large ships suitable for overseas trade. The result was that the native merchant marine was limited to small vessels for coastal commerce among the Japanese islands. Overseas trade expansion was thus brought to an abrupt end, and thousands of Japanese abroad were permanently cut off from their homeland and left to lose their identity in the native populations of the towns of Southeast Asia.

Despite this policy of extreme national isolation, the Tokugawa were wise enough not to cut off all contact with other nations. They preserved Nagasaki as a window looking out on the rest of the world. Chinese merchants were allowed to visit and trade there under careful supervision, and the Dutch trading post at Hirado was moved to a small island in Nagasaki harbor, where the Dutch merchants were kept in virtual year-round imprisonment.

The measures the early Tokugawa took to ensure the continuance of their regime were indeed drastic. They stifled the normal social and economic development of the country and so isolated Japan from the rest of the world that she began to drop far behind Europe in scientific and industrial achievements. Even Japan's population stopped growing after about 1700 and remained relatively static at about 30 million people during the remaining century and a half of Tokugawa rule.

It must be admitted, however, that the Tokugawa were supremely successful in establishing the political stability they sought. Between the middle of the seventeenth century and the middle of the nineteenth, no revolution, disturbance, or incident in any way threatened their rule. The peace of the land was broken only by occasional and sporadic outbursts of man and nature—a great fire in Edo, a destructive earthquake, the last great eruption of the now-extinct volcano of Fuji in 1707, an occasional outburst by impoverished city dwellers (the worst was in Osaka in 1837), scattered riots by still more impoverished peasants demanding relief from crushing taxes or unjust officials—but nothing on a national scale and nothing which could shake the existing political or social order.

Perhaps the best idea of the carefully guarded political tranquillity of the time can be gained from the story of the only political incident that at least emotionally shook the nation during these two hundred years and became the favorite literary and dramatic theme of modern Japan. This was the incident of the "Forty-seven Ronin," which took place between 1701 and 1703. A minor daimyo was so grievously insulted by an important official of the shogun's court that in a rage he drew his sword and wounded his tormentor. To have drawn his sword within the castle grounds of Edo was an offense punishable by death, and the Edo authorities ordered the unlucky man to commit suicide and confiscated his domain. His feudal retainers lost their status as full-fledged samurai and became ronin, which was a term for a masterless samurai who had lost his normal place in society.

Forty-seven of these ronin vowed to take vengeance upon the lord who had caused their master's downfall, but realizing that the government would be watching for just such a move on their part, they decided first to lull its suspicions. They bided their time for two years, while their leader took up a life of debauchery and degradation to indicate that nothing was to be feared from him. Then, on a snowy winter night, they assembled at

Edo, broke into the residence of their lord's old enemy, and avenged themselves by taking his head and the heads of several of his samurai. By this act they of course flouted the authority of Edo, but their self-sacrificing loyalty to their master made them at once national heroes. After much debate the government finally permitted them to atone for their crime by the honorable death of *seppuku*, commonly called *harakiri*, which is suicide by the painful method of cutting open one's abdomen. This they did, and today the simple graves of the forty-seven *ronin* stand side by side in a quiet little temple compound in Tokyo.

The two centuries of strictly enforced peace under the watchful eye and firm hand of the Edo government have left an indelible mark upon the people. The bellicose, adventurous Japanese of the sixteenth century became by the nineteenth century a docile people looking meekly to their rulers for leadership and following without question all orders from above. They grew accustomed to firmly established patterns of conduct. A thousand rules of etiquette, supplementing instructions from their rulers, governed all their actions. As a result of this rigid regimentation of society, the Japanese became a people who lived together in their cramped islands with relatively few outward signs of friction. Nowhere in the world was proper decorum more rigorously observed by all classes than in nineteenth-century Japan, and nowhere else was physical violence less in evidence in everyday life. At the same time, few people have been more dependent on orders from above and on long-established rules of conduct. When thrown on their own judgment away from their normal environment, they have seemed to be more at a loss than peoples accustomed to greater freedom of action at home. The Japanese, of course, are as emotionally excitable as any people, and in an unfamiliar situation to which their accustomed patterns of courteous conduct do not apply, they have sometimes reacted violently. This may be one explanation for the contrast between the courtesy and docility of the Japanese at home and their cruelty and excesses as conquerors abroad during the first half of the twentieth century.

The long peace of the Tokugawa era was, of course, in many ways a blessing. At the same time, the Tokugawa held back the wheels of normal social and economic progress and fixed on the nation an antiquated political and social order. They preserved in Japan a feudal structure and mentality far longer than these could have lasted in a freer society or one more open to pressures from abroad. What had been essentially a conservative political and social system when founded in the early seventeenth century was preserved almost intact until the middle of the nineteenth century. Then a Japan still intellectually and socially bound by this antiquated system was suddenly confronted again by the Europeans, who during the intervening two centuries had made tremendous strides forward in almost all fields of human endeavor.

7 ❀ SIGNS OF CHANGE BEHIND
THE FEUDAL FACADE

Despite the best efforts of the Tokugawa to prevent any change that might undermine their safely isolated political system, it was, of course, impossible to stop all natural processes of evolution and growth within Japanese society. It was relatively simple to maintain outward political forms, but the internal workings of the society and the economy could not be held to a rigid pattern. During the sixteenth century, Japanese society and the economy had developed beyond the bounds of a strictly feudal system, and even the ruthless Edo regime could not force them back into this mold.

Actually, the unity and long peace of the Tokugawa period made the perpetuation of a feudal economy all the more impossible. National unity wiped out many of the petty economic restrictions that had existed in the days of the Ashikaga. Trade was possible on a greater scale than ever before, and despite the division of the land into many daimyo domains, Japan became essentially a single economic unit. Thus the economic foundations were laid for Japan's modernization when it was opened again to contact with the outside world in the nineteenth century.

The factor which most inexorably produced the development and unification of the economy was the centralization of political control in Edo, especially the *sankin kotai* system, which required the daimyo to maintain large establishments at the capital and make costly annual trips between their respective domains and the city. All this called for heavy expenditures outside their domains which could only be paid for by excess produce, usually in the form of rice but also of other special crops and manufactured goods. Another factor was that the economically advanced heart of the country and all the major cities were in the hands of the shogun. Individual domains might put sharp restrictions on their local merchants or engage in their own little state monopolies, but the merchants of the large cities could operate on a national scale under the shogun's protection. Relieved of the feudal fees and restrictions of earlier ages, they no longer needed the old, closed guild organization. Guilds gradually disappeared, and independent merchant firms and freer associations of merchants or manufacturers took their place in a greatly expanded economic system.

Although the Tokugawa, the daimyo, and the whole samurai class clung tenaciously to the concept that agriculture was the only true source of wealth and continued to measure their incomes in terms of *koku* of rice, in the cities and towns of Japan a vigorously expanding merchant class was creating a commercial economy far beyond anything to be expected in a politically feudal land. Kyoto, the old imperial capital, was restored to economic vigor as a major center of fine handicrafts, as it has remained ever since. Osaka, strategically located at the eastern end of the Inland Sea, became the great commercial entrepôt for all of western Japan, and many daimyo maintained business establishments there to market their surplus agricultural produce and perform other economic services. Edo, with its large population of samurai consumers, in time outstripped both these older cities, and in the eighteenth century, when its population reached 1 million, it was probably the biggest city in the world, as its successor, Tokyo, is today. Under these conditions, a fully developed money economy spread throughout Japan, and much of Japanese agriculture became oriented toward the national market. Paper credits of all sorts were developed and commonly used in big transactions, and great rice exchanges with daily fluctuating price quotations grew up at the two economic capitals, Osaka and Edo.

The ruling class had placed the merchants at the bottom of the social scale, but these same merchants came increasingly to dominate economic life. Already by the late seventeenth century, there were large numbers of sharp and experienced merchants and moneylenders in the cities. Some had become extremely wealthy, like the Mitsui, who were to survive to grow into the largest private economic empire in the world in the first half of the twentieth century. In an expanding money economy, the daimyo and samurai had a growing need for cash, and as the Tokugawa period progressed, many of them fell hopelessly in debt to rich city merchants. This in time even led to some blurring of the sharp line between samurai and merchant, both through intermarriage and through occasional shifts in class status. The urban merchants, on the whole, were cautious and conservative, fully aware of their dependence on the feudal military authorities. A more aggressive breed of small entrepreneurs, however, began to emerge from rural areas in the late eighteenth and early nineteenth centuries. Their appearance was a sign of substantial economic progress in rural Japan.

Occasional famines, frequent peasant riots, and the Malthusian limit to the population after 1700 all suggest basically grim conditions in peasant Japan. On the other hand, there seems to have been steady progress in material wealth, in the specialization of crops and agricultural technology, and in overall economic integration. The sharp line drawn by Hideyoshi and the Tokugawa between warriors and peasants had also had its beneficial aspects. While some daimyo domains continued to have rural samurai, in most areas the peasants were left to run their villages autonomously, so long as they kept the peace and paid their taxes. The land increasingly became divided into small family-size units, privately owned, for all practical purposes, by the peasants themselves; crops were grown increasingly for sale rather than subsistence; and supplementary labor came to be hired for wages. In other words, the basic rural system was developing far beyond the earlier feudal pattern.

Rural Japan also shared in a great expansion of literacy and learning during the Tokugawa period. The warriors of the sixteenth century had been largely illiterate, but under the influence of Confucianism and the prevailing bureaucratic form of government of Tokugawa times, the samurai quickly developed into a well-educated class of administrators and intellectuals. The city merchants, responding to the needs of a more complex economy, also became largely literate, and even among the richer peasants literacy became common. The daimyo domains developed educational institutions for their samurai, but the townsmen and peasants had to rely on small private academies, called "temple schools." It is estimated that by the end of the Tokugawa period, literacy among males was about 45 percent and among females, 15 percent. Such levels compared well with those of Europe at that time and were far ahead of any other part of Asia.

❁

The merchants, not the warrior-administrators, obviously dominated Tokugawa Japan economically, but their real supremacy is perhaps best seen in the cultural field, for the arts and literature of the period were more an expression of a city bourgeoisie than of a feudal warrior class. The cities dominated Tokugawa culture, and in the cities the gay amusement quarters were the centers of social life. Here came the tired businessman and the "slumming" samurai for the free social contact with women denied them by the overly formalized patterns of society, which confined women of breeding strictly to their own homes. This was the background for the development in more modern times of the *geisha*, the professional female entertainer carefully trained in the arts of singing, dancing, and amusing conversation.

To a surprising degree, the art and literature of the time revolved around the amusement quarters. Artists of the Tokugawa period loved to portray the streets of these quarters and the famous beauties who lived there; and the great seventeenth-century novelist Saikaku made the demimonde the normal subject of his amusing and somewhat risqué novels. Thanks to the greatly increased use of printing in the Tokugawa period, the novels of Saikaku and the works of other popular writers had a great vogue with city dwellers.

The drama of the age, like the novel, reflected the tastes of the city merchant class. A puppet theater developed in the seventeenth century, and, closely parallel to it, a new dramatic form known as *Kabuki*. Both are still alive and have their devotees. Kabuki stressed realism of action and of setting. It utilized the revolving stage with great success, and the settings it developed were in many respects far superior to those of the West. In sharp contrast to the slow-moving and sedate Nō drama of the Ashikaga period, the Kabuki maintained a high degree of emotional tension and dealt freely in scenes of violence and melodrama. The greatest of the Tokugawa dramatists, Chikamatsu (1653–1724), drew equally from great historical themes and the social drama of contemporary city life, such as double suicides by blighted lovers.

The most popular poetic form of the Tokugawa period, the *haiku*, was also well suited to the wit and sophistication of an urban population, though it really displayed more of the Zen spirit than that of the city bourgeoisie, and was, in any case, a very natural outgrowth of the classical "short poem." The *haiku* was even briefer—a reduction from thirty-one syllables to a mere seventeen—but in the hands of a master like the seventeenth-century poet-monk Basho, it could be a superbly clever creation, conjuring up a whole scene and its emotional overtones in a simple phrase or two. Its brevity, however, made it even more limited as a literary form than the old "short poem," and the thousands of faddists who took up *haiku* writing during the Tokugawa period often reduced it to little more than an amusing word game.

Art in the time of Hideyoshi and the early Tokugawa showed in many respects a radical departure from the major trends of Zen art of Ashikaga days. The calm and serenity of the simple landscape paintings were lost in a burst of magnificence and splendor—fitting expression of the military and political might of the age. Great efforts were put into erecting and decorating beautiful palaces. Gorgeous decorative screens and panels, with brightly colored scenes and designs laid on backgrounds of gold leaf, were the typical artistic creations of the time. The expansive spirit of the age is well illustrated by the greatly increased scale of landscape gardening and by the elaborateness of architecture. This Baroque age of Japanese architecture is exemplified by the magnificent temple-mausoleums of the early Tokugawa shoguns erected in a beautiful forest and mountain setting at Nikko, north of Edo. On the other hand, the deep religious spirit which earlier had produced serene statues of Buddhas and fine portrait statues of monks had been lost by the late sixteenth century; and sculpture had become largely the ornamenting of palaces and temples with a superabundance of elaborate carvings.

The art of the early Tokugawa period was in many ways already a popular art as contrasted with that of Ashikaga times, but it steadily grew even more markedly popular. The work of the sculptor became largely the production of small, often amusing trinkets for popular use, and the subject matter of the graphic arts became increasingly the city people and their life. While many great artists continued to paint works to meet the tastes and beautify the residences of the upper classes, others produced pictures to fit the tastes and pocketbooks of the bourgeoisie. This was particularly evident in the development of the technique of wood-block printing, which made it possible to reproduce many copies of a single colored picture and to sell them at reasonable prices. The subject matter was at first famous actors, well-known courtesans and other beautiful women, sometimes with pornographic touches, and then in time beautiful or famous scenes—the precursor of the picture postcard. This was the world's first art for the masses, and it reached a glorious culmination in the early nineteenth century in the landscapes of two great masters, Hokusai and Hiroshige. The wood-block print, as exemplified in their works, became the form of Japanese art best known in the Occident.

The increased industrial output of the Tokugawa period resulted in a great gain in the semi-industrial arts. The making of fine pottery and beautiful porcelain ware, at first under the guidance of Korean potters brought back by Hideyoshi's armies, became a great industry with high artistic standards. Gorgeous silk brocades were produced by the expanding textile industry, and lacquer ware of great decorative distinction was made in quantity. In pottery making, weaving, and lacquer work the Japanese maintained their esthetic standards despite increasing production during the Tokugawa period, and in these fields and in many other industrial arts they have continued up to the present day a balance between large-scale production, technical excellence, and esthetic value which is almost unmatched in the modern world.

The development of a complicated commercial economy and a sophisticated urban culture were not the only ways in which the foundations for a modernized Japan were being laid during the Tokugawa period. Great advances were also being made in knowledge and in intellectual sophistication.

For one thing, interest in Europe and things European was reviving. Christianity and possible foreign aggression had become such dead issues by 1720 that Yoshimune, the one strong shogun of the eighteenth century, felt free to remove a long-standing ban on the study of the West and the importation of European books—with the exception, of course, of anything dealing with Christianity. Soon a small but energetic group of students of European science appeared, working through the medium of the Dutch language, which they learned from the Dutch at Nagasaki. Within a few decades, these students of "Dutch learning," as it was called, had compiled a Dutch-Japanese dictionary and had translated into Japanese a text on anatomy. By the middle of the nineteenth century there were Japanese scholars well versed in such Western sciences as gunnery, smelting, shipbuilding, cartography, astronomy, and medicine. Few in number though they were, they formed a valuable nucleus of scholars to help in scientific study on a much larger scale when the opportunity finally came.

The development of a strong national consciousness during the Tokugawa period was another way in which the stage was set for Japan's modernization. Why nationalism should have appeared so early and developed so fully in Japan, long before it became significant in other Asian lands, is an interesting question. Nationalism in Japan, as in Europe, was the product of a long, slow evolution. A sense of national identity seems to have been stirred as early as the first great period of cultural borrowing from China, inspired probably by a feeling of inferiority resulting from the sharp contrast between a small and backward Japan and an incomparably larger, older, and more advanced China.

It should be noted, however, that the Koreans and other East Asian peoples stood with regard to China in a similar position to that of Japan, but did not develop the same national consciousness. Perhaps their closer proximity to China, their more successful reproduction of its political and social institutions, and the occasional military conquest they suffered at the hands of their great continental neighbor combined to produce in them willing acceptance of a status as autonomous but subordinate members of the Chinese cultural and political empire. The Japanese, in contrast, lived across the sea from China, were never conquered by Chinese armies, diverged sharply in feudal times from Chinese political and social patterns, were an extraordinarily homogeneous people living within clear, sea-girt boundaries, and were protected (as were the Koreans) from complete cultural absorption by a strong linguistic barrier. For these various reasons, they never seem to have been able to identify themselves completely with China, and as time passed they increasingly tended to compensate for the many ways in which Japan was obviously less important than China by flaunting their distinctiveness and taking pride in whatever they could call their own. The early nationalism of Northern Europe may well have been stimulated by a similar consciousness of distinctiveness, tinged with feelings of inferiority toward the older lands of the Mediterranean. In fact, the story of the development of Japanese nationalism may be a valuable example for the understanding of nationalism everywhere.

Attitudes of national self-consciousness were already clear in Japan by the Kamakura period, when Nichiren and other religious leaders injected a strong nationalistic note into their teachings. They were clearer in the political writings of the early Ashikaga period, when a scholar wrote a history in support of Go-Daigo's cause in which he argued that the unique virtues of the Japanese political system derived from the fact that Japan was a land of divine origin, ruled by an imperial line of divine ancestry.

Shinto priests, who again began to play a part in the intellectual life of Japan during the feudal ages, did much to build up this sort of national consciousness. For centuries Shinto had been completely overshadowed by Buddhism, and its many deities had been given humble recognition as local manifestations of universal Buddhist deities. But during the feudal period Shinto began to free itself from Buddhist domination and to take on new intellectual vigor. Shinto philosophers, by adopting many Buddhist and Chinese concepts, developed a philosophy to accompany the original simple nature cults of the religion. In the process, these priests came to claim superiority for Shinto over Buddhism, even reversing the old theory of the relationship by defining the Buddhist deities as foreign and therefore inferior manifestations of supreme native Japanese gods.

During the Tokugawa period, two hundred years of self-imposed isolation greatly strengthened the national consciousness of the Japanese. The expulsion of the Europeans and the suppression of Christianity in the early seventeenth century generated a violent xenophobia which did not decline much during the next two centuries. Strangely enough, even the Tokugawa patronage of Confucianism helped strengthen nationalism, for interest in Confucianism led to a revival of historical studies, and the study of Japanese history took scholars back to the myths and legends of ancient Japan as related in the early histories, the *Kojiki* and *Nihon shoki*. One important school of historians was founded by the second head of the great Tokugawa branch family at Mito. In the seventeenth century, this group began a monumental history of Japan, written in classical Chinese, which was not finally completed until the early years of the twentieth century.

Scholars who turned to a study of the old myths and traditions and reintroduced them to the educated public contributed even more to the growth of nationalism. In the latter part of the eighteenth century one of them, Motoori Norinaga, produced a commentary on the *Kojiki* which did much to make this early history the primary text of Japanese nationalism. He and others like him looked to the primitive pre-Chinese period of Japanese history for unique native virtues that would explain to their own satisfaction the superiority to China which their unreasoning nationalism now led them to feel.

The intellectual revival of Shinto was paralleled in the first half of the nineteenth century by the appearance of new popular Shinto sects. Some were founded by women, and several stressed faith healing. All these sects added many Buddhist concepts and practices to basic Shinto principles, but they were often strongly colored by nationalism as well. These popular Shinto sects were not only a sign of growing national consciousness; they also indicated that Buddhism was no longer able to meet all the spiritual needs of the lower classes. Converts flocked to the new sects in great numbers, and today some of them count their adherents in the millions.

The interest of historians and Shinto scholars in the early days of Japanese history naturally revealed the high place the imperial family had once held in Japan, and nationalists tended to emphasize the divine ancestry of an unbroken imperial line as one of the unique virtues which accounted for Japan's supposed superiority. Together with the greater attention and more adequate support the Tokugawa gave to the imperial court, this made most Japanese aware again that there was an emperor in Kyoto, and that in theory he was the supreme ruler of the land. The emperor and his court of course remained politically impotent, but the imperial line emerged from obscurity. The emperor in fact became a figure of such nationwide importance that some people began to wonder why a shogun was actually ruling. In the late eighteenth century, a scholar in Kyoto so boldly expounded the right of the emperor to rule that Edo was forced to take disciplinary action against him and his courtier pupils.

During the eighteenth century and the first half of the nineteenth century, Tokugawa rule continued serene and unchallenged, but beneath an unchanging surface, forces were at work remaking the foundations of the nation. Although the Tokugawa were able to preserve an antiquated political system and an absurdly outdated political and social philosophy until the middle of the nineteenth century, behind this feudal facade, true feudal forms of government had been largely replaced by what was in effect a highly developed, even if class-bound, bureaucracy. Respect for the imperial line had been so restored that a native alternative to rule by a feudal military class was at least imaginable. Rapid economic growth had produced an advanced commercial economy, capable of ready transformation into a more modern economic order. Literacy was widespread, and the nation was intellectually prepared for complex new ideas. Despite the division of the land into a large number of feudal domains, the people had developed a strong sense of national consciousness and were ready to act as a modern nation-state. Indeed, Japan had spiritually become a modern nation in many ways, ready to take over and utilize the more efficient political institutions and means of production being developed by the nation-states of the West.

Perhaps the greatest question of all modern history is why Japan alone among the non-Western countries of the world had so developed by the nineteenth century that she was able to transform herself into a modern nation-state and adopt with success not just the technology, but the political and economic institutions of the contemporary West. Much of our understanding of the successes and failures of other non-Western peoples in attempting to do the same in the twentieth century depends on our understanding of the Japanese achievement. Japan's unique history in the nineteenth century was unquestionably determined in large part by what she had become in the course of the Tokugawa period. And Tokugawa Japan in turn was undoubtedly a late phase, or one might call it an aftermath, of what had been a long feudal experience. It is significant that the great technological, institutional, and ideological transformation of modern times, which, for lack of a more precise term, we simply call "modernization," started in a Western Europe just shaking itself free from a similar long feudal experience. Since only Europe and Japan ever developed fully feudal societies, it may be reasonable to assume that feudalism, or more probably its aftermath, has something to do with the development of attitudes and institutions conducive to success in modernization.

8 ✤ THE CREATION OF A
MODERN STATE

By the middle of the nineteenth century, political and social changes were long overdue in Japan. The political system, in many ways reactionary even in the early seventeenth century, was by now more than two hundred years out of date. The growth of nationalism and the development of a full-fledged commercial economy had made Japan ready for an entirely new political and social order. But so well had the early Tokugawa succeeded in creating a system capable of preserving political stability that the machine was still running relatively smoothly. It took an outside force to disrupt it. This force was provided by the Westerners, who came not only from Europe, but also from their newer home in America.

In the last years of the eighteenth century the Russians, who had crossed the vast land expanse of Siberia and reached the Pacific, began to attempt to establish contact with the Japanese. At about the same time the English, who had supplanted the Portuguese as the chief traders in East Asian waters, began to try to rewin entry into Japan. But the Americans were most interested of all in opening Japanese ports. Their whaling vessels frequented the North Pacific and the waters around Japan, and American clipper ships, bound for China on the great circle route across the Pacific, passed close to the islands. The Americans wanted permission for their ships to enter Japanese ports in order to take on water and replenish their stores, and when steamships came into use, the desirability of coaling stations in Japan became obvious. Not infrequently, also, American and European sailors were wrecked on the shores of Japan. The law of the land decreed death for any foreigner entering the country, and although this was no longer commonly enforced, mariners stranded in Japan who eventually got out by way of Nagasaki usually had tales of cruelty to tell.

In the first half of the nineteenth century the Americans, English, and Russians repeatedly sent expeditions to Japan in an effort to persuade the Japanese to open their ports to foreign ships, and the Dutch urged the Tokugawa to accede to these demands. But Edo stood firm on its old policy. A few students of "Dutch learning" bravely advocated the opening of Japan, but the vast majority of the people, long accustomed to isolation from the rest of the world, were bitterly opposed to allowing foreigners into their land. It was obvious that Japan would not voluntarily open her doors.

The American government eventually decided to try to force the doors open. For this purpose, it dispatched a considerable naval force under Commodore Perry. Perry steamed into what is now called Tokyo Bay in July 1853. After delivering a letter from the President of the United States demanding the inauguration of trade relations, he withdrew to Okinawa for the winter, with the promise that he would return early the next year to receive a reply. Edo was thrown into consternation over this sudden crisis, and the remaining decade and a half of Tokugawa rule, known as the *bakumatsu*, or the "end of the *bakufu*," was a period of great turmoil. The Japanese were appalled by the size and guns of the American "black ships," as they called them, and they were amazed by the steam-powered vessels which moved up the bay against the wind. They realized that their own shore batteries were almost useless and that Edo and the coastal shipping which provisioned it lay defenseless.

The government split into two factions—conservatives who advocated the expulsion of the foreigners, and realists who saw that Japan could do nothing but bow to the American demands. In their own indecision, the Edo authorities did a most unusual thing. For the first time in over six centuries of military rule, the shogun's government asked the opinion of the emperor on an important problem of state. It also invited counsel from the daimyo. Conservative Kyoto and the daimyo, most of whom were safely removed from the immediate threat, were of course strongly in favor of repelling the foreigners. The Edo government was indeed caught on the horns of a dilemma when Perry's fleet returned to Tokyo Bay in February 1854. The emperor and the nation as a whole demanded a policy which Edo was quite incapable of carrying out. Under the threatening guns of the American ships, Edo had no choice but to sign a treaty with the United States, opening two ports to American ships and permitting a certain amount of closely regulated trade. The two ports were Shimoda, at the end of a peninsula near Edo, and Hakodate in Hokkaido, both insignificant ports in relatively remote places, but adequate for the provisioning of American ships. An American consul was also permitted to reside at Shimoda.

Once the door had been pushed open a crack, there was no closing it. Within two years Edo had signed treaties with England, Russia, and Holland, and in 1858 Townsend Harris, the first American consul, negotiated a full commercial treaty, including the unequal provision that Americans would enjoy extraterritoriality in Japan, that is, the right to be tried by their own consular courts, as had become the practice in Western treaty relations with China. The European powers soon made similar treaties with Japan, and the door was now wide open.

Foreigners were permitted permanent residence at five ports and also at the great cities of Osaka and Edo. Relatively free trade relations were also sanctioned. Foreign merchants began to set up business concerns not far from Edo at the fishing village of Yokohama, which grew rapidly and within a few decades developed into one of the great port cities of the world. A second Western merchant enclave at Hyogo across the bay from Osaka similarly grew into the great modern port city of Kobe. Both Yokohama and Hyogo were at first essentially Occidental towns, protected by Western soldiers, in much the same pattern as the so-called foreign "concessions" in China.

The Tokugawa realized that because of their own military impotence, they could do nothing to check the foreigners. Rather belatedly they initiated reforms designed to modernize their military establishment, and built a small Occidental-type navy. However, the Kyoto court and the vast majority of the feudal domains, which still had seen nothing of the overpowering military might of the West, showed little interest in military moderni-

HOKKAIDO

Sapporo

Hakodate

SEA OF JAPAN

Sendai

Niigata

HONSHU

Kanazawa

Tokyo
Yokohama *TOKYO BAY*

Nagoya

Kyoto
Kobe Nara
Osaka

Shimoda

Hiroshima

Shimonoseki

PACIFIC OCEAN

Fukuoka

SHIKOKU

Nagasaki

KYUSHU

Kagoshima

MODERN JAPAN

0   200 Miles

zation and remained completely unreconciled to Edo's yielding to the foreigners. The cry of "expel the barbarians" (joi) grew in all quarters of the land.

The Tokugawa branch family at Mito led the opposition within the Edo government, and in 1860 men from Mito assassinated the "great elder" who had concluded the new commercial treaties and had been energetically attempting to reassert Edo's control over the daimyo. Other irreconcilable conservatives from the Satsuma domain in southern Kyushu murdered an Englishman near Yokohama in 1862, and the next summer the forts of the large western Honshu domain of Choshu began firing on Western shipping in the narrow straits at the western end of the Inland Sea near Shimonoseki. This action was in response to a general order for the expulsion of the foreigners, which the Kyoto court, rising to a new sense of authority, forced the Edo government to accept. The emperor even took the unprecedented step of summoning the shogun to Kyoto, and the shogun, showing how far Edo had already gone in surrendering authority to the emperor, meekly complied.

The Tokugawa regime was obviously foundering not because the machinery of government had broken down, but because Edo had lost the confidence of the nation. Ruling in theory as the military arm of the emperor's government, it had shown itself unable to fulfill its basic duty of defending the nation, and it had acted counter to a specific imperial order. It was vulnerable to attack under the popular twin slogans of "honor the emperor" (sonno) and "expel the barbarians." Even some of its own supporters, influenced by historians and Shinto propagandists, were beginning to doubt its right to monopolize political power. Its once overwhelming military power had grown flabby in two centuries of disuse, and its councils were divided by doubts. Discontented Kyoto courtiers and ambitious samurai in some of the large outer domains of western Japan, which had never become fully reconciled to Tokugawa dominance, pressed the attack on the shogunate, eager to share in its power. Their slogan was "the union of court and military," suggesting a sharing of Edo's power with Kyoto, and through Kyoto with the outer daimyo. But some of the malcontents began to aim at a complete overthrow of the shogunate.

The lead in these subversive activities was taken particularly by young samurai, mostly of relatively humble origin, from Satsuma and Choshu, and secondarily from Tosa in Shikoku. It is not easy to explain why men from these three domains played such a decisive role in Japanese history at this crucial moment, while most of their peers in the other two hundred and sixty or more autonomous units of Japan stood by in relative inactivity. But at least a partial explanation is possible. These three domains were among the largest, and only the big units had much chance to take effective action in the crisis. Satsuma and Choshu in particular had unusually large samurai populations, and being on the somewhat backward periphery of Japan, their old feudal solidarity was probably less eroded than in the more centrally located domains. These two also had nursed particularly strong anti-Tokugawa traditions. Most important, perhaps, they both happened to be among the few domains that were financially solvent, and therefore they were able to purchase superior new Western arms for the impending conflict.

The dynamic young leaders who won control of both domains at this time pushed them into daring action: they carried out intrigues at the Kyoto court and challenged Edo authority. The long Tokugawa peace was finally broken when loyalist forces struck back and drove the Choshu elements out of Kyoto in 1863. The situation thereafter deteriorated rapidly, and Edo was forced to marshal great armies to attempt to force Choshu into submission. A first campaign in the winter of 1865–1866 ended in a compromise settlement, and a second the next summer ended in a clear defeat for Edo. A single domain had challenged its authority and won. The end of the shogunate was obviously at hand.

One of the reasons for Choshu's success was Satsuma's benign neutrality during the second campaign, which had been brought about by a secret alliance between the two. A year and a half later, their forces, aided by Tosa and some other domains, including even "related daimyo," carried out a coup d'état in Kyoto on January 3, 1868, and announced the "restoration" of imperial rule. The new shogun, who had been selected from the Mito line, where for many years pro-imperial sentiment had been strong, was inclined to yield, but some of Edo's supporters decided to resist. The new coalition defeated them in the environs of Kyoto and pushed on to Edo, where only minor resistance was encountered. Some northern domains put up a fight in defense of the old order, and the Tokugawa navy held out in Hokkaido until the spring of 1869, but there was no general effort on the part of the Tokugawa and their supporters to preserve Edo's rule.

The Tokugawa shogunate, which had seemed so firm a mere two decades earlier, had been swept away with surprisingly little bloodshed. Its theoretical foundation and rigid feudal structure had become so hopelessly outdated by the middle of the nineteenth century that, once the system started to crack, it collapsed suddenly and completely.

To create a new central government to take the place of the shogunate, however, was no easy task. The new leaders were a small group of court nobles and samurai from a few western domains, none of whom had had any experience in running a national government. Their aim of "restoring" imperial rule harked back to a vague historical memory of a millennium earlier, but they had no specific plan. They had fallen heir to a collapsing, antiquated governmental mechanism that was bankrupt to boot. The bulk of the domains stood aside in distrust or unconcern, and the nation as a whole was deeply resentful of the disruptive presence of foreigners.

The new imperial government naturally centered around the person of the emperor, for it had been the revived theory of imperial rule that had justified the overthrow of the Tokugawa. The coup d'état and its aftermath came to be referred to as the "Meiji Restoration," named for the new "year period" adopted in 1868, which became in time also the posthumous name for the young emperor who had ascended the throne the year before. There was no thought, however, that this boy of fifteen would actually rule. The Japanese had become too accustomed to political figureheads and collective leadership for this. The psychology of the Restoration leaders is not easy to recapture today, but they seem to have combined a deep devotion to the emperor and a fanatical belief in imperial rule with an unconscious assumption that they themselves, of course, would be making the decisions. The Meiji emperor came to be an influential force in the government, but he and his successors remained basically symbols of authority rather than actual rulers.

The old Fujiwara aristocracy around the emperor included some able men. Until his death in 1883, Iwakura was the most powerful member of the new government, and later Prince Saionji and Prince Konoe rose from this background to become prime ministers. But most Kyoto courtiers lacked the experience and the drive to become forceful leaders in the new government. Some of the outer daimyo participated in its work, but for the most part they were no more than figureheads even in their own domains. The higher posts in the new government went to imperial princes, court nobles, and daimyo, but the real leadership was largely in the hands of the young samurai of Satsuma, Choshu and a few other domains—men such as Okubo and Saigo of Satsuma and Kido of Choshu, who had cut their political teeth on internal domain politics and on intrigues against the Tokugawa. Mostly from the lower strata of the samurai class, they were a group of extraordinary ability, the products of an age of turbulence and rapid change, when only the ablest and most flexible could hope to succeed. Ranging in age from twenty-seven to forty-one in 1868, they were remarkably young, and thus able to adapt to new conditions. And exercising power far beyond what their status in the samurai class would have entitled them to under the old regime, they believed strongly in rewarding talent over birth and were open to other new, revolutionary social concepts.

The changes these men brought to Japan proved to be indeed revolutionary, but their Meiji Restoration, unlike the nineteenth-century revolutions of Europe, had not welled up from below. Nor was it like the Chinese revolution and other Asian revolutions that were to follow. In China the Manchu dynasty was in sad decay in the nineteenth century, but the country had to go through decades of economic and political disruption at the hands of the predatory Western powers before the imperial system had so disintegrated that revolutionaries with the Occidental theory of republicanism were able to overthrow it. In much of the rest of Asia, a sense of nationalism had to grow slowly in response to colonial domination and Western concepts before revolutionary changes took place. In Japan, instead, a small group from the lower fringes of the old ruling class, armed with a native "revolutionary" political concept, had been able to sweep away the old central government with little bloodshed, and take over the nation almost intact. Coming from the top down, the "revolution" was carried out without widespread destruction.

The Japanese also had another advantage over the Chinese, whose age-old assumption that theirs was the only land of true civilization made it extremely difficult for China to adapt herself to outside ideas. The Japanese, because of their old pattern of borrowing from China and their continuing awareness that things could usefully be learned from abroad, had no difficulty in realizing that the strong nations of the West offered valuable economic and political models. They quickly seized on the idea that the best way to make their country secure from the West was to modernize it along Western lines, and they were willing to do anything necessary to achieve this goal.

The new leaders had been united by their anti-Tokugawa feelings and their enthusiasm for the imperial cause, but they had also rallied at first under the slogan of "expel the barbarians." Some of them, in fact, had joined in attacks on the Westerners in Japan, but long before they came to power in 1868 they had learned the hopelessness of this approach. In 1863 a British squadron had bombarded Kagoshima, the capital of Satsuma, in retribution for the murder of the Englishman by Satsuma warriors the year before. In the same year, Western naval vessels attacked the Choshu forts near Shimonoseki that had been firing on Western merchant ships, and completely destroyed them in 1864. The samurai of Satsuma and Choshu learned their lesson at once, and, demonstrating an amazing ability to reorient their thinking, dropped all belief in a narrow policy of isolation and immediately began to study the techniques of warfare that had made the West so strong.

Satsuma, with advice from the British, soon launched its own small modern navy, and the young officers who began their naval careers in Satsuma became the men who created and dominated the Imperial Japanese Navy until well into the twentieth century. Similarly, Choshu, abandoning the concept of a small warrior class, started to create mixed peasant and samurai rifle units trained in European military techniques. The success of this effort was clearly demonstrated when these modernized forces successfully fought off the assembled might of the Tokugawa in 1866. The samurai officers of these units went on to become the dominant element in the officer corps of the Imperial Japanese Army. Thus, the samurai of Satsuma and Choshu, far from remaining champions of antiforeign conservatism, had already started the military and social revolution that was soon to sweep away the last vestiges of the feudal order.

Once in control of the national government, the new leaders naturally threw themselves into developing a more efficient national army and navy in close imitation of those of the contemporary West. This was only to be expected of men who were themselves for the most part military men by tradition and early training and who had personally experienced the humiliation of being forced to bow to superior Western military might. They were understandably obsessed with the idea of creating a Japan capable of defending herself against the Occident. At the same time, however, they were surprisingly broad-minded in their approach to the problem, for they realized that to achieve military strength Japan also needed political, economic, social, and intellectual renovation. The concept was epitomized by the popular slogan *fukoku kyohei*, "rich country, strong military."

New organs of central government and new patterns of national union were of course necessary, because the old institutions of the shogunate had been destroyed, and the old feudal divisions made Japan no match for the Western powers. Edo had for so long been the real political capital of Japan that the new leaders made it their own headquarters. In September 1868 it was renamed Tokyo, or "eastern capital," and the emperor and his court were moved to the great Edo castle the next spring. The new government, though supported by the military power of Satsuma, Choshu, and their allies—a small minority among the hereditary warrior class of Japan —found its chief financial base in the income from the huge shogunal domain, which it largely appropriated for itself. It also resorted to forced loans from the rich merchants, as the shogun and daimyo had been in the habit of doing when in need.

In their search for a pattern of "imperial government," the new leaders restored titles and offices from the remote period of rule by the imperial court in the eighth century, but these titles and offices naturally had no life in themselves. The new leaders also experimented hesitantly with the representative institutions of the West by calling together a body of representatives from the domains, but it proved meaningless. They even experimented with the American concept of the separation of powers among executive, legislative, and judicial branches, but this proved more confusing than helpful. More practically, they began to develop embryo "ministries" in response to specific needs. But in essence they fell back on the old Japanese technique of collective leadership. Important decisions were simply made by informal groupings of the new leaders themselves. A few of them, like Iwakura the court noble, held high posts, but most of them were samurai of relatively low status from Satsuma, Choshu, and a few other domains, who at first occupied only second-level positions as councillors and as vice-ministers or department heads in the various new ministries, even though they participated in the major decisions.

The most important job facing the new government was to get rid of the large number of autonomous feudal units into which the bulk of Japan was divided and the class system that stood in the way of modernizing the government, the economy, and—most important—the military establishment. In March of 1869, only a little over a year after they had come to power, the new leaders started the task of doing away completely with the feudal system under which they had grown up and which had given their class a dominant place in society. They persuaded the daimyo of Satsuma, Choshu, Tosa, and Hizen to offer their domains to the emperor, and the other daimyo of Japan felt morally obliged to follow suit. Thus, at one bold stroke the division of Japan into feudal principalities came to a sudden end, at least in theory.

Actually, the daimyo, as expected, were appointed governors of their old domains, with one-tenth of their former revenues as personal salaries. But two years later, in a much more sweeping move, the government abolished the domains completely, and divided the country into a number of prefectures (ken) directly controlled by Tokyo. This action marked the definite end of the daimyo as feudal lords. The government made them an economic settlement by giving them fairly generous lump sum payments in the form of government bonds, which helped ensure their support of the new regime. These bonds became an important source of banking capital, but the daimyo themselves faded into genteel and affluent obscurity.

Getting rid of the daimyo was a far easier task than stripping the samurai of their social, economic, and political privileges. Constituting about 6 percent of the total population, they were a wide upper stratum that had monopolized not just the military power, but most political and intellectual leadership, and had enjoyed the economic privilege of hereditary, even if often niggardly, salaries. Choshu had already led the way toward depriving the samurai of their status as an aristocratic caste of warriors, and the new government felt itself strong enough in early 1873 to carry out what was in the Japanese context perhaps its most revolutionary reform— universal military service. Under the able leadership of young officers, such as Yamagata of Choshu, an army of peasants was recruited and organized, first on the French and subsequently on the German model. Meanwhile the government had lifted all class restrictions on roles in society and in 1871 had decreed legal equality for all Japanese, including the outcasts called eta, who constituted about 2 percent of the population. In 1876 the samurai were even ordered to stop wearing swords, which had been their badge of social superiority.

The samurai's loss of his cherished position as an aristocratic warrior-administrator was accompanied by the loss of his privileged economic status. Samurai hereditary stipends, inadequate though most of them were, had been cut in half in the reform of 1869, and finally in 1876 the government forced the samurai to commute their remaining stipends into lump sum payments of still further reduced value. Even then, the payments to samurai and daimyo constituted an extremely heavy financial burden on the new government. A complete cutting off of the feudal aristocracy would have been cheaper in the short run, but perhaps this relatively generous treatment is one reason why modern Japan had no continuing problem with the *ancien régime*, as did France.

Because of their strong traditions of political leadership and their high educational standards, samurai still monopolized the positions of leadership in the new government. They also filled the officer corps of the new army and navy and provided the bulk of the policemen, helping to account for the high prestige the police enjoyed. Many became business leaders, and others dominated the new educational institutions and intellectual life. But most of the samurai were unable to adjust to the new conditions and sank into the working masses. In any case, the distinction between samurai and commoner origin lost its significance within a generation or two and became merely a matter of casual historical interest.

It was not possible, however, to disinherit so large a privileged class without some turmoil. Irreconcilable conservatives among the samurai often defied the new government in its first decade of rule. Significantly, these troubles occurred largely in the same western domains from which the new leaders had come. Perhaps their authority seemed less valid in areas where their relatively lowly origins were well remembered. The most serious as well as the last of the samurai revolts came in 1877 in Satsuma itself. There some 40,000 discontented conservatives rallied around Saigo, who had withdrawn from the government in dudgeon four years earlier. In bloody fighting, the government's new peasant conscripts managed to crush the rebels, proving even to the diehards that the old order had indeed passed.

Within ten years of coming to power, the new government had thus cleared away the antiquated political and social system and had achieved unchallenged control over the country. The development of modern political institutions, a new social and intellectual order, and a new economic system to support modernized military power, however, was a much slower and harder undertaking.

Unlike the modernizing countries of the middle of the twentieth century, Japan found no outside financial or technological aid on which to lean. In view of the predatory nature of Western imperialism, the Japanese were understandably fearful of foreign loans and used them only very sparingly. Loans, in any case, were obtainable only at particularly high interest rates, because Japan seemed to the West a poor risk. Expert knowledge could be bought by hiring Western experts, but to do this the Japanese had to pay unusually high salaries even by Occidental standards, because Japan did not seem to Westerners a desirable place to live. In other words, Japan had to lift herself economically by her own bootstraps.

One accident of history, however, benefited her. A silk blight in the 1860s in Europe had created a strong demand for Japanese silk and silk eggs. The enterprising peasants of the chief silk-producing areas in the mountains of central Japan rose to the challenge, and as a result, Japan developed a favorable balance of trade with the West. In the 1870s, as the artificial stimulus of the European silk blight faded, peasant entrepreneurs adopted the relatively simple process of reeling silk by mechanical power, and thus produced a more uniform and superior silk thread to that of other Asian countries. This gave Japan the lion's share of the silk market in the West, and silk remained her largest export until well into the twentieth century.

Already in the 1870s, however, the balance of trade had turned against Japan. In 1866 the European powers had forced on the shogunate a tariff rate fixed at the low level of 5 percent, and this had opened the country to an increasing flood of Western cotton textiles and other manufactures, which began to undermine many traditional industries. There was a desperate need to industrialize the country if Japan were to protect herself from Western economic domination and build the sort of economy that could support a military establishment that would provide security from the West. Some of the leaders also hoped that modern factories would provide jobs for the samurai, who were in serious financial straits.

The shogunate and some of the daimyo domains had experimented on a small scale with strategic industries such as munitions and shipbuilding, and also with some consumer industries such as cotton spinning and weaving. The new government continued and expanded these efforts. It built pilot plants which led the way in the mechanization of silk reeling and the industrialization of cotton spinning, cotton weaving, and a number of other light industries. Aside from silk reeling, however, most of these industrial efforts lost money. It always takes considerable time and effort to overcome the inevitable initial hurdles in developing new industries.

The government was more successful, however, in establishing a stable base for future industrialization and economic growth. It created a modern currency system in 1871, with the yen as the basic unit, valued during most of the next half-century at about half an American dollar. It developed a modern banking system, based heavily at first on the government bonds of the daimyo. It led in developing communications—creating a modern postal system, tying the country together with a telegraph network, modernizing port facilities, and in 1872 laying the first railway line between Tokyo and its port of Yokohama. This was a small beginning on what in time was to grow into the world's busiest and perhaps most efficient railway system.

In order to set up a modern budgetary system, the government shifted in 1873 from the old form of agricultural taxes as percentages of produce to taxes on agricultural land assessed in fixed monetary terms, regardless of the size of the harvest. In the process of this change, legal sanction was given to the private ownership by peasants of their individual plots that had been developing informally during the Tokugawa period. Inflation in the late 1870s reduced the burden of these fixed taxes and allowed the peasants to put new capital investments into their lands, and this, together with the stimulus of improved transportation, the elimination of the remaining feudal barriers to trade and to the spread of advanced native agricultural technology to the more backward regions, and some increase in the area under cultivation, resulted in a steady and marked increase in agricultural production over the next few decades.

The Japanese economy was undoubtedly beginning to modernize and expand, but by the late 1870s the government was in serious financial difficulties. It had had to take over shogunate debts and indemnity payments to the Western powers; attempts to renovate the government and economy had proved costly, and most of its industrial ventures were still losing money; a modernized military establishment was extremely expensive; foreign expert advice came at a very high price; attempts to develop the frontier island of Hokkaido required further outlays; and the liquidation of the old order through payments to the daimyo and samurai, as well as the cost of the Satsuma rebellion, were a heavy financial drain. The new paper currency depreciated seriously in value, and a dangerous inflation loomed.

Strong financial measures were obviously called for. These were undertaken by Matsukata, one of the samurai leaders from Satsuma, who was appointed finance minister in 1881 and carried through a program of stern retrenchment. He slashed the budget and sold off to private owners most of the government's plants in nonstrategic industries. The reforms worked, and the government was back on a sound financial footing well before the end of the decade.

Another result of Matsukata's reforms was the concentration of Japan's nascent industrial resources in the hands of the few persons able to buy them from the government. Since few people had enough money to buy factories that were in any case still losing money, the payments received were far less than the original outlays. But in terms of the prices paid for the factories, they were bargains, and they soon began to bring in profits. In part this may have been the result of more flexible and imaginative private management, but it was also a sign that the Japanese had built up enough skill and experience to get over the initial difficulties of industrialization. The first boom came in cotton spinning in the mid-1880s, and this was followed by surges in one industrial field after another. Japan was well on the way to industrialization by the end of the century, but in part because of Matsukata's sales, the financial benefits of this development became concentrated in the hands of a relatively small group of private businessmen, some of whom were later to develop into the great financial magnates the Japanese call *zaibatsu*, "the financial clique."

The industrialists and businessmen of Meiji Japan were not, as one might imagine, simply the descendants of the great urban merchants of Tokugawa days. Most of these proved unable to adapt to the new age. They were too tied to traditional industries and old-fashioned ways of doing business. Only a few, like the seventeenth-century house of Mitsui, became an important element in the new economy. Some of the new businessmen came from among the aggressive rural entrepreneurs who had appeared in the latter part of the Tokugawa period. For example, Shibusawa, from a prosperous peasant business family in the environs of Edo, after winning samurai status in the closing years of the shogunate, became a leader in the cotton spinning industry, in banking, and in a host of other fields. Others were men of obscure origin, talented adventurers who seized the opportunities offered by a time of rapid change. The bulk of the new business community, however, came from the samurai class. Such men took advantage of their greater educational attainments and their connections with samurai in government to forge ahead in the business world. Some of them had had experience as business agents for their daimyo. Such was the case of Iwasaki of Tosa, who, starting in the field of shipping, built up his firm of Mitsubishi to be second only to Mitsui.

Japan's success in modernizing her economy in the second half of the nineteenth century is naturally a relevant story for the many countries in the world trying to do the same today. This story has usually been interpreted as showing the importance of government leadership in industrialization, but this is to misunderstand it. The government did indeed take the lead in many fields, but Japan's industrial success actually came after the government had withdrawn from most industries. The Japanese story is basically a classic economic tale. The government first had to build a stable economic foundation: it had to provide sound currency, adequate banking institutions, a modernized tax and budgetary system, and political stability. Moreover, a considerable expansion of agricultural production had to precede any real success in industrialization. And the latter, when it came, was overwhelmingly in the hands of private entrepreneurs, and it appeared in the same stages as in the West— first in light industry, such as textiles, and only later in heavy industry.

The need to industrialize Japan's economy may have been obvious enough, but the Meiji leaders showed surprising perspicacity in realizing the importance both of learning the technology and ideas of the West and of creating an educated public to support a modernized economy and society. Some of them, such as Ito of

Choshu, had themselves studied in Europe before the end of the shogunate. During the last few years of the Tokugawa, the Edo government and some of the daimyo had sent envoys and students abroad to learn the skills and science of the West, and the new government greatly expanded this program. In fact, the first two decades of its rule were essentially a time when the Japanese studied, borrowed, and gradually assimilated those elements of Western civilization which they chose to adopt.

This period of learning from the West was comparable only to the great period over a thousand years earlier when the Japanese had imported Chinese civilization, but this time the process of learning from abroad was carried out on a much larger scale and more systematically. Students were carefully chosen on the basis of their knowledge and capabilities, and the countries where they were to study were selected with equal care. The Japanese determined to learn from each Western country that in which it particularly excelled. For example, they went to England to study the navy and merchant marine, to Germany for the army and for medicine, to France for local government and law, and to the United States for business methods. The world was one vast schoolroom for them, but they chose what and where they would learn and how they would use the knowledge to change life in Japan.

The new government also hired scores of Occidental experts and teachers at high salaries in order to attract real talent, and since, unlike contemporary modernizing countries, they paid for these people out of their own meager financial resources, they utilized their abilities to the full. Hundreds of missionaries, mostly from America, also provided free instruction in the English language and numerous other fields. Although the old ban on

Christianity was not officially dropped until 1873, American Protestant missionaries had entered Japan as early as 1859, and they founded many pioneer schools. While the missionaries continued to teach gratis, the government replaced its own expensive foreign experts and teachers as quickly as possible with Japanese they had trained or with returned students. Before the end of the century, foreigners in the government or in government schools had become very rare, except in the field of foreign languages.

The Meiji leaders clearly saw the importance of an educational system in a modern state. They realized that a technically competent populace was a prerequisite for modern power. The army and navy needed men who could read and who knew the rudiments of Western science. Modern industry also required a literate working force and large numbers of more highly trained technicians as well, if it was to build prosperity for the nation and the sinews of its defense. In 1871 the government created a Ministry of Education and embarked Japan on an ambitious program of universal education. It naturally took time to build the thousands of schoolhouses required, to train the tens of thousands of teachers needed, and to develop the financial resources for both. By the early twentieth century, however, virtually all Japanese children were in school, and the educational pyramid had become stabilized in the form of a six-year compulsory elementary school, followed for progressively smaller and more select groups of students by a five-year middle school, then an elite three-year higher school, and at the top, a three-year university. Tokyo University was founded in 1877 out of earlier elements, and it was joined in time by other so-called imperial universities and eventually by a host of private universities.

The educational system, unlike those of the West, was thus almost entirely created *de novo*, and except for some missionary institutions and private universities (which did not compare in prestige with the imperial universities), it was almost entirely in government hands. Thus it was free of the aristocratic aura and religious domination of many Western educational systems of the time. It was, in fact, a far more rationalized, secular, and state-oriented educational system than existed at that time in most of the West. Education was regarded primarily as a tool of government, to train obedient and reliable citizens for service in the various skills needed in a modern nation. It was narrowly tailored to meet the national needs foreseen by the leaders: a literate working and military force, a broad group of technicians, and a small leadership elite produced by the imperial universities.

One result of this highly rational system was to change Japanese society within a generation or two from one in which prestige and function were largely determined by birth to one in which both were determined almost entirely by education. Thus Japan, starting as a still essentially feudal society in the middle of the nineteenth century, had become a much more egalitarian society than England by the early twentieth century. A less happy result of central government control of education was its use for indoctrination. The lower levels of education became increasingly a means for teaching the people what to think rather than how to think. The heavy burden of rote memory work imposed by the writing system may have heightened this tendency. In any case, Japan has the dubious distinction of pioneering in the modern totalitarian technique of consciously inculcating obedience and uniformity through a standardized and closely controlled educational system.

❋

After crushing the Satsuma rebellion in 1877, the new regime was politically secure at home, and Matsukata's reforms in the early 1880s gave it new economic stability. The time had obviously come to create a more permanent and fully elaborated political order than the somewhat makeshift and fast-changing system that had existed until then. Having more than two centuries of clearly established and stable political institutions behind them, the Japanese leaders yearned to re-create a stable and well-defined form of government.

The Western concept of a constitution to delimit such a system, though a new idea to them, had strong appeal. For one thing, constitutions and representative institutions seemed to contribute to the strength and stability of the most advanced nations of the West, and therefore they might be of value to Japan too. Equally important, the adoption of a constitutional form of government with representative institutions was considered the best way to impress the West with Japan's progress. In the minds of Japanese of the time, the need to win diplomatic equality with the West, that is, to get rid of extraterritoriality and tariff limitations, came second only to winning military and economic security. As early as 1872, Iwakura himself had led a large part of the leadership group on a mission to the United States and Europe, in part to observe the West, but also to try to win back diplomatic equality. By the 1880s there was a strong demand for treaty revision among all educated Japanese, but in order to get the treaties revised, it was clearly necessary for Japan to win the respect of the Occident.

From the start, the new leaders had been intrigued by the representative institutions of the West. Already in 1868 they had induced the emperor to issue a brief "Charter Oath" that mentioned "deliberative assemblies" in a vague way, and since then they had from time to time tried to draw up plans for a national assembly. They also experimented cautiously by arranging for the election of prefectural assemblies in 1879, and municipal assemblies the next year.

In 1874 Itagaki, a samurai from Tosa and a leading member of the government, irritated at the rejection of his ideas, left the leadership group and started a popular party oriented toward representative government. His movement was at first basically an expression of samurai discontent, parallel to the more violent samurai outbursts in Satsuma and elsewhere, but prosperous peasants and city merchants soon joined the movement, and by the late 1870s a considerable "freedom and people's rights movement" (*jiyu-minken-undo*) had developed. It was buttressed by the work of intellectuals such as Fukuzawa, a samurai from a Kyushu domain, who led in popularizing the liberal political concepts and value systems of the West, though he is best remembered today as the founder of Keio, a great private university.

In 1879 the emperor requested all the councillors to submit their personal proposals for constitutional government, and in 1881 one of them, Okuma of Hizen, made a radical proposal for the immediate adoption of the British parliamentary system. The proposal, together with Okuma's attack on another of the leaders over alleged scandals in the sale of government properties in Hokkaido, precipitated a crisis. The upshot was a reorganization of the government which got rid of Okuma, who then followed Itagaki's lead by starting another pop-

ular opposition political movement. He also followed
Fukuzawa's lead by founding Waseda, another great private university. As a result of the crisis, the government
also made a clear decision to move slowly over the next
several years to adopt a constitution and create a national
assembly by 1890, but to base the assembly more on the
conservative Prussian model than on the democratic
model of England.

The shaping of the final form of the new government
fell to a slightly younger group than the original Restoration leaders. The three dominant early figures, Saigo and
Okubo of Satsuma and Kido of Choshu, were all gone
by 1878, and the leading court noble, Iwakura, died in
1883. This left men like Ito and Yamagata of Choshu
and Matsukata of Satsuma in control. A fairly small and
clear-cut group, these men dominated Japanese politics
as a sort of oligarchy during the next few decades and
came to be known as the genro, or "elder statesmen."
Ito in particular took charge of drafting the new constitution. He visited Europe, especially conservative Germany and Austria, to learn the latest in Western political theories, and he also busily set about creating the
political institutions that were to accompany the new
constitution.

In 1885 a modern cabinet system, under a prime minister, was adopted, with Ito himself in the top post, and
thereafter for a number of years the oligarchs themselves
revolved in the cabinet posts. In the same year a fully
modernized civil service system was adopted. Tokyo University was designed to be the chief source of the higher
bureaucracy, as it has remained ever since, but in the
1890s the superabundance of university graduates forced
the adoption of a selection system through rigid but fair
examinations. Work also went ahead on modernizing Ja-

pan's legal structure, since a system that corresponded with Western legal concepts was necessary if there was to be any hope of persuading the Western powers to relinquish their extraterritorial privileges. French models were used at first and then German, but it was a big and complicated task, and the finished codes were not issued until 1899.

A central concern of the leaders was to protect the imperial prerogatives—and of course their own power through the control of these prerogatives—against challenges from what seemed to them less informed and able men hoping to exercise power through representative institutions. From the 1870s until the early 1880s Japan had endured a craze of Westernization: all things Occidental, ideas as well as styles, were in vogue. But in the late 1880s there was a swing away from this blind imitation of the West, the first of a series of swings of the pendulum that have characterized Japanese attitudes toward the West during the past century. This explains the issuance in 1890 of a very traditional, Confucian-style document under the title of "The Imperial Rescript on Education," and may account for some of the conservative tone of the constitution. But this conservatism by twentieth-century standards was only to be expected. The men shaping the constitution were all products of a feudal background, deeply devoted to the concept of "imperial rule," and by then well accustomed to exercising autocratic authority themselves. They were not inclined to give their power away to others whom they felt were less qualified to rule.

The leaders strengthened the court positions immediately surrounding the throne and established in 1888 a Privy Council, which was to act as a bulwark of imperial authority. They also created in 1884 a new nobility to people a House of Peers, which was to balance the elected lower house. The old court aristocracy and the daimyo, the latter in accordance with the size of their former domains and their service to the cause of the Restoration, were divided into five noble ranks, and the samurai leaders assigned themselves places in the peerage which were subsequently raised until several of them achieved the highest rank of Prince.

The constitution itself was finally promulgated on February 11, 1889, as a gift to the people by the emperor. It dwelt at length on the prerogatives of the emperor, who was described as "sacred and inviolable" and the source of all authority. The duties and rights of subjects were described in detail, though their rights were somewhat circumscribed by phrases such as "within the limits of the law." The great innovation of the constitution was the creation of an entirely elective House of Representatives, but the electorate for it was limited to men paying 15 yen or more in direct taxes. They numbered at the time only about 450,000, which was about 6 percent of the adult male population. This was roughly the same proportion as the old samurai class, though the new electorate consisted largely of peasant landowners and other people of nonsamurai origin. The lower house was held in check by the equal authority of the House of Peers, and the two together, traditionally called the Diet, had only very restricted powers, for they were limited largely to the voting of taxes and the budget.

While the new Japanese constitution was reminiscent of earlier stages of Western democracy and was not unlike the political systems then existing in some of the less advanced parts of Europe, it was a far cry from the democracy of the time in England, France, or the United

States. This situation has led many historians to view the constitution as an unnatural, reactionary reversal of the normal flow of democratic progress and to consider it a defeat for democracy in Japan. But it is doubtful that Japan could have successfully governed herself at that time by a much more fully democratic system, and it is hard to imagine an effective political leadership in Japan during that period which would have designed a much more liberal constitution.

The real question is why the oligarchs gave the elected representatives of the people a real share in political power and designed a constitution with enough ambiguity, probably in part on purpose, to permit considerable evolutionary development within it. It was certainly not because of the strength of the demands for popular government, which the oligarchs could have disregarded with impunity. More likely, it was because of their own assumptions that a constitution and representative institutions, as in the West, could contribute to a stronger, more stable political system by marshaling popular support for the government and permitting discontent a relatively innocuous oratorical safety valve.

The leaders were also fully aware that nothing would more favorably impress the nations of the West than a constitutional form of government in Japan with representative institutions and clear and just legal procedures like those of the West. In this they were quite correct. The successful modernization of their government along Western lines was a major reason why on July 16, 1894, even before Japan had demonstrated her new military strength in the Sino-Japanese War, Britain relinquished extraterritoriality as of 1899, when the new law codes went into effect. The other nations quickly followed suit, and by 1911 Japan had also won back full control over her own tariffs, and was thus completely out from under the unequal treaties that the West had imposed on her through superior military power. Japan had become the first non-Western nation to win diplomatic equality with the Occident.

9 ✸ EMPIRE AND DEMOCRACY

Even after the new constitution went into effect in 1889, the Japanese of course continued to learn much about Western science and technology and to be influenced by Occidental institutions and concepts, but for the next several decades the internal evolution of the modernized system they had set up loomed much larger than further foreign borrowings. This evolutionary development led in many different directions. On the one hand, Japan became a great imperialistic power abroad; on the other, she moved far toward parliamentary democracy at home. Such seeming contrasts were hardly unique: both France and Britain were great empires and at the same time democracies. But in Japan, less established in her new social and political forms and moving at a more rapid evolutionary pace, the clash between conflicting trends proved in the long run more upsetting.

Japan's only organized effort at foreign conquest had occurred three centuries before under Hideyoshi, but early in the Meiji period there was a demand for a military expedition against Korea, ostensibly to chastise her for an insulting response to Japanese overtures, but in reality to provide honorable employment for the dispossessed samurai. It was largely over this issue that Saigo and Itagaki left the government. As a sop to the war party, a much less hazardous expedition was mounted in 1874 against a few aborigines in Taiwan (Formosa) who had killed some Okinawan mariners. When the Chinese government paid Japan an indemnity for this incident, it unwittingly confirmed Japan's claim to sovereignty over the Ryukyu Islands, which were fully incorporated into Japan in 1879 as the prefecture of Okinawa.

By the 1890s Japan was in a position to play a larger and more aggressive role abroad. In the West at that time it was generally accepted that great nations had a right to rule over lesser ones for their own good as well as for the economic benefit of the colonial masters. National prestige and security were also felt to depend on foreign conquests. The late nineteenth century in particular was a high point in the mad scramble for empire and a time when everyone was looking forward to dividing up the "Chinese melon." It is not surprising that the Japanese leaders, with their own military background and their decades of learning from the West, accepted these Occidental points of view. They could also see that Korea was an area of obvious strategic importance to Japan.

In 1876 Japan had employed Perry's technique against the shogunate to force Korea to sign her first modern treaty and open herself to foreign contacts. Since then, the Japanese had exercised increasing political influence as modernizers in the peninsula; and because Korea recognized a vague sort of Chinese suzerainty, this brought Japan into rivalry with the great continental empire. In the summer of 1894, both Japan and China dispatched troops to Korea because of the outbreak of a rebellion there, and this brought on war between the two. To the amazement of the Western powers, the now thoroughly modernized forces of the small island nation triumphed easily over the Chinese giant. The Japanese swept through Korea and into Manchuria, destroyed the Chinese fleet, and occupied the port of Weihaiwei in North China. The Treaty of Shimonoseki of April 17, 1895, brought an end to the Sino-Japanese War. In it, China ceded to Japan the island province of Taiwan, the nearby Pescadores Islands, and the Liaotung Peninsula in southern Manchuria, paid a large indemnity, accepted the full independence of Korea, and accorded the Japanese the same unequal diplomatic and commercial privileges the Westerners had extorted.

In this age of rampant imperialism, the Westerners, far from condemning the Japanese for their aggressions, applauded them as being apt pupils. They also taught the Japanese how ruthless the game of imperialism could be and how unwilling Westerners were to accept other races as full equals. Russia, France, and Germany banded together to force Japan to return the Liaotung Peninsula to China, and then three years later these same powers cynically seized new slices of China, the Russians taking the Liaotung Peninsula for themselves. Even Britain followed suit by taking Weihaiwei, the port the Japanese had occupied in North China.

The Japanese swallowed this humiliation, but they began to feel that a clash was inevitable with Russia, which was already dominant in Manchuria and was extending her influence into Korea. Not wishing to face again a coalition of European powers, they sought a Western ally. This they found in Britain, which was not averse to seeing her Russian rival embroiled in war in

East Asia and was eager to share in distant areas her growing burden of world naval supremacy. The resulting Anglo-Japanese Alliance of 1902 was the first entirely equal military pact between a Western and non-Western nation.

The stage was now set for a confrontation with Russia. Choosing their time in February 1904, the Japanese set a new pattern for modern warfare by first crippling Russian naval strength in East Asia and then declaring war. Russia was far stronger than Japan, but was under the disadvantage of having to fight the war at the end of a single-track railway several thousand miles long. Her military operations were further hampered by revolutionary movements at home. The Japanese were consistently victorious, bottling up the Russians in the Liaotung Peninsula ports, which fell after costly assaults, and driving their other armies northward through Manchuria. Russia sent her European fleet from the Baltic Sea around Africa to the Pacific, but the entire Japanese navy fell upon it in the straits between Japan and Korea and annihilated it. Although Russia was being soundly trounced, Japan was so exhausted that she welcomed the peace arranged by President Theodore Roosevelt, who greatly admired Japanese efficiency and pluck. A treaty signed in Portsmouth, New Hampshire, terminated the Russo-Japanese War on September 5, 1905. In it Russia acknowledged Japan's paramount interests in Korea, transferred to Japan her lease of the Liaotung Peninsula and the railways she had built in southern Manchuria, and ceded the southern half of the large island of Sakhalin, north of Hokkaido, in lieu of an indemnity. Japan, the military ally of Great Britain, the victor over Russia, and the possessor

SIBERIA

OUTER MONGOLIA

Amur R.

MANCHURIA

SAKHALIN

KURILE ISLANDS

INNER MONGOLIA

Vladivostok

• Peking

SEA OF JAPAN

LIAOTUNG PEN.

KOREA

JAPAN

Weihaiwei

SHANTUNG

• Tsingtao

CHINA

Nanking •

Yangtse R.

Hankow •

Shanghai •

EAST CHINA SEA

BONIN ISLANDS

FUKIEN

RYUKYU ISLANDS   OKINAWA

PACIFIC OCEAN

• Canton

PESCADORES ISLANDS

TAIWAN

Hong Kong

THE JAPANESE EMPIRE

▓▓ **Extent of Japanese Empire**

—+—+— **Manchurian Railway Lines**

SOUTH CHINA SEA

0   300 Miles

PHILIPPINE ISLANDS

of an expanding colonial empire, was becoming a true world power.

Relieved of Chinese and Russian competition in Korea, Japan quietly annexed the whole of the peninsula in 1910 without the slightest protest from the Western powers. There, as in Taiwan, she embarked upon an ambitious program of economic development and exploitation, which brought railways, school systems, factories, and other outward aspects of the modern world to these lands. The Koreans and Taiwanese, however, were subjected to the repressive rule of an efficient but often ruthless colonial administration and an omnipresent and often brutal police force. Particularly in Korea, where annexation had come later and had encountered the proud traditions of a homogeneous people who had had their own centralized, Chinese-type bureaucratic state for more than a thousand years, Japanese colonial rule proved extremely oppressive and was hated by the Korean people.

World War I gave Japan another chance to expand, this time with little risk or effort. As the ally of Britain, she soon declared war on Germany. Little interested in the outcome of the war in Europe, Japan happily proceeded to pick up German colonies in the East, taking Tsingtao on the China coast and all the German interests in the surrounding province of Shantung, and seizing the German islands in the North Pacific—the Marianas, Carolines, and Marshalls—which were later assigned to Japan in the form of a mandate by the Versailles peace treaty. With the eyes of the rest of the world turned toward Europe, Japan also found this a good time to win more concessions from the Chinese, and in 1915 presented China with the so-called Twenty-one Demands. Although the Chinese succeeded in resisting the most sweeping of these, which would have turned China into a virtual protectorate, Japan did win broad new economic rights in Manchuria, Shantung, and the coastal province of Fukien opposite Taiwan.

Thus only fifty years after the Restoration, Japan emerged from World War I as Britain's chief rival for domination in China. She went to the peace conference at Versailles as one of the Big Five among the victors and an accepted world power. The Meiji leaders, who had set out in 1868 to create a Japan that would be militarily secure from the West and fully equal to it, had, within the very lifetimes of their more long-lived members, done exactly that. Few generations of political leaders anywhere have proved as successful within the limits of their own goals.

Japan's growth as a military power was matched by her economic advances. The new industries were beginning to pay by the late 1880s, and the Sino-Japanese and Russo-Japanese wars both proved economically stimulating. World War I was even more of a boon, because it cost Japan little, but gave her the markets of Asia, cut off by the war from the factories of Europe. Japanese businessmen took full advantage of this opportunity to make deep inroads into rich markets previously monopolized by the Europeans.

During these decades Japan succeeded in one new field after another in the light industries. The rapid descent of Japan's numerous though small rivers was fully exploited to bring electric power to all corners of the land. Municipal water and gas systems were widely developed, and streetcar systems became common. In all ways Japan was becoming a modern industrialized land, and at a pace more rapid than that of the West.

As the first non-Western land to adopt the industrial and commercial techniques of the West on a significant scale, Japan found herself in a unique position in the economic world. Western technology and cheap Oriental labor made an excellent combination for low-priced production. The rest of Asia had cheap labor but as yet lacked technical skills; Europe and America had high technology and far greater natural resources than Japan, but also much higher standards of living and therefore correspondingly higher wages. This discrepancy between Oriental and Occidental standards of living and the lag in the industrialization of other non-Western lands gave the new Japanese industries and commercial enterprises an exceptional chance for rapid growth. Producing for its own relatively poor citizenry and for the even poorer populations of the rest of Asia, Japanese industry became oriented particularly toward cheap and sometimes shoddy consumer goods. Textiles accounted for more than half of factory employment at the end of the nineteenth century, and predominated in the export trade. Heavy industries such as steel and shipbuilding were developed to some extent, but largely for strategic reasons. It was not until the 1930s that the Japanese could begin to compete with the industrially much more experienced Western nations in the heavy industries, and not until after World War II that they became competitive in complicated machinery and the fine industries.

Japan found herself provided with an ample and also competent supply of labor. Unlike many other non-Western nations, the lower classes were already familiar with working for wages, and Japan's relatively advanced traditional industries had made them skilled workers. The population, responding to modern medicine and transport facilities, doubled to 60 million within a little over a half century after the Meiji Restoration, and rural Japan, already saturated with people in the Tokugawa period, became a seemingly inexhaustible reservoir for cheap urban labor.

The contrast with the United States was sharp. There the mechanization of farming released workers for urban labor, but at the same time greatly increased the scale and prosperity of agriculture. This pattern was possible only where land was abundant and labor scarce. In Japan there was a minimum of land and an abundance of labor. Since there was little unused land, except in Hokkaido, and the average size of a farm in the other islands was only 2 1/2 acres, the increased rural population had to drain off to the cities, but the new industries could not grow fast enough to absorb it all. Thus city wages remained inexorably tied to the inevitably low living standards of the miniscule Japanese scale of agriculture. Farm girls between the termination of their schooling and marriage in their twenties became the bulk of the workers in textile mills. Herded into dormitories, they provided a cheap but docile and efficient working force. Younger sons, forced to migrate to the cities, became in time a more permanent urban working class, but tied as they were to their rural backgrounds and returning to their old homes for subsistence in hard times, they were at first little more than an urbanized peasantry.

Japan's great industrial success thus did not bring a rapid rise in living standards for the lower classes. Population growth was too great, and the drag of a dense, impoverished peasantry too strong. All classes did benefit from cheaper and better manufactured goods, such as inexpensive cotton cloth, rubber-soled footwear, rubber boots, and bicycles, and they also benefited from modern services, such as public schooling, improved medicine, electric lighting, and cheap and convenient railway service. But there was little improvement in such basics as food and housing.

Another reason why the masses failed to share fully in Japan's great economic advance was because the leadership had other, more pressing objectives. True to the early slogan of "rich country, strong military," they devoted their attention to a rapid development of the industrial plant and to building up Japan's military power.

The heavy concentration of private economic power in the hands of the great zaibatsu enterprises contributed to the emphasis on industrial growth rather than consumption. So did the parsimonious, saving habits of most Japanese, presumably a legacy of the Confucian morality and economic limitations of the Tokugawa period. The zaibatsu families, in view of their great wealth, must be rated as conspicuous underconsumers. They did not go in for yachts, foreign banking accounts, and villas abroad, but assiduously plowed back their profits into expanding their economic enterprises. And the common people, largely through post office savings accounts, showed a comparable propensity for saving that has continued to the present.

The great concentration of private economic power had not been merely the product of Matsukata's sale of government industries in the 1880s. A more important cause was government financial aid and patronage for those they regarded as best able to build the economic sinews Japan needed. These were often men with whom the government leaders were closely connected by previous background or marriage, and much of this favoritism would be judged scandalous by contemporary standards. For example, Iwasaki got his start in building up the Mitsubishi interests through ships and funds provided him by the government in connection with the Taiwan campaign of 1874 and the Satsuma rebellion of 1877. But scandalous or not, such collusion between the government and private business interests did help to produce rapid economic growth.

Another result of this situation was the development of a relationship of cooperation and trust between government and big business, a sharp contrast with the American tradition of suspicion and hostility. Japanese businessmen readily accepted guidance and control from the government, which after all had been traditional in Tokugawa times too. Such guidance and control, of course, took modern forms, such as mergers and cartels sponsored or encouraged by the government. The Mitsui and Mitsubishi shipping interests, for example, merged in 1885 to form a single strong Japanese shipping enterprise more capable of competing with Western firms. Similarly, the cotton spinners, in order to strengthen their hand in buying cotton on the world market, formed a strong cartel in the 1890s under Shibusawa's leadership. The net result of such tendencies was that the Japanese showed more conscious effort and greater skill in shaping the national economy than had as yet appeared in the West.

Despite government guidance and cartel arrangements, the individual economic enterprises grew to be not only huge, but powerful. Mitsui and Mitsubishi were the two largest and set the pattern for the unique Japanese institution of zaibatsu combines, or conglomerates, as they might be called today. Commonly there was a central, family-controlled "holding company," which through large blocs of shares controlled major industrial and commercial firms, which in turn controlled lesser affiliates. The whole structure was not unlike that of the Tokugawa shogunate, with its fiefs and subfiefs. There were feudal overtones too in the personal relations within the combines. Loyalty was strong, for young business-men joined a combine for life and rose by moving around among its various units, and a system of inter-locking directors further strengthened solidarity.

Unlike the great industrial empires of the West, a zaibatsu combine was not concentrated in a single field, but was spread throughout the whole of the modern sector of the Japanese economy. Combines usually cen-tered around great banking institutions, but they were also likely to include manufacturing, mining, shipping, and foreign trade. Broadly based as they were, they could best afford to finance promising new fields in the econ-omy, and thus their share in the whole economy tended to grow. They also developed great rivalries with one another, and the economic and political battling be-tween Mitsui and Mitsubishi became legendary.

Political and intellectual development after 1889 was no less marked than the economic, but it was much more uneven and less predictable. By the end of the century, many of the basic social and educational reforms of the Meiji leaders were beginning to have a major impact on society. A fully literate citizenry was emerging, and higher education expanded rapidly with each passing decade. A large and self-confident business community was developing, together with a huge new urban class composed of the well-educated white collar worker, which the Japanese came to call the "salary man." Most important, the new generation of Japanese were post-Tokugawa people, products of the new education who lacked the common feudal background of the old political leadership.

Men like Fukuzawa had popularized the utilitarianism of England, social Darwinism, and the philosophy of Rousseau, and toward the end of the century the socialist doctrines of Europe also began to seep into Japan. By the 1880s a strong native Christian church had developed which, together with the missionary educational institutions, had a much greater impact on Japanese ethics and ideals than the relatively meager number of converts would suggest. The revulsion against Westernization of the 1880s also produced various forms of ultranationalistic thought, which merged easily with military expansionism by calling for Japan's defense of Asia against enslavement by the West. Newspapers and magazines of all sorts proliferated in number and expanded greatly in distribution, as a mass reading public developed and began to show the characteristic Japanese mania for reading.

This greatly increased intellectual ferment may help explain the revitalization of Japanese literature at this time. In the first few decades after the Meiji Restoration, the chief activity had been the translating of Western books, but around the turn of the century Natsume Soseki and other vigorous new writers, inspired by Western authors but also deriving much from the Tokugawa literary tradition, began to create a new prose literature which was in time to make the modern Japanese novel one of the great currents in contemporary world literature. These novelists drew heavily on their own personal experiences and showed a deep concern with the private life of the individual. There was already discernible in them a clear sense of alienation from society, which illustrated the psychological strains many Japanese were beginning to feel, caught as they were in the rapid transition from old to new and the pull between native tradition and modern values associated with the West.

In this fast-changing economic and intellectual environment, it is not surprising that the political system the Meiji leaders had perfected by 1889 did not work quite as they had expected. The House of Representatives proved much more obstreperous than they had imagined it would be, and they also discovered to their dismay that they had given it more power than they had intended. A provision that the previous year's budget remained in effect if the new one was not voted—the political trump card of their conservative German advisors—proved to be of little value in a rapidly growing economy. The previous year's budget was never enough, and to get new taxes and appropriations the leaders found they had to make more concessions to the elected representatives of the people than they had counted on.

Perhaps the most surprising development in Meiji Japan had been that, in a country which was entirely lacking in any sort of democratic traditions or institutions, a strong grass-roots demand for a democratic sharing of power had manifested itself. In part this was a sign of the great prestige of Western ideas at the time, in part proof of the universal appeal of the democratic ideal. But a more important reason was probably the very size of the old samurai class, with its strong tradition of political participation. The great majority of the former samurai had found no place in the new leadership, and many of these men clamored for a share in political power. They easily became critics of the new regime, and quite a few went into newspaper work as a way to attack the government. (They thus account for the old and deep tradition of opposition to the government in the Japanese press.) Naturally the concept of political parties and elected assemblies appealed to some of these outsiders as a way to win a place for themselves in the political leadership. That men of peasant and merchant background soon joined them in these political demands is evidence of how much the samurai ethos had spread to the educated elements among these other classes during the Tokugawa period. In general, the motivations behind the demand for representative government in Japan were not unlike those that had resulted in England's long parliamentary growth—not democratic theory so much as a desire for a share in power.

Itagaki, one of the original oligarchs, had embraced concepts of representative government as early as 1874 and had stirred up the widespread—even if politically impotent—"freedom and people's rights movement." The expulsion of Okuma from the oligarchy in 1881 and the concurrent promise to create a national assembly led Itagaki, Okuma, and their respective followers into another flurry of political party building. Elections for the prefectural assemblies from 1879 on and for municipal bodies after 1880 gave these political outsiders considerable grass-roots electoral experience, and to the dismay of the government leaders, they dominated the first election for the House of Representatives, held on November 25, 1890.

The opposition elements in the Diet coalesced into two major parties, the Liberals (Jiyuto), who were Itagaki's followers, and the Progressives (Kaishinto), who supported Okuma. Their one clear avenue to power sharing was to cut the budget, which they immediately proceeded to do. In the following four years there was a continuous battle between the party men and the oligarchs over the budget. The latter frequently dissolved the Diet and forced new elections, in the hope that this form of chastisement would produce a more cooperative membership. They sometimes used the prefectural governments and the police to try to buy elections or suppress opposition candidates, but even in the second general election of February 1892, the most violent and corrupt in Japanese history, the loyal government supporters failed to win a majority. The parliamentary creation of the oligarchs proved such a nuisance that some of them wished to abolish it, but they could hardly do this without losing face before the West and endangering their chances for winning back diplomatic equality. Ito in particular, probably because of pride of authorship, was insistent that they carry through with their experiment in "constitutional government."

The Sino-Japanese War, like all later wars, gave the government some respite from the fray, because the Japanese Diet members, like their parliamentary counterparts in more democratic countries, proved to be chauvinistic supporters of taxes and budgets in wartime. Following the war, a pattern of compromise was worked out. Ito took Itagaki into his cabinet in return for the support of the Liberals in the Diet, and in 1896 Matsukata worked out a similar deal with Okuma and the Progressives. While the oligarchs believed strongly in keeping the cabinet "transcendental," that is, above the politics of the Diet, they were willing to make some concessions, particularly to these two former members of their own group. The parties, for their part, were willing to compromise in this way because they were violent rivals for whatever power the House of Representatives exercised, and the chief objective of their members, after all, was not some distant democratic ideal but winning an immediate share in political power. The new parliamentary system was working neither very smoothly nor in accordance with Ito's original plan, but at least it had survived its perilous infant years. For the first time, a parliamentary body in a non-Western country was becoming an established and meaningful part of the political process. In fact, it was showing signs of following the same line of evolutionary development taken by the mother of parliaments in London. But many ups and downs lay ahead.

In 1898, when none of the oligarchs proved willing to take the prime ministership, they gave Okuma and Itagaki a chance to form an essentially party cabinet, but this experiment proved abortive because of the rivalries between the two parties and the refusal of the bureaucracy to give them full cooperation. Yamagata, who as the creator of the Japanese army was one of the more conservative of the oligarchs, then put his hand to pushing back the parliamentary clock. He formed an entirely "transcendental" cabinet, strengthened the laws that controlled public meetings and political activities, increased the exclusiveness of the civil service system in order to keep political appointees out of high bureaucratic jobs, limited the army and navy ministers to generals and admirals on active service in order to keep civilian appointees from controlling the armed services, sought—though without success—to put new life into a government party, and changed the election laws.

This last reform led in two different directions. On the one hand, the tax qualifications for the suffrage were lowered, so that almost a million persons now qualified. On the other hand, electoral districts were made much larger than before; they were now usually a whole prefecture, with up to 13 members elected from each. In theory this was to attract broader-gauged, more statesman-like candidates, but in reality its purpose was to make electioneering more difficult and, through the roughly proportional system that resulted, to make more room for a balancing government party between the two opposition parties.

Yamagata's reforms served as a brake on the development of party control over the government, but he found that even he could not govern effectively without majority support in the Diet. In 1900 his colleagues therefore permitted Ito to try a more imaginative approach to the problem, one which Ito had advocated for some time. It was based on the principle so colorfully expressed by the American dictum, "If you can't lick 'em, join 'em." He and his chief bureaucratic supporters joined with the Liberals to form a new party, named the Seiyukai. Then, as party president, he took over the prime ministership for the fourth time and included in his cabinet a few of the old party politicians. This seemed to him the best way to get the needed support of the Diet, and the politicians naturally saw it as a heartening expansion of their role in government.

Ito's solution, which worked more or less smoothly for over a decade, gave Japanese politics more stability than it had had in the first decade of "constitutional government." He himself, however, did not last long in the anomalous position of both oligarch and party leader. Yamagata, who had emerged as his chief rival for leadership within the oligarchy, was outraged at Ito's role as party president and got the House of Peers to vote down his budget. In 1901 Ito gave the prime ministership to General Katsura, one of Yamagata's protégés and like him from Choshu. Katsura tried to carry on Yamagata's hard-line attitude toward the parties and dissolved the Diet in 1902 and again in 1903. The Russo-Japanese War of 1904–1905 gave him a respite from the political battle, but by then he had come to realize that compromise was necessary, and he worked out an agreement with the Seiyukai for its support in return for a promise that the prime ministership would go to the Seiyukai leader when Katsura left the post.

Ito himself had meanwhile faded from the political scene. He had passed on the party presidency in 1903 to his own protégé, Prince Saionji, and accepted for himself the prestigious post of president of the Privy Council. He later became resident general in Korea, but was assassinated in 1909 by a Korean patriot. Saionji, like Ito, was a somewhat ambiguous figure as party president. A descendant of the old Fujiwara court aristocracy, he had had a decade of study in France, became a liberal newspaperman, then a bureaucrat, then the head of a political party, and ended his career as the last generally recognized member of the genro, or "elder statesmen."

The leading politician within the Seiyukai party, who actually engineered the deal with Katsura, was Hara. He was a man of quite high samurai origin from north Japan, who had paralleled Saionji's career as a newspaperman critic of the government, bureaucrat, and supporter of Ito, but as an outsider from the north, he channeled his ambitions exclusively into the parliamentary route to power. While Saionji, as Seiyukai president, alternated as prime minister with Katsura between 1906 and 1912, it was Hara who shaped the Seiyukai into a sort of permanent government party, loyally supporting either Saionji or Katsura and obtaining in return government patronage, which helped it win every election handily. A fairly stable, even if temporary, balance was thus struck between the powers of the politicians in the lower house and the oligarchs and their bureaucratic henchmen.

This period of relative political calm was shattered in December 1912 when the army torpedoed the second Saionji cabinet by withdrawing the army minister in retaliation for Saionji's refusal to accept army demands for the creation of new divisions. Katsura came back as prime minister for the third time, but he failed this time to win Seiyukai support and ran into a violent public outcry led by the politicians and newspapers. This they called the "Movement to Preserve Constitutional Government." In desperation, Katsura tried to form a new party, the Doshikai, out of dissident Dietmen from the Okuma tradition and his own bureaucratic supporters, but he fell far short of a majority in the lower house. He was replaced in February 1913 by Admiral Yamamoto, of Satsuma origin, and died a broken man before the year was out. The crisis subsided when Yamamoto won Seiyukai support by accepting its policies and six of its members into his cabinet.

The Meiji emperor had died in the summer of 1912 and the new "year period," named Taisho, had started. There was therefore a sense that a new era had dawned, and the parliamentary blowup that winter, which has been called the "Taisho Political Change," did indeed presage a new stage in Japan's political evolution. For one thing, the new emperor was mentally incompetent —in fact he had to be replaced in 1921 by his son as prince regent. There could be thus even less thought than before that the emperor would indeed rule. The emptiness of the concept of "imperial rule" was in fact made clear during the Taisho Political Change when the

Seiyukai rank and file simply refused to bow before a direct "imperial" request that it cooperate with Katsura. The strategy of an "imperial" request was never again used in Japanese politics.

Even more significant was the obvious breakup of the old oligarchy, or rather the disappearance of the old unity in the greatly enlarged bureaucracy that was supplanting it. The army had acted on its own to disrupt the government. This was possible because Yamagata had seen to it that the constitution specified that the armed forces were directly under the emperor and thus theoretically independent of the civil government. His ruling in 1900 that only generals and admirals on active service, and therefore under army or navy discipline, could head the service ministries had also given the armed services in effect a veto over the cabinet, as the army had demonstrated.

On the other hand, the politicians had shown conclusively that no prime minister could rule without strong party support in the Diet. The newspapers and the public in general had also shown that they understood "normal constitutional government" to be rule by a cabinet which was more or less responsible to a parliamentary majority, a far cry indeed from the system the oligarchs thought they had devised in 1889.

Finally, Katsura's attempt to create a substitute government party for the Seiyukai showed that two could play at this political game. Though a failure in 1913, the new party, like the Seiyukai in 1900, had received an infusion of able men from the bureaucracy, and under the leadership of one of them, Kato, who had served as minister to England and foreign minister, it grew into a strong rival of the Seiyukai. In 1914, the year Hara succeeded Saionji as Seiyukai president, Kato became president of the Doshikai, which was renamed Kenseikai in 1916 and finally Minseito in 1927.

The five years following the Taisho Political Change were a period of transition. Yamamoto's Seiyukai-dominated government gave way in 1914 to one led by Okuma, who was in theory acting as an ex-oligarch, but was in actuality dominated by Kato and his Doshikai. Between 1916 and 1918 General Terauchi, another Yamagata protégé from Choshu, made an anachronistic and unsuccessful attempt to restore "transcendental" cabinet rule. Finally, in September 1918, Yamagata, seeing the writing on the wall and favoring Hara over Kato, agreed to Hara's appointment as prime minister, signaling the acceptance by the old leadership of responsible party rule as the new stage of "constitutional government."

Hara was the first man to win his way to the prime ministership completely through parliamentary politics. Of considerably higher social origin than most of the Meiji oligarchs, he symbolized his status as a politician rather than a bureaucrat by refusing any title of nobility, remaining what some called "the great commoner." Though a high-handed leader, he was a master politician, with a keen sense of the type of pork barrel politics that so characterized nineteenth-century American politics. In three earlier cabinets he had effectively used the position of home minister, with its control over the prefectural governments and the police, to weaken Yamagata's strong following among local government officials and build up a following of his own. He skillfully used the budget to reward electoral districts that voted for his party with public works and the construction of higher schools. He frustrated army wishes to change the trunk railway lines for strategic purposes from narrow to standard gauge, and used the railway budget instead to build politically more profitable small branch lines.

While Hara had achieved responsible party government in the British parliamentary sense, he was no liberal by modern standards. This was hardly to be expected of a man of his background. He showed no eagerness to achieve universal manhood suffrage, which elements in the public had long been demanding. Instead, he contented himself in 1919 with a substantial reduction of the tax qualifications for the suffrage. The result was an expansion of the electorate to over 3 million. He also adopted the Anglo-American electoral system of one seat per electoral district, which eliminated proportional representation and made it much easier for a majority party to maintain its supremacy. This the Seiyukai proceeded to do in the elections the next year by winning 278 out of 464 seats in the lower house.

Hara's strong rule was tragically ended by an accident of history—his assassination in November 1921 by a demented youth. His successor, Takahashi, had been an able finance minister but proved a weak prime minister. There followed between 1922 and 1924 a brief reversion to partly "transcendental" cabinets under three short-lived, nonparty prime ministers, two admirals and a bureaucratic protégé of Yamagata. When the latter's supporters in the Diet fared disastrously in the general election of May 1924, Japan swung back to the full pattern of responsible party governments, this time with an alternation of parties in power like that of England. Kato of the Kenseikai was appointed prime minister in June 1924, and after his death in January 1926, the Kenseikai kept control of the cabinet for more than a year. By 1927, it was the Seiyukai's turn, under its new leader, General Tanaka, a career military man who had switched to parliamentary politics as the only way to ultimate political power. Two years later the cabinet went back into the hands of the Minseito, as the Kenseikai had been renamed, and in 1931 back to the Seiyukai.

The Kenseikai during its years as an opposition party before 1924 had committed itself to popular causes, and under Kato in 1925 it abolished the tax qualifications for the suffrage. Japan thus achieved universal manhood suffrage only thirty-five years after the first parliamentary election, a far shorter time than England had required to reach this level of democracy in 1867. In the 1925 election reforms, the Japanese also adopted a compromise between Yamagata's large electoral districts of 1900 and Hara's one-seat districts of 1919. In this so-called "middle-size electoral district system," 3 to 5 representatives were elected from each district, allowing for a certain degree of proportional representation. It is this system which is still in operation in Japan.

Within less than four decades after 1890, Japan had gone through an evolutionary development that had taken centuries in England. On the surface, at least, it had achieved the full British parliamentary system. But beneath the surface, there were great differences. The powers of the House of Peers were undiminished. The Privy Council and the court bureaucracy could still speak for an emperor whose authority, as described in the constitution, appeared almost autocratic. The military guarded a jealous independence of the civil government. There was no deep emotional commitment to democratic principles on the part of most Japanese, and many of them viewed with distaste the open clash of private interests in elections and in the parliamentary process, preferring the older ideal of a harmonious, unified society, ruled through consensus by loyal servants of the state. In particular, the great financial influence over the politicians on the part of the zaibatsu and other business groups seemed morally unacceptable to people still influenced by Tokugawa prejudices against the merchant class. It was generally believed that Mitsui interests dominated the Seiyukai, and Mitsubishi, its rival party. Though this was a great exaggeration and oversimplification of the actual situation, party politics seemed to many Japanese inherently corrupt.

Just when the party governments were coming to power, moreover, Japan began to encounter great and perplexing new problems. The two decades that followed World War I were not a happy time for any of the industrialized nations, and Japan faced her full share of difficulties. Adjustments after the booming economic conditions of the war proved difficult. An inflationary spiral had set in which led to widespread rioting over rice prices in August 1918, the worst breakdown of internal order since the Satsuma rebellion. The return of the industrial power of Europe to Asian markets after the war also produced more competition than some of the unsoundly expanded industries of Japan could meet. A long period of deflation began. Unfortunately, the Japanese governments of the time, like their counterparts in the West, handled the problems of deflation with ineptness and uncertainty. The net result was that the growth of production in Japan during the twenties was only 33.4 percent, which is not low by world standards, but is little more than half the average growth in Japan during the other decades between 1890 and World

War II. As the decade progressed, the problems grew worse. Between 1925 and 1931 the prices of rice, the chief agricultural product, and silk, the major export, plummeted by over half. By 1927 a flood of bank failures was sweeping Japan. The worldwide depression that started in 1929 made matters still worse for a country like Japan, which depended heavily on foreign trade, and the government compounded its difficulties by attempting to go back on the gold standard in 1930 and 1931, the worst possible time for such a move.

Another economic problem was also becoming more severe. This was the development of what the Japanese came to call the "dual structure" of the economy, divided between the highly productive modern industries on the one side and agriculture and the traditional, low-productivity handicraft industries and services on the other. Rural Japan, where half the population still lived, was entirely in the lower half, left behind by the industrial progress of the cities and resentful of its declining relative position. Tenant farmers in particular began to show signs of serious discontent. Perhaps as much as 30 percent of the land had been tenant-operated already in 1868, and the establishment of fixed money taxes in 1873 resulted in a sharp upswing of tenancy rates to 45 percent by 1908, after which a now-alarmed government managed to hold it fairly level. The economic conditions of the twenties, however, aggravated the plight of tenant farmers. There was a great upsurge in tenant-landlord disputes after World War I, and the first organization of tenant farmers was founded by Christian social workers in 1922. Urban labor, which was beginning to free itself from its agrarian background, was also becoming restive. A forerunner of the later labor unions had been formed by Christian leaders in 1912, and after 1918 there was a rapid increase in labor disputes, strikes, and the organization of unions. More than 300,000 workers were involved in labor disputes in 1919, and before the end of the twenties a like number had formally joined unions.

The military and political upheavals in Europe also produced a flood of new intellectual and social influences in Japan. The triumph of the democracies over the autocracies in World War I contributed to a feeling that democracy was indeed the wave of the future, and this no doubt helped in the achievement of party supremacy and universal manhood suffrage. The liberalizing social trends of the postwar West also combined with the great economic growth of the war years in Japan and the economic uneasiness of the twenties to produce a loosening of old social patterns, at least in urban areas. The great Kanto earthquake and fire of September 1, 1923, helped accelerate the rate of social change. The great cataclysm, which destroyed half of Tokyo and most of Yokohama and took some 130,000 lives, helped sweep away old ways and cleared the ground literally for new cities and figuratively for a new society.

Downtown Tokyo became a city of wide thoroughfares and of many great steel and reinforced concrete buildings, resembling in sections the cities of Europe and America more than those of Asia. The Marunouchi district around the main Tokyo railway station became the pride of the nation and a symbol of the new modernized Japan. Other cities followed Tokyo's lead, and soon modern office buildings of steel, school buildings of concrete, large movie houses, an occasional great stadium, and sprawling railway stations became the typical architecture of Japanese cities.

Family solidarity, paternal authority, and male dominance remained salient features of Japanese society, but increasingly the younger generation in the cities joined the worldwide revolt of youth and began to question time-honored social customs. College students embraced the freer social concepts of the West, and there was a growing demand on the part of youth to be allowed to have marriages of love rather than marriages arranged by families through go-betweens. Women office workers became a feature of the new social system, and under Occidental influence, many middle class Japanese men began to treat their wives almost as social equals. The women of Japan began slowly to free themselves from their traditional position as domestic drudges.

The mass culture of the modern West also began to manifest itself in Japan. The symbol of the twenties, as in the United States, was the "flapper," called by the Japanese the *moga*, a contraction of the English words "modern girl." Moving pictures, either from Hollywood or made in Japan on Hollywood patterns, had a tremendous vogue, and American jazz and Western social dancing became popular with the more sophisticated. Taxi-dance halls appeared; all-girl musical review troupes rivaled the popularity of the movies; Western and Chinese restaurants became numerous; and there was a mushroom growth of so-called cafés, which were small "beer joints" where gramophones ground out American jazz and emancipated young men enjoyed the company of pretty young waitresses of doubtful morals.

The Japanese threw themselves into Western sports with enthusiasm. Baseball and tennis were already extremely popular. Now they concentrated on track and field sports as well, with a view to making a better showing at the Olympic Games, and they actually came to dominate the Olympic swimming events in the 1930s.

Golf links were built for the rich, and the middle classes took up skiing. Baseball, however, was the great national sport, and university and middle school baseball games drew crowds comparable to those attending major college football and big league baseball games in the United States.

Thousands of books poured off the Japanese presses, and the literature of the whole world became available in cheap translated editions. Great Tokyo and Osaka newspapers grew to have circulations in the millions. Higher education was sought by more and more young men from all classes, and higher education for women finally achieved a slow start. A growing taste for Western music was evident in the organization of symphony orchestras and in huge audiences for visiting Western musicians. The city people of Japan were beginning to share in the popular culture of the modern West, and in doing so were moving even further away in spirit and habits from rural Japan.

The Russian Revolution also stimulated a sudden upsurge of interest in Marxism. There had been earlier Leftist stirrings. Christians and university intellectuals had tried to start a Socialist party in 1901, but it had been immediately suppressed, and a well-known anarchist had been executed in 1911 for an alleged plot to assassinate the emperor. Leftist movements now grew on a significantly larger scale. Radical student groups appeared in the great universities, such as Tokyo, Kyoto, and Waseda, and produced figures who were to be prominent in radical politics of the next several decades. A Communist party was organized in 1922, and though repeatedly suppressed by the police, invaded the labor union movement with some success. With the enfranchisement of urban labor and the poorer peasants in the electoral reform of 1925, legal parties of the Left were founded. As elsewhere in the world, however, they tended to splinter on ideological grounds, and in any case, the radical intellectuals who dominated them were few in numbers, and tenant farmers and urban labor remained for the most part politically apathetic. Still, the so-called proletarian parties were able to win eight seats in the election of 1928, the first after the adoption of universal manhood suffrage.

A somewhat menacing sign for the future was the increasing alienation of the intellectual classes, which had first become apparent among the novelists a couple of decades earlier. The parliamentary politicians had developed no coherent democratic philosophy to accompany the evolutionary growth of the British parliamentary system. They were not theorists themselves and in any case were impeded by the prevailing myth of imperial rule. A constitutional scholar, Minobe of Tokyo University, worked out a tortuous justification for parliamentary supremacy based on German legal theory, though his so-called organ theory, which defined the emperor as an "organ" of the state, had no great popular appeal. Many intellectuals, perhaps showing the idealism and unconscious elitism of both their Tokugawa Confucian heritage and their German legal and philosophical training, inclined toward Marxist theories and turned away from Japanese politics and society as these were actually developing.

The twenties were thus an unsettled period not just in the economic field, but socially and intellectually as well. The party politicians, who had concentrated on winning power from the oligarchy and its bureaucratic successors, were not oriented toward the new problems.

Like their predecessors in British politics and their contemporaries in the United States, they were slow to see and deal with the problems of modern industrial society. A few small starts in social and labor legislation had been made around the turn of the century and these were somewhat expanded, though quite inadequately, in the twenties. More typical of the reaction of the politicians to the new radicalism was the adoption of a strengthened Peace Preservation Law outlawing any advocacy of change in the basic political system or of the abolition of private property. Ironically, this law was passed in 1925, the same year that universal manhood suffrage was adopted.

Perhaps the most poignant aspect of the malaise of the twenties was the loss of a sense of national goals and national unity. The goals of the Meiji leaders—security and equality—had been won. Now both these and the men who had formulated them were gone. Yamagata died in 1922, and the last of the original "elder statesmen," Matsukata, in 1924. Only the late joiner, Saionji, remained. Leadership had passed into the hands of a much broader and more disparate group, with much less unified backgrounds or objectives. There were the party leaders, some bureaucrats in origin and others pure politicians; there were the great bankers and industrialists; there was a powerful civil bureaucracy; there was the officer corps of the army and navy; and finally there was a literate, vociferous voting public with a wide range of attitudes. A precarious political balance had been achieved through parliamentary politics and its relationship with the still somewhat independent power of the military and high bureaucracy, but there were deep differences in vision as to what Japan was and should be not just among the leaders, but throughout the nation.

As in the critical years at the end of the Tokugawa shogunate, the deepest divisions were over foreign policy. This had not been true earlier. The Diet had continually opposed the budget increases the armed forces desired, but it had enthusiastically supported the Sino-Japanese and Russo-Japanese wars. Popular opinion also backed imperial expansion, and the chauvinistic dangers of a mass society could readily be seen in the violent popular outburst against the police that broke out in Tokyo in 1905 because of disappointment that Japan had not obtained an indemnity from Russia in the Treaty of Portsmouth. It was also the party leader Kato who as foreign minister in 1915 pressed the Twenty-one Demands on China.

In the twenties, however, two sharply diverging roads seemed to lie ahead: to continue to strengthen the military and expand the empire in the way that had proved so successful in the past, or to adopt the political and economic internationalism that had captivated parts of the West at the end of World War I. Japan obviously needed foreign markets to pay for the huge imports of raw materials required to support her expanding industrial economy. Foreign markets could be obtained either by conquest in the nineteenth-century style or by friendly international intercourse in the new way, but not very well by a mixture of the two.

The problem posed itself with particular urgency in China. By the twenties Japan had become the dominant external power best able to take advantage of China's weakness. But the situation in China was changing. The Chinese people, with a newly awakened sense of nationalism, were beginning to boycott foreign merchants whose governments were considered to be pursuing an aggressive policy against their country. Consequently, military intervention in China cost the double price of lost markets and increased military expenditures. Periodic outbursts of antiforeign violence swept the land, and in the mid-twenties the Nationalists, under Chiang Kai-shek, unified most of the country under their control. The Chinese were also starting to build competing railway lines in Manchuria, which threatened established Japanese interests.

The basic answer of Japan's postwar governments to the foreign policy problem was to chose the road of peaceful trade rather than imperialist expansion. The politicians and businessmen, supported by the general public, opted for this course, and the bureaucrats and military were induced, though sometimes with misgivings, to go along.

Japan had emerged from World War I with a firm hold on the former German interests in Tsingtao and Shantung, and an expeditionary force of 72,000 men in eastern Siberia. The latter was the bulk of a joint Japanese-American intervention in July 1918, designed to help the White Russians keep their country in the war against Germany, but the Japanese military obviously looked on the effort as an excellent chance for imperialist fishing in troubled waters. Hara managed to withdraw the Japanese army from Siberia, and he also gave Japan's assent to a conference the United States wished to call in Washington in the winter of 1921–1922, in order to put a ceiling on naval expansion and settle problems in the Western Pacific.

At the Washington Conference, but in a separate agreement with the Chinese, Japan consented to give up Tsingtao and the bulk of her rights in Shantung. In the major agreements, she accepted the moralistic American position on the "open door" for the trade of all nations in China and the "territorial integrity" of the country, which were considered to be largely empty rhetoric in any case. She also accepted a ratio in capital naval vessels of 3 to 5 with the United States and Britain, in return for British and American agreements not to build fortifications between Pearl Harbor and Singapore. This left Japan in overall naval inferiority to the two great English-speaking powers, but clearly supreme in her own part of the world.

In China, Japan sought to maintain her long-established privileges in Manchuria and elsewhere, and General Tanaka as prime minister even intervened militarily in Shantung in 1928 to stop for a while the northward advance of the Nationalists. But Japan's policies were basically conciliatory. Shidehara, as foreign minister in the Kenseikai-Minseito cabinets of 1924–1927 and 1929–1931, pursued a liberal policy of accommodation to China's nascent nationalism and cooperation with the United States. At home, military budgets were reduced more than half between 1919 and 1926, and four divisions of the standing army were eliminated.

The 1920s thus were a troubled time for Japan, but on the surface it seemed that the Japanese, having developed through their own evolutionary procedures a rough approximation of the British parliamentary system, would go on paralleling the English by developing a freer society at home and turning away from military conquest abroad.

10 ✿ MILITARISM AND WAR

The "liberal" twenties, which are characterized by the Japanese as the period of "Taisho democracy," were followed in the thirties by a violent swing back toward military expansion abroad and authoritarian rule at home. Why this should have happened is one of the great questions of modern Japanese history, and is not easily answered. But Japan's case was by no means unique. Two great Western nations experienced the same sort of reaction—Italy a little before Japan, and Germany at much the same time. The underlying causes in all three cases seem not to have been entirely dissimilar.

In view of Japan's earlier background of authoritarian leadership by a military elite and the fact that her frantic modernization had started as a reaction to the military threat of the West, it is not surprising that Meiji Japan had been both militaristic and authoritarian. It is also not surprising that, even though the dominant postwar political and social trends were toward a more liberal system at home and less imperialistic policies abroad, many Japanese continued in the older ways of thought. Most families remained authoritarian; the old Confucian ideal of social harmony still had a greater appeal than the individualism of the West and the admitted clash of interests in parliamentary politics; there was still an easy acceptance of hierarchy and strong elitist assumptions on the part of leaders of all sorts; and respect for the military and pride in their imperialistic achievements pervaded the nation.

Japan in fact was becoming a deeply divided nation by the twenties—divided by the "dual structure" of the economy, divided in ways of life and thought between the cities and the countryside, divided between those more influenced by the great changes modernization had brought and those living a more traditional life, and divided between the better educated and those who had received only the new mass education with its heavy indoctrination. The liberal political, social, and intellectual trends of the twenties were strongest among the better educated classes of the cities and weakest among the rural products of elementary education.

Peasants and residents of the thousands of villages and small towns, who still constituted the bulk of the population, looked at what was happening in the cities with wonderment and often with disapproval. More conservative elements throughout society regarded the liberal and sometimes radical political theories of the city intelligentsia and the antics of the moga with growing hostility and resentment. Army and navy officers, rural landowners, lower middle class citizens, and many petty government officials found it quite impossible to accept the growing challenge to the old patterns of political and social authority. These people too were members of the new generation and products of the new education, but

with them the nationalistic and militaristic indoctrination of the school system had weighed more heavily
than the opening of new horizons and the influences
from abroad. They were in complete sympathy with the
authoritarian rule at home and the strong expansionist
program abroad of the Meiji leaders. The postwar triumph of the party men, who seemed to them but the
spokesmen for selfish moneyed interests, and the halt
these leaders had brought to the expansion of Japan's
armed forces and empire appeared to be little more than
treason. They had inherited from the Meiji leaders a
desire to see Japan continue to expand her military
power and domain, but too narrow an indoctrination apparently had robbed them of some of the pragmatism
and flexibility those leaders had shown.

Even during the Meiji period, there had been signs
of what was later to be called ultranationalism, but it is
hard to distinguish between it and the intense nationalism that pervaded the whole country. At first it had
manifested itself as part of the general protest movement
of outsider samurai against the government, which was
more spectacularly evident in the samurai uprisings of
the 1870s and in the longer-lasting "freedom and people's rights movement." Slowly this ultranationalism
separated itself from the liberal political movement. It
at first stressed support for revolutionary movements
against Western domination in other Asian lands, and
then it moved on to champion the expanding empire of
Japan's own military forces as the best way to stop the
West's subjugation and perversion of Asia.

The leadership in this ostensibly pan-Asian but more
significantly imperialistic movement came at first from
activists in western Japan who, being closest to the continent, were perhaps more conscious of the problems in

other Asian countries. An organization called the Genyosha was founded in Fukuoka in northern Kyushu in 1881, and this in 1901 spawned another organization called the Kokuryukai. This name has been dramatically translated in the West as the "Black Dragon Society," but it was actually based on the Chinese name for the Amur River, and was meant to suggest that Japan's natural strategic frontiers were on this northern boundary of Manchuria.

These imperialistic pressure groups in time became involved in reactionary political causes at home, and the whole movement became larger and more influential after World War I. Certain conservative bureaucrats of high standing founded intellectually more respectable nationalistic societies, and several popular propagandists of ultranationalism appeared. These men for the most part harked back to the authoritarian and agrarian traditions of the past, and like the Restoration leaders before them, they drew the cloak of imperial sacredness around their own ideas. They claimed that what they advocated was the true *kokutai*, or "national polity," and asserted that they represented the real "imperial will." While both terms had for long been in use, it was at this time that they became widely popularized. Despite these atavistic tendencies, some of the ultranationalists also drew on the current socialist theories of the West, and the whole movement derived considerable inspiration and also respectability from the success of the Fascists in Italy and later the Nazis in Germany. These European examples showed that liberal democracy was not necessarily the wave of the future.

The ultranationalistic movement, however, was fundamentally anti-Western, and this coloration was strengthened by the realization that, despite Japan's status as a world power, Westerners were still not willing on racial grounds to accept Japanese as full equals. At the Versailles peace conference in 1919 Japan had argued for the inclusion of a clause on "racial equality," but this had been blocked by the United States and Britain. This was because there was strong opposition in America, Canada, and Australia to Oriental immigration. Moreover, throughout the Occident there had been for decades much racist talk of the "yellow peril." In the United States, Orientals had much earlier been declared ineligible for naturalization on racial grounds, and California and other western states put their children into segregated schools and denied them the right to own land. To ease the strains of this situation, Japan and the United States worked out in 1908 a "Gentlemen's Agreement," which brought a virtual end to Japanese immigration. Despite this, Congress in 1924 passed an Exclusion Act which specifically applied to Japanese as aliens ineligible for citizenship. This was deeply resented by Japanese of all types as a gratuitous insult. Though really a part of American rather than Japanese history, it is worth noting that anti-Oriental racism in the United States was to reach its peak in the early days of World War II, when the whole Japanese population of the West Coast, loyal, native-born *nisei* citizens and their inoffensive, elderly, immigrant parents alike, were driven out of their farms and homes and herded into concentration camps.

The organized ultranationalistic movement remained relatively small in Japan and never proved politically dominant, as in Italy and Germany. Its significance was that it helped stimulate a much broader but more inchoate reaction to the liberal trends of the twenties. This grew largely out of the unsatisfactory economic conditions of the time and the disunity and sense of loss of direction. Intellectuals felt alienated from society; urban labor was restless; small businessmen, merchants, and artisans felt outclassed and overwhelmed by the great new industries; and the collapse of agricultural prices in the late twenties produced conditions of dire want for many peasants. All these groups resented the growing economic domination of big business and its political influence over the parties. It was at this time that the term *zaibatsu* became popularized as a pejorative. The Meiji dream seemed to have faded into a confused and sordid reality, dominated by greedy capitalists, corrupt politicians, and decadent young people in the cities. The obvious Western backgrounds of industrial capitalism, parliamentarianism, and the liberal urban social trends made them all the more suspect to many Japanese. Like men in other times and other places, such people understandably, even if unrealistically, looked back to old ideals and old ways for correctives to new and unfamiliar problems.

It was natural for the reaction, when it came, to center around the military. After all, the military, thanks to Yamagata, had preserved a semi-independent position within the government, from which it could more easily take action. It also symbolized not just the success of Meiji Japan, but the older tradition of elite, military leadership. Japanese found it easy to believe that army and navy officers, the salaried military servants of the state, were more honest and dependable, or as they put it, more "sincere," than were rich industrialists and self-seeking politicians. And the military officers themselves, segregated educationally from other Japanese at a relatively early age and deeply indoctrinated in a proud military tradition, believed this fully. They were also deeply unhappy over national policies that cut their appropriations, relegated them to a secondary role in foreign affairs behind the international trader, and seemed to be sapping the country of the moral fiber on which they felt military strength depended. Given their ideas, their traditions, and their position within the government, they were the obvious leaders for the reaction.

It was also not surprising that the military received broad, even if inarticulate, support from the peasants and other little men not caught up in the new life of urban Japan. Here was a vast reservoir of the attitudes and ways of the traditional, collectivist society. It is true that the parties that now dominated politics had their oldest and strongest roots among the richer peasants. But rural society, as a whole, was much less changed from Meiji days—even from Tokugawa days—than the rest of Japan. The peasantry, moreover, had a special affinity with the military. The modern mass education had quickly spread the strong nationalism of the upper classes of the late Tokugawa period to all Japanese, but more remarkably, it had soon convinced the descendants of peasants, who for almost three centuries had been denied swords and other arms and had been exploited by a military caste above them, that they too were members of a warrior race. Making up the great bulk of the conscripts, the peasants found their experience in army barracks as educational as the time spent in primary school. Both inculcated in them the glory of Japan's great military traditions and the ideal of death on the battlefield in the service of the emperor. For most peasants, service in the army or navy was the one exciting release from an otherwise humdrum life of crushing farm labor, and the "reservist organizations" of military men who had completed their active service were important bodies in the countryside.

The army and navy officers, for their part, constituted no Junker class holding itself aloof from the common people. The samurai coloring of the officers of early Meiji days had been largely lost. By the twenties, military officers, like most other Japanese leaders, were the products of an educational system, not of a social class. The army and navy were among Japan's most modernized institutions, but in their ideas, many officers were closer to the peasants than were other leaders. Basically prejudiced against party politicians, big businessmen, and city ways, they also showed a special concern for the peasantry as the manpower on which military strength depended. They were deeply worried that the rural depression of the late twenties would undermine the health of the poorer peasants. There was thus a genuine resonance in emotional attitudes between the military and rural Japan.

The militaristic and ultranationalistic reaction that swept Japan in the thirties was atavistic in that it looked back to a simpler, more harmonious, more agrarian, and more authoritarian past, rather than to the rational solution of the new problems of an industrialized society. It might therefore never have won out if the parliamentary leadership of the twenties had proved more competent in handling the new economic and social problems, or if there had been a better formulation of a democratic philosophy to support the emerging political system. It is also often argued that the traditional parties would have stayed in power if they had known how to embrace the new radicalism and the newly enfranchised lower classes, but this is doubtful. There was still relatively little political consciousness among tenant farmers and urban laborers, and in any case, the old parties continued to win elections with ease in the thirties. The vote in elections was not their problem. Much more important was the lack among most Japanese of any strong belief in democracy or any emotional commitment to it. Authoritarian leadership, if it was honest or wise, did not seem repugnant or dangerous. In fact, many yearned for the emotional security of the old days. The ideal of harmony through consensus in a collectivist society seemed attractive, even if the means of achieving it in a pluralistic, modern society were not clear.

Even so, the militarists might not have won out if they had not offered a seemingly better solution to the great economic and international problems that Japan faced at the end of the twenties. The population had reached 60 million by 1925 and was growing at the rate of a million a year. Japan was becoming increasingly dependent on imported food and raw materials and foreign markets to pay for imports. Emigration offered no solution to the population problem, because the relatively empty lands, such as the United States, Canada, and Australia, barred Japanese immigrants. The Asian and African empires of the European powers were for the most part not open to Japanese exports, and the worldwide depression was cutting other markets and producing a rash of protectionist policies.

Under these conditions, it could be argued that there was grave danger in relying on international good will and free trade to achieve economic security for Japan. This might do for great continental lands like the United States and the Soviet Union and for worldwide empires like those of Britain and France, which had adequately diverse resources and big enough markets under their own control. But it would not suffice for a small, overcrowded land like Japan. To survive world depressions and secure a place in the sun, Japan needed a bigger empire than she had. Nearby China—and especially the rich northeastern provinces in Manchuria, which Japan already partially controlled—would be the natural core for such an empire. History was to prove that the Japanese who argued this way were drastically mistaken on economic as well as military grounds. Japan's foreign trade and economy recovered brilliantly in the thirties, and in retrospect her empire can be seen to have been a net economic handicap rather than an asset. But at the time, the argument was convincing to many. Thus once again it was a foreign policy issue that proved most decisive in determining the course Japan was to take.

Cause and effect in history are not easily unscrambled. Many of these arguments and much of the swing of public sentiment back toward earlier ideals appeared after the Japanese government had already started to return to more aggressive foreign policies and more authoritarian rule at home. Thus they served as much as justifications for changes already made as causes for these changes. Military officers and other conservative leaders were undoubtedly influenced by the spirit of the time, but they did not wait for it to carry them and Japan back to the ideals they believed in. They took direct political and military action on their own to achieve this goal, and their acts in turn helped build up public attitudes that made further steps more possible. Thus public attitudes and political actions worked on each other to produce a progressively greater reaction in both areas.

The first sign of the shift of the political tide came in 1928. In June of that year, young officers of the Kwantung Army, the Japanese military force in Manchuria, blew up a train in order to kill the local warlord and Japanese puppet, Chang Tso-lin, whom they considered incompetent and uncooperative. The new emperor, who after five years as prince regent had succeeded to the throne late in 1926 and who still reigns under the year name of Showa, had come to maturity at the height of postwar liberalism and had even been allowed to study briefly in England in 1921. He was outraged at this act and demanded of his prime minister, General Tanaka, that the officers be disciplined. The army refused Tanaka's request, claiming that to discipline the officers would hurt army prestige, and that, according to the constitution, the emperor and not the civil government had "supreme command" over the military, and therefore the civil government had no right to intervene in army affairs.

The incident was very revealing in three ways. As far as is known, this was the first important political action a Japanese emperor had tried to initiate in modern times, and it failed. The army also successfully defied the civil government, even though the prime minister was a man who himself had recently been in charge of the army. And the crisis, which helped commit Japan to a more intransigent stand in Manchuria, had been precipitated by middle-grade officers in the field, who were felt by the army to be justified in their actions because of its tradition of giving wide discretionary powers to the man on the spot. But none of these things probably would have happened if the mood of the military and of the nation had not already changed considerably from what it had been only a few years earlier.

This change of mood was revealed again in 1930 at the time of the London Naval Conference. Following up the naval agreements at the Washington Conference of 1921–1922, the government now agreed to the extension to heavy cruisers of the 5–5–3 ratio with the United States and Britain (or 10–10–6 as it was now called), and accepted a 10–10–7 ratio on light cruisers. The navy, which wanted a 10–10–7 ratio for heavy cruisers too, bitterly opposed the agreement and was cynically supported in this by the Seiyukai as a way of attacking the Minseito government. The cabinet won the fight, but it was a Pyrrhic victory. There was a strong popular reaction against it, and the navy resolved to take a more aggressively independent position in the government.

The full turn of the tide came in 1931 in another case of "direct action" by middle-grade officers in Manchuria, but on a larger scale than in 1928. On the night of September 18 they blew up a small section of the South Manchurian Railway that Japan owned, and claiming it had been done by the Chinese, used this as a pretext to overrun all of Manchuria in a series of rapid military pushes. Obviously they could not have done this without tacit approval from the start of elements of the high command in Tokyo, and the whole of the army closed ranks behind them. The emperor and the leaders of the civil government tried to keep the "incident" under control, but found themselves helpless. The navy, jealous of the glory the army was winning, stirred up a fight with the Chinese in Shanghai late in January 1932, but its landing party got in over its depth and had to be rescued by three army divisions. The army started to form Manchuria into a separate puppet state, and in September 1932, Japan recognized this as the nation of Manchukuo, under a puppet, Pu-yi, who had abdicated the Manchu throne of China as an infant in 1912.

The United States in January 1932 enunciated a policy of "nonrecognition" of Japanese conquests, which it held to right up to World War II. The League of Nations sent a commission of inquiry to Manchuria, which brought in a report condemning Japan. When the League adopted this report, however, Japan simply withdrew in March 1933, and thus contributed to its rapid decline. Undeterred by foreign criticism, the Japanese army in 1933 and 1934 continued a series of smaller "incidents" that established its control over the eastern part of Inner Mongolia and areas in North China around Peking.

The so-called Manchurian Incident created a war psychosis in Japan. The populace was swept by a nationalistic euphoria over the spectacularly easy conquest of Manchuria, an area far larger than Japan itself, with a population of 30 million hard-working Chinese. The army, and behind it the whole of Japan, became committed to an expansionist policy on the continent. The "incident" also made clear what had been hinted at in the murder of Chang Tso-lin in 1928. The emperor and the government leaders could not control the army. In fact, it was the army that was establishing Japanese foreign policy through *faits accomplis*, and all the civil government could do was to serve as an unhappy apologist for this policy before the world. A sort of dual government was emerging, with the military holding the upper hand so far as foreign policy was concerned.

The army is commonly spoken of in the singular, but it was itself a complex, pluralistic aggregate of individuals and factions. The leadership tended to divide between the modernizers, who sought to build a more fully mechanized force, and those who emphasized the "spiritual power" of the emperor's army, rather than mechanization, as the true source of its strength. The latter might be compared to the Maoists of China of a later date. Eventually they came to be known as the "imperial way faction" (*kodoha*). While the modernizers were not at all averse to military expansion and army control of foreign policy, it was the "imperial way" leaders who most strongly backed the activist officers in the field. Another division was that of age between younger and older officers. In part this was the product of a natural irritation on the part of younger officers at the slowness of promotions, but it was also the result of a generational gap between men a little closer to the samurai background of the Meiji leadership and the products of a narrower, more specialized education and a greater degree of indoctrination. These twin pressures produced what was called the "young officers problem." Field-grade and even company-grade officers often acted with extraordinary daring and independence, and usually were protected by the "imperial way" firebrands among their superiors. They openly bullied more conservative or cautious generals and took "direct actions" on the continent that determined Japan's overall foreign policy.

A small fringe of extremists among the younger officers even adopted terrorist tactics at home by reverting to the sort of assassinations for political purposes that had been common during the last troubled years of the Tokugawa. These men were for the most part young zealots who had become disciples of one or another of the popular ultranationalist propagandists. Younger officers of this type plotted a "Showa Restoration" in the spring of 1931. This and a second plot that autumn were quashed by the military authorities, but young army extremists did succeed in February 1932 in assassinating the finance minister who had just left office and a leading Mitsui executive, and on May 15 (in the so-called 5-15 Incident), they assassinated the Prime Minister, Inukai. Similar plots were nipped in the bud in 1933 and again in 1934. The army leadership, of course, did not support the radical philosophies these young men had espoused, much less their rash actions. But the generals were willing to make use of these acts to put pressure on the civil government for political change. The general public also proved extraordinarily tolerant of these violent deeds. They were taken as evidence of the evils of the times and the inability of the government and economic leaders to reform society. Showing somewhat the same attitude Japanese have in more recent years evinced toward extremists of the Left, the public openly admired the "pure" motives of the young men and condoned their crimes as mitigated by the "corruption" of those who were killed. Trials of the terrorists tended to turn into public propaganda forums for their ideas.

The army's direct action abroad had changed Japan's foreign policy and had influenced the mood in the country, and these changes, together with the "direct action" at home of a few extremists, helped bring a great shift in the direction of domestic political development. Inukai of the Seiyukai had become prime minister in December 1931, following the Manchurian Incident, in a macabre last act of party rule. He was the most liberal man to reach the prime ministership before the end of World War II: he had originally gone into party politics with Okuma in 1881 and had developed into a staunch ideological champion of parliamentary government. The now-aged remaining "elder statesman," Prince Saionji, who had a special, even if only tacitly recognized, role as a spokesman for the emperor in the selection of prime ministers, was convinced by Inukai's assassination that for the sake of "national unity," it was necessary to return, at least temporarily, to the earlier system of "transcendental" cabinets. Since the navy was less controversially involved in the crisis than the army, he selected as prime minister Admiral Saito, who had been the most "liberal" of all the Japanese governor-generals in Korea.

Saito still had seven party politicians in his cabinet, and Admiral Okada, who succeeded him in 1934, appointed five. But Okada also included in his cabinet several of the so-called revisionist bureaucrats, who were personally ambitious men willing to cooperate closely with the new foreign policies of the army. He also took the supervision of Manchurian affairs from the foreign ministry and put it under the army ministry, and he opened civil service posts to military officers, starting what turned out to be an increasing direct penetration of the civil government by the army and navy.

Another big turning point in domestic politics was precipitated by the February 26 Incident (or 2–26 Incident) of 1936. A group of young extremist officers used elements of the First Division in Tokyo to try to sweep away all the top government leaders of whom they disapproved. They managed to kill the current Finance Minister and former Prime Minister, Takahashi; the Lord Privy Seal, who was the former Prime Minister, Admiral Saito; and one of the three top generals of the army; but they only wounded the Grand Chamberlain, Admiral Suzuki; while Saionji and the current Prime Minister, Admiral Okada, managed to escape, though the latter's brother-in-law, who happened to resemble him, was killed through mistaken identity.

This "incident" was the biggest military challenge to

the government since the Satsuma rebellion. The army saw that it had to crack down on this sort of insubordination, and it firmly suppressed the incipient coup d'état and dealt severely with the leaders. This was possible because the more conservative modernizers among the army leaders, who were by then known as the "control faction" (toseiha), were indeed in control of the army. They had been winning out over the "imperial way faction" and had taken strong measures to bring it under control after a lieutenant-colonel of that faction had cut down one of the top three generals at his desk in 1935. After the February 26 Incident, effective discipline was restored in the army, and there was no further violent factional fighting or rank insubordination by the younger officers. But, from the army's point of view, there was no longer any need for that sort of "direct action" either. By then the military had achieved preponderant control over the civil government as well as over Japan's foreign policies.

Following the February 26 Incident, Hirota, one of the revisionist bureaucrats from the foreign ministry, supplanted Okada as prime minister. While he still retained four party men in his cabinet, it had a decidedly more conservative cast than the preceding cabinet, and he cooperated in the further penetration of the civil government by the military. He also restored Yamagata's old ruling that only generals and admirals on active duty could head the service ministries. This ruling had been scrapped by the politicians in 1913, following the political crisis of that year, though no government in the interim had seen fit to make use of this potentially liberalizing reform.

In February 1937 Hirota was followed by General Hayashi, who for the first time had no party men in his cabinet. The parties thus had lost even a foothold in the cabinet and had sunk into frustrated impotence. The two main parties still could win elections. Five months after the outbreak of the Manchurian Incident, they had between them won 447 out of the 466 seats in the lower house. A few days before the February 26 Incident of 1936, they were able to win 379 seats, and even in April 1937 they carried 354 seats. The new Leftist movement was also doing well at the polls. The Social Mass party (Shakai Taishuto), which was an amalgamation of the more moderate Leftists who were willing to support the army's expansionist policies, won 18 seats in 1936 and doubled its showing to 37 the next year. But despite overwhelming majorities in the Diet and occasional daring speeches by some Diet members, the parties had lost virtually all political power. The public, while voting for them, emotionally supported the army's foreign policies and the belief that the "crisis" required cabinets of "national unity." The parties, in an effort to hold on to whatever political power they could, had employed the same strategy of practical compromises they had used to come to power, but now the process worked in reverse. Each successive compromise had left them with diminished influence.

The powerful civil bureaucracy, divided between mutually jealous ministries, fought to maintain its prerogatives, but did not unite to try to block military domination of the government as a whole. Instead, the revisionist members of the bureaucracy jumped on the army bandwagon. Only the high court officials around the emperor held out against military domination in favor of the older Meiji concept of national unity, and for this stand they were singled out for attacks by assassins. Saionji sought to stem the army's tide in January

1937 by trying to engineer the selection as prime minister of a former general who had cooperated well with the parties in the twenties, but he ran up against a stone wall of army opposition. In June 1937 Saionji attempted to create a truly "transcendental" cabinet by selecting as prime minister his own protégé from the old court aristocracy, Prince Konoe. But Konoe proved to be a weak and ambivalent leader, and the outbreak of war with China a few weeks later swept the nation to new paroxysms of militaristic enthusiasm. Saionji, realizing that after his death all the "elder statesmen" would be gone, also sought to create a substitute body of all the retired prime ministers, dubbed the "senior ministers." Starting in July 1940, four months before Saionji's death at the age of 91, this group took over the duty of naming prime ministers.

Konoe, who had resigned in January 1939, returned in July 1940 for a second round as prime minister, and between his two terms the post was held by an old ultranationalist bureaucrat, a general, and an admiral. The cabinet, however, had by then lost most of its role as the highest decision-making body in the government. From 1938 on, this function was taken over in part by a smaller group of key cabinet ministers and still more by various liaison bodies between the military and cabinet, which tended merely to ratify decisions already made by the military. Finally, in October 1941 General Tojo established unquestioned military control over the civil government in his dual capacity as head of the army and prime minister.

As the military leaders strengthened their holds on the civil government and a crisis psychology increasingly pervaded the nation, Japan began to take on some of the totalitarian coloring of the Fascists and Nazis in Europe. The army and navy had no love for industrial capitalism itself, and many officers tended toward the National Socialist thinking of contemporary Europe. The zaibatsu leaders and most other businessmen, on the other hand, looked with alarm at the adventurist policies of the military abroad and their soaring budgets at home. But neither side proved doctrinaire in its attitudes, and a sort of marriage of convenience ensued.

The army found itself unable to develop its new Manchurian empire economically without the businessmen and was forced to invite them in. The result was the development of a new set of so-called Manchurian zaibatsu. The army also was less interested in the economic theories of socialism than what it called "total mobilization" or a "national defense state," and for this it was easier to use the existing economic system than to change it. There was no nationalization of the economy, or any real attempt to improve the lot of the peasantry, about which there had been so much talk by the military. Instead, as the crisis deepened into actual war, the government extended thoroughgoing controls over the economy not unlike those developed by the Western democracies during World War II. On the other hand, the great zaibatsu industries naturally grew and profited greatly, as the industrial sinews of the country were strengthened and Japan rushed frantically into a booming wartime economy.

There were greater and more clearly totalitarian changes in the field of personal freedom and thought than in the economy. The Peace Preservation Law of 1925 had made it a crime to advocate the overthrow of the "national polity" or the system of private property, and after 1931 laws such as this were enforced with new vigor and thoroughness, at home by the "special" police, often called the "thought control" police, and throughout the empire by the military police. Hundreds of Leftist political and labor leaders and university students were thrown into prison and forced to recant their "dangerous thoughts." Professors were dismissed for their theories, and in 1935 Minobe, whose "organ theory" about the emperor had been generally accepted by sophisticated Japanese in the twenties, was accused of *lèse majesté*, and was dismissed not only from his university post, but from his appointive seat in the House of Peers, and his writings were banned. This sort of McCarthyism in government was outdone by volunteer McCarthyism on the part of ultranationalist enthusiasts, whose tactics of abuse and intimidation proved very effective in silencing most dissenters in what was still a relatively tightly knit and conformist society.

The other side of the coin was indoctrination. The Japanese government had engaged in this from the start of its modernization, but now the effort was stepped up progressively and spread not just through the schools but also through the mass media. Textbooks were repeatedly revised to bring them in line with the spirit of the time. There was, however, no *Mein Kampf* of Japanese totalitarianism. An effort was made to produce a great spiritual guide, resulting in the appearance of a book called the *Fundamentals of National Polity* (*Kokutai no hongi*), but this was a strange amalgam of old, outmoded ideas. It stressed the ancient mythology and the superiority of Japan to other countries because of the uniqueness of her unbroken imperial line. There was a great deal about the "imperial will," but also much about the Confucian virtues of harmony, loyalty, and filial piety, as well as

Japan's own medieval "way of the warrior." It was deeply anti-Western and even more against individualism, which was alleged to be responsible for all the Western vices from democracy to communism. But there was little to give guidance to the movement.

The *Kokutai no hongi* was characteristic of much of the thought of the time, which grew steadily in emotional intensity, but not in intellectual content. Its positive ideas were at best vague. Traditional virtues were extolled, and great devotion was expressed to the "imperial will," but otherwise it fell back largely on vague, undefined terms like "Japanese spirit," "national polity," and assorted catch phrases, such as one dug out of ancient Chinese philosophy and thought to mean "the whole world under one roof" (*hakko ichiu*). This conveniently could be interpreted as referring innocuously to the brotherhood of mankind or more menacingly to worldwide Japanese domination. On the negative side, the thought of the time was somewhat more explicit. Its "enemies" were clear: greedy capitalists, corrupt politicians, individualism, internationalism, and a vaguely menacing but at the same time effete West. These were all lumped together in obloquy, each helping to discredit the others through their common Western background in a sort of institutional guilt by association. All Westerners were looked upon with suspicion, and by the late thirties children sometimes referred to any Westerner encountered on the street by the English word "spy."

These political and intellectual trends had their effects on society too. Anything considered "un-Japanese" was condemned, though the term proved as slippery to define as "un-American." Ballroom dancing was frowned upon as an immoral Western custom, but no one dreamed of abandoning Western military technology. Baseball remained popular, but golf was criticized as a Western luxury sport. A not very successful effort was made to stem the flood of English words into Japanese conversation and writing. Bilingual street and railway signs were remade with the English omitted. Students, labor unions, and newspapers were curbed with increasing rigorousness. And women, while encouraged to come out of the home and fill the manpower needs of a wartime economy, were at the same time told to be nothing more than the obedient wives and dutiful mothers of Japanese tradition.

The trends toward a totalitarian society were unmistakable, but unlike Germany and Italy, no organized mass totalitarian movement emerged. In 1940 Konoe did paste together a large number of organizations into an "Imperial Rule Assistance Association" (*Taisei yokusankai*), but as its ponderous name suggests, it had no life. All the parties were forced to dissolve and enter its parliamentary branch, but even in the wartime elections of April 1942, candidates with its official blessing could garner no more than 64 percent of the votes, the rest going to stubborn holdouts. Something closer to a mass organization was created during the war by reviving the traditional Tokugawa system of neighborhood associations (*tonarigumi*) to supervise rationing, spread information, and ensure absolute conformity.

What ideology the reaction of the thirties had was directed back in history toward the ancient imperial mystique and the virtues of Tokugawa times, but there was of course no turning back to a premodern society or even to Meiji times. What had emerged was a far cry from the social solidarity of earlier days or the natural unity of ideals and objectives of the Meiji leadership. The latter, if they had survived to see it, would have been horrified at the artificial unity forced on a now very diverse society by a military dictatorship, itself divided between a largely autonomous army and navy, controlling a supine civil government, disregarding the expressed wishes of the emperor, and embarked on a perilous course of adventure abroad.

The parallels were more with the emerging totalitarian states of Europe, particularly those of the Right, rather than with earlier Japan. As an at least partially modernized country, with an educated populace and a pluralistic society, Japan could scarcely reestablish the old unity and harmony of a simpler, more static age. Nor could there be a traditional and generally accepted autocracy. Educated men inevitably had their own ideas, and they either would demand a share in decisions or else the government had to control them very carefully, limiting not only what they did, but what they said and wrote. As in the modernized West, the premodern types of autocracy were no longer viable, and totalitarianism had become the only real alternative to democracy. Modernization, moreover, had brought the means to transform premodern autocracy into modern totalitarianism: mass education, mass communications media, modernized police and military power, and a great centralization of both economic and political controls.

There were great differences, however, between the Japanese experience in totalitarianism and those of the Italians and Germans. The Japanese people, being closer to an authoritarian past, may have been more docile and more easily led; and the opponents of the new trends were not well enough entrenched in their liberal ways and ideologies to put up much resistance. In any case, there was no revolutionary change, no sudden, wrenching break with the past, and no liquidation of large numbers of opponents. The changes came by small steps, none seemingly definitive in itself. Japanese totalitarianism thus appeared less harsh and more moderate—and in any case it was a truncated experience which never developed into a fully totalitarian system. Most surprising, it was all achieved within the framework of the 1889 constitution, and this alone accounts for many survivals from the dream of the Meiji oligarchs as well as from the parliamentary system that had evolved out of it.

The constitution had indeed proved a flexible and ambiguous document. It had accommodated the development of the British parliamentary system and then a military dictatorship with totalitarian leanings. This was its virtue in the twenties and its fatal flaw in the thirties. The theory of imperial rule without the reality had left an essentially headless system. It had never really been clear who was in charge—who would choose the prime minister or the other high officials around the emperor who acted in his name. This situation had raised no problems at first because a well-entrenched group of oligarchs occupied these posts and made the decisions; but when they disappeared, no one person or group clearly took their place. A difficult and perilous transition had been made by the twenties to a system in which it was generally recognized that a parliamentary majority ultimately determined the choice of leaders. But this system was far from complete, and islands of autonomous power remained within the government. In fact, politics was, in a sense, a shifting balance between a series of elites— the parties, the court, the civil bureaucracy, the military, and big business. And the theory remained that all of these were only carrying out the "imperial will." The door was open for the military to assert that it better represented the "imperial will" than did self-seeking politicians, and only a minor readjustment in the balance between elites could put the military in the saddle and bring a total change in Japanese politics at home and abroad.

The foreign policy of the military had one serious inconsistency. While giving full rein to Japanese chauvinism, it assumed that Japan's neighbors would not only welcome her as a deliverer from Western oppression, but would content themselves with being serfs in Japan's "Greater East Asian" empire. Nationalism, however, was mounting rapidly, especially in China, and the realities of colonial rule by Japanese in Korea and Manchuria made them no more attractive as imperial masters than the white race. As Japan's empire grew, so also did the Chinese determination to resist. Japan's period of dominance in East Asia and her drive for empire had come too late in world history for the same easy success that imperialistic adventuring had met in the nineteenth century. The politicians and businessmen in the twenties had correctly read the signs of the new nationalism in China, but the military leaders, insofar as they saw these signs, were goaded by them instead to try to seize as much empire as they could while it still seemed possible to do so. In 1931 they had appeared to be successful in this policy, but then time began to run out for them.

World War II, which was in reality the first true "world war," started in China in 1937. On the night of July 7, fighting broke out accidentally between Chinese and Japanese troops on maneuvers near Peking. Unlike earlier incidents, this was not an engineered plot, and the Japanese military command in North China tried to settle it locally. The Chinese government, however, with far greater self-confidence than it had had in 1931 and with a more nationally aroused citizenry behind it, demanded a basic settlement of differences between China and Japan. The Tokyo government followed suit in demanding a "basic settlement." During this impasse, Chinese planes attempted to bomb Japanese warships in the river at Shanghai on August 14, but hit the city instead. This led to a major land battle around Shanghai, while the fighting in the north continued to spread.

The Japanese government decided that the only answer to such Chinese intransigence was a quick knockout blow. It proceeded to mount a major military effort, though it euphemistically called the resulting war "the China Incident." The army swept south and west from its bases in North China. Meanwhile, in heavy fighting, the crack divisions of Chiang Kai-shek's army were finally defeated around Shanghai, and the invaders pressed on in December to capture Nanking, the capital, where the Japanese soldiers were permitted to indulge in an orgy of rape and pillage. But the Chinese continued to fight and the Japanese doggedly pushed on, seeking the elusive knockout blow. Hankow in the center of the country and Canton in the far south were captured by the autumn of 1938, and most of Inner Mongolia and North China were overrun. Thus the Japanese controlled all the largest cities, all the major ports, the bulk of the railway lines, and most of the more productive and heavily populated parts of the country. But the Nationalist government continued to fight on from its provisional capital at Chungking in the mountain-girt fastnesses of west China, while a troublesome guerrilla resistance developed around the Chinese Communist center of Yenan in the northwest.

The Japanese set up a puppet regime in North China,

and in March 1940 they persuaded Wang Ching-wei, once a major leader among the Nationalists, to head a new, subservient national government in Nanking. But the Chinese masses were not won over to anything more than sullen acquiescence, and the military resistance continued. There seemed to be no end to the war. Chinese nationalism would not bow, and even the great Japanese war machine could not stifle it. Japan thus became the first of the modern military powers to find itself frustrated by guerrilla techniques in a less developed country and caught in the quagmire of Asian nationalism.

The situation was made more threatening for the Japanese and more hopeful for the Chinese by the growing storm clouds of war throughout the world. While the Japanese navy had for long regarded the United States as its chief potential enemy, the army expected the struggle to be with the Soviet Union. For this reason, Tokyo in November 1936 entered into an Anti-Comintern Pact with Nazi Germany, which Italy joined the next year. In the summer of 1938 a large-scale, twelve-day battle did take place with the Soviets on the eastern border of Manchukuo, and the next spring and summer there was a still larger, five-month battle on its western frontiers. The Japanese were worsted in both contests, showing that they needed to press the mechanization of their forces still faster.

The outbreak of the war in Europe in the summer of 1939 at first seemed encouraging to the Japanese. It helped draw world attention away from East Asia, as had happened in World War I to Japan's economic and military benefit. The collapse of France permitted the Japanese in September 1940 to extend military control over northern French Indo-China, that is, North Vietnam, in order to block the railway line from there into southwest China. At the same time, they were emboldened to form a full Tri-Partite Alliance with Germany and Italy. In July 1941 they extended their military control over the rest of Indo-China to secure its potential naval bases in the south. Japan's "New Order in East Asia," which had been announced in November 1938 to embrace Japan, China, and Manchukuo, was expanded to a dream of Japanese hegemony over the whole of East Asia. The concept was cloaked by a euphemism—the "Greater East Asia Co-Prosperity Sphere"—and eventually found administrative expression in 1942 in a Greater East Asia Ministry.

The war in Europe, however, served to arouse the American government and public to the great potential danger of a world in which a hostile Germany held sway over all Western Europe and a hostile Japan over all East Asia. Washington hitherto had limited itself to a policy of verbal protests and the doctrine of nonrecognition of the results of Japanese aggression on the continent. Now it began to take more substantive countermeasures while building up its own military strength. In July 1939, just before the European war broke out, the American government denounced its commercial treaty with Japan, thus freeing its hand for further economic moves. In July 1940, it adopted a policy of licensing scrap iron and oil shipments to Japan in order to cut down on the flow of these materials, which were essential to the Japanese war machine, and when Japan seized southern Indo-China in July 1941, Washington, together with the British and the Dutch, adopted a total oil embargo.

Japan was now caught on the horns of a dilemma. Both her army and navy were dependent on imported oil and had only about a two-year supply on hand. Victory in China must come soon, or Japan's armed forces would grind to a halt. Japan had to act quickly and decisively. Two choices were open. One was to bring an end to the war in China by generous concessions, withdraw her troops as the United States demanded, and settle back to profit economically from the war in Europe, as she had done with such splendid results during World War I. Here was clearly the course of economic self-interest. With the factory power of Europe temporarily cut off from Asia and threatened with more permanent destruction, Japan could take another great step forward toward the establishment of an economic empire in Asia without the attendant costs of conquest, if she could but disentangle herself from the war in China.

But economic self-interest was not to carry the day. Withdrawal from China seemed to the military a national loss of face that could not be tolerated. It also would have been interpreted in Japan as an open admission that the military's program of economic security through conquest had failed. There would have been an inevitable shift in sympathies which would have endangered the military's hold on the government. The United States, moreover, was unrealistically insistent that no settlement could be discussed until Japan had relinquished the fruits of her aggression since 1931. Japan would have to yield first and discover what the terms were later.

The alternative was to sail south, break the tightening economic blockade by seizing the resources of Southeast Asia, particularly the oil of the Dutch East Indies, the present Indonesia, and thus achieve at one great blow the much-vaunted Greater East Asia Co-Prosperity Sphere. Tokyo had secured its rear for such a move by signing a neutrality pact with the Soviet Union in April 1941. The Japanese had been terribly embarrassed when their German allies, who had a similar agreement with the Soviets, invaded Russia in June, but early Nazi successes seemed to put the Soviets even further out of the picture. The one great danger in the policy of southern conquest was that it would undoubtedly precipitate war not just with Britain and the Netherlands, which had little military strength in East Asia and were desperately fighting to survive in Europe, but with the United States, which was an incomparably bigger economic power than Japan. But so long as Germany remained undefeated, the United States, it was felt, would not dare to concentrate much of her military might in the Pacific. Germany thus would be the first line of Japan's defense. If she won, Japan was safe. If she lost, she would at least have fought a rear-guard action in behalf of Japan by tiring their mutual enemies and giving Japan time to bring China to her knees and to build an invulnerable economic and military empire, protected by the vast expanses of the Pacific and Indian oceans and containing enormous natural resources and many hundreds of millions of industrious people.

Japan faced an agonizing, fateful decision. As the result of small initial wagers in 1931 and 1937, she had now been forced into a position in which she either had to withdraw ignominiously from the game and lose what was already won, or else make a win-all, lose-all play. Konoe and other civilians in the government tried desperately to find some compromise with Washington, but ran into a rigidly moralistic American stance. The emperor made clear his disapproval of the war policy. But to the military, in the summer and autumn of 1941, the chances for success seemed good, and the rewards of victory promised to be the creation of the most populous and perhaps the richest empire the world had ever seen. The Japanese military miscalculated, not so much on military, geographic, or economic factors, as on the human equation. They counted heavily on their own moral superiority, the "Japanese spirit," and the supposed degeneracy and pacifism of the Western democracies, particularly America, which they believed to be corrupted by too many luxuries. They were convinced that Americans did not have the will to fight a long war, especially if early Japanese successes showed how great the costs would be.

Repeating the strategy used against Russia in 1904, the Japanese started the war with a brilliantly successful surprise attack on Pearl Harbor in Hawaii at dawn on Sunday, December 7, 1941. They crippled the American navy with this single, sharp blow, virtually eliminating its battleship fleet. They missed, however, the aircraft carriers, which were to prove in the ensuing war far more important weapons. The attack on Pearl Harbor cleared the way for an easy conquest of Southeast Asia and the islands north of Australia. It was indeed an unqualified military success for Japan, but it was also a psychological blunder. It united the American people, who had been bitterly divided over the question of participating in the wars in Europe and Asia, and they took up arms determined to crush both Japan and Germany.

Japanese planes sank Britain's two major naval vessels in East Asia off Malaya early in the war, and the Japanese then invaded Singapore from the land and captured this great bastion of the British Empire on February 15. By March 1942 the Dutch East Indies were for the most part under their control. Resistance by the combined American and Filipino forces ended in the Philippines in May, and the same month the conquest of Burma was largely completed. Meanwhile Thailand, the only independent nation in the area, had bowed to the prevailing military winds and had joined Japan as a passive ally.

The United States, however, threw herself into rebuilding her naval strength and dispatched what forces she could to the Pacific to try to hold the line against Japan. In May American and Australian naval units fought the Japanese to a draw in the Coral Sea northeast of Australia, and the next month the American navy, with the benefit of superior intelligence facilities, administered a sharp defeat to a Japanese fleet preparing to seize Midway Island west of Hawaii. In September a Japanese effort to cross the island of New Guinea to its south coast was stopped, and in a bitter jungle campaign between September and February, the Americans turned the Japanese back at Guadalcanal northeast of Australia. Japanese forces had thus reached the limit of their conquests within the first year of the war, but it was a long time before the Americans could make serious inroads into the vast empire they had seized.

Japan had entered the war with the United States with her economy already in high gear after four years of war with China, and her manpower resources fully mobilized. The great conquests in Southeast Asia and the Pacific stretched both very tight. Meanwhile the United States, with twice the population and more than ten times the economic power of Japan, started to build up overwhelming superiority. The "Japanese spirit" did indeed prove strong, and Japan's forces fought ferociously and often to the last man, but bit by bit they were outclassed on land, on the sea, and in the air. American

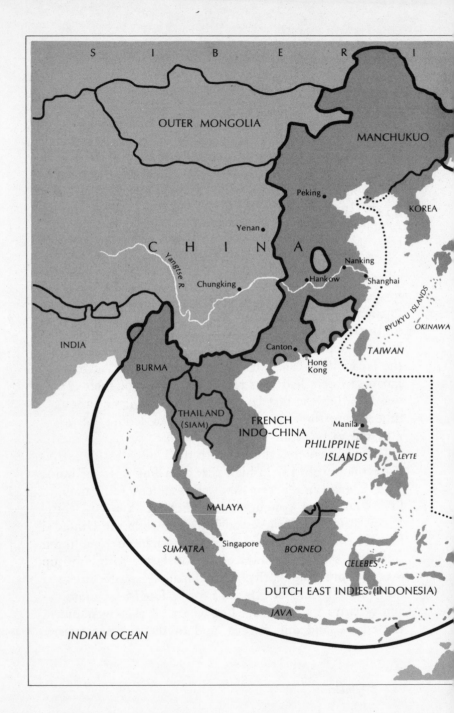

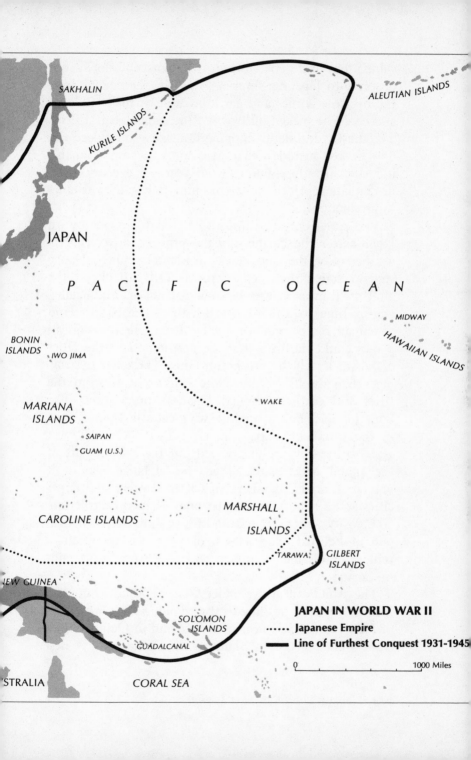

SAKHALIN

ALEUTIAN ISLANDS

KURILE ISLANDS

JAPAN

P A C I F I C   O C E A N

MIDWAY

BONIN
ISLANDS   IWO JIMA

HAWAIIAN ISLANDS

MARIANA
ISLANDS

WAKE

SAIPAN
GUAM (U.S.)

CAROLINE ISLANDS

MARSHALL

ISLANDS

TARAWA   GILBERT
ISLANDS

NEW GUINEA

SOLOMON
ISLANDS

JAPAN IN WORLD WAR II

.... **Japanese Empire**

──── **Line of Furthest Conquest 1931-1945**

GUADALCANAL

0   1000 Miles

AUSTRALIA   CORAL SEA

submarines and aerial mines in harbors cut slowly but deeply into Japanese shipping, until by the end of 1944 the overseas armies and garrisons were virtually isolated and could be picked off by the Americans one at a time. The drastic decline in shipping tonnage also reduced the flow of raw materials to Japan, and as a result, Japan's industry, already suffering from years of overwork and inadequate replacement of machinery, began to decline in production.

The Americans had already started to move toward Japan across the Pacific in a two-pronged drive. In November 1943, the navy began an island-hopping advance straight across the Pacific with a costly attack on the atoll of Tarawa in the Marshall Islands in mid-Pacific, and by June 1944 it had reached the much larger island of Saipan in the western Pacific. From there American planes could start a systematic destruction of the cities of Japan, largely by fire bomb raids. These, by destroying urban dwellings, drove the workers away from the cities and further crippled Japanese production. The bombing raids culminated in two great attacks on Tokyo in the spring of 1945, which together took well over 100,000 lives by fire and wiped out the greater part of the capital. Most of the other cities of Japan were dealt with in a similar manner; only Kyoto among the larger cities and a handful of smaller ones escaped destruction. The costly American seizure of Iwo Jima north of Saipan in February and March of 1945 was to obtain a refuge for disabled bombers returning from these raids on Japan.

The American army, under General MacArthur, had meanwhile been pushing westward along the north coast of New Guinea and nearby islands, and in October 1944 went ashore on Leyte Island in the Philippines. A desperate sortie by the remainder of the Japanese fleet failed to turn the tide, and after a long and arduous campaign, Manila was retaken in February. The two prongs of the American offensive then converged in April 1945 on Okinawa, which was to be the staging area for an invasion of the main islands of Japan. The Japanese fought back desperately, flinging their remaining planes at the American ships in remarkably effective suicide attacks. Harking back to the "divine wind" that had saved Japan from the Mongols in 1281, they called these attackers the *kamikaze*. But the vastly superior military weight of the Americans triumphed, and the island was completely overrun by June, with a staggering loss of life—some 110,000 Japanese military men and 75,000 Okinawans, about an eighth of the island's civilian population.

Meanwhile, Germany had accepted defeat on May 8. Clearly, Japan too had lost the war. But there was no break in civilian morale. The people stoically accepted starvation conditions and the mounting war disasters. They appeared resigned to fighting on to the end. Some high civilian leaders around the emperor, however, had seen the hopelessness of Japan's position already in 1944 and had started to maneuver toward ending the war. General Tojo had been persuaded in July of that year to pass the prime ministership on to another general, and a few days after the invasion of Okinawa, the latter was replaced by Admiral Suzuki, who had almost died at the hands of the army extremists in the February 26 Incident in 1936. In June the emperor, returning again to the initiative, called on the Supreme Council to find a way to end the war, and the government tried to get the Soviet Union to mediate. The United States had repeatedly spoken in terms of "unconditional surrender" for Japan as well as Germany, but she, together with Britain and China, issued on July 26 the so-called Potsdam Proclamation, in which the conditions for Japan's "unconditional surrender" were wisely elaborated. Japan was to be stripped of her empire and occupied until she had remade herself into a peaceful, demilitarized nation, but she would retain her national identity and the people would be free to decide on their future form of government.

The end was in sight, but the Americans, without stopping to think fully about what they were doing, proceeded on August 6 and 9, 1945, to drop on the cities of Hiroshima and Nagasaki the two atom bombs they had at long last completed, wiping out in two big puffs close to 200,000 lives and ushering in the horrors of the nuclear age. An argument could be made for having used the first atom bomb on Hiroshima in order to shock the Japanese leaders into surrender, because the decision even then hung precariously in the balance, but there was certainly no justification for using the second bomb. Meanwhile the Soviet Union had invaded Manchuria on August 8, and found the vaunted Kwantung Army of the Japanese little more than a hollow shell. At the Yalta Conference in February, Stalin had promised his allies to enter the war against Japan within three months after Germany's surrender, and he was eager to enter the fray before it ended, in order to have a say in the postwar settlement with Japan.

In the midst of all these disasters, the leaders around the emperor remained deeply concerned about the old concept of "imperial rule." On August 10 they accepted the terms of the Potsdam Proclamation, but only on the understanding that it did not prejudice the emperor's position as a "sovereign ruler." The American reply to this condition was ambiguous, and the Supreme Council split 3–3 over it. The emperor then made the decision for surrender, the first important political decision a Japanese emperor had made since ancient times, and he himself broadcast the surrender announcement to his people on August 14. The war was over. An imperial prince was made prime minister to help ensure the acceptance of the decision by the military. On September 2, Japan formally surrendered to General MacArthur on board the battleship *Missouri* in Tokyo Bay.

11 ❁ OCCUPATION

In the late summer of 1945 Japan lay in ruins. Some 2 million of her people had died in the war, a third of them civilians; 40 percent of the aggregate area of the cities had been destroyed, and urban population had dropped by over half; industry was at a standstill; even agriculture, short of equipment, fertilizer, and manpower, had declined. The people had poured all their energies into the war, blindly trusting their leaders and confident that "Japanese spirit" would prevail. Now they were physically and spiritually exhausted. Many were in rags and half-starved, and all were bewildered and mentally numbed. The "divine wind" had failed. For the first time in history, Japan was a conquered nation. The Japanese faced the prospect with trepidation, but, as the emperor had put it, they must "bear the unbearable."

The almost seven years of American occupation and tutelage that followed were to prove a unique experience not just for Japan, but in world history. Never before had one advanced nation attempted to reform from within the supposed faults of another advanced nation. And never did the military occupation of one world power by another prove so satisfactory to the victors and so tolerable to the vanquished. There was, of course, much to complain about on both sides. But the occupation turned out to be a far less unpleasant experience than the Japanese had anticipated, and in retrospect it came to be seen as an important, constructive phase of Japanese history.

The Japanese and Americans share the credit for this happy outcome. The latter, far from proving the vicious, cruel conquerors the Japanese had expected, showed themselves to be basically friendly and fair-minded, and they threw themselves with enthusiasm into the task of trying to reform Japan. The Japanese, far from being the fanatical fighters the Americans had come to know on the battlefield, proved at home to be a docile, disciplined, cooperative people. When the emperor and his government surrendered, the army of occupation became the unchallenged locus of authority, and the people obeyed it without question. Perhaps American conquerors were easier to accept than any others because of the long influence of American teachers and missionaries in Japan and the great admiration of many Japanese for the United States—despite all the wartime propaganda—and because of, rather than despite, the overwhelming victory of the American forces. Even the leaders, though resentful of American domination and dubious of some American reforms, realized that open resistance was useless and that only through cooperation could they hope to influence the policies of the occupation and help bring it to an early end. The net result of all these attitudes was a remarkable degree of cooperation, respect, and even good will between victors and vanquished.

The American occupation brought a massive flood of new attitudes and institutions comparable only to the Western impact in the nineteenth century, but much more sudden and pervasive. The effects were greatly heightened by the changes war and defeat had brought within Japan and in her relationship with the outside world. The disastrous failure of the foreign policy of the military and the terrible suffering of the war years produced a revulsion against military leadership and any form of militarism. The Japanese longed for eternal peace and swung rapidly from seeing themselves as a warrior race to becoming the most passionate of pacifists. The people were horrified to learn that, far from being welcomed as the deliverers of Asia from Western oppression, they were bitterly hated throughout China, Korea, and the Philippines and disliked in other Asian lands. Japanese soldiers, who had left home as heroes, were spat upon by resentful city crowds as they returned dispirited from overseas. "Nationalism" and "patriotism" became dirty words. Even for more hard-headed Japanese, the military's solution for Japan's great economic problem stood entirely discredited. In the postwar world, Japan, with its narrow geographic and economic base, could not hope to be a competitor with the new superpowers, the United States and the Soviet Union. In their disenchantment with past policies, the Japanese mentally downgraded their country not just to a second-class power, but to a third-rate nation. Clearly, Japan could not conquer and hold her own economic empire. If the destitute, overcrowded country was ever to reestablish a viable economy, it would have to be through trade in an internationally open and peaceful world. Even former military expansionists turned rapidly into sincere internationalists.

The physical, social, and spiritual disruption brought by the war and defeat had also helped clear the ground for a new beginning. Fear of the American conquerors soon turned into hope that they would lead Japan to a better day. If the militarism and authoritarianism of the past had proved so wrong, then the democracy the Americans extolled or the socialism or communism of other Western lands, all of which Japan's recent leaders had condemned, must be right. The average Japanese, feeling that he had been duped and misled by the government, was free of the sense of guilt common among the Germans. He could thus accept change more easily. Japan lay entirely open to new influences.

The Americans rushed in to fill the spiritual and political vacuum. General MacArthur had been designated the Supreme Commander for the Allied Powers, or SCAP, pronounced "scap" for short. He was a good choice from the point of view of domestic American politics. As the viceroy in Japan of a Democratic administration and the hero of the Republican opposition, MacArthur enjoyed the confidence of both sides and thus helped keep occupation policies from becoming embroiled in American politics, as happened with China policy. He was also a good choice from the Japanese point of view. He was undoubtedly a forceful and able leader, and his messianic pose and turn of phrase gave inspiration to the Japanese at a time when they desperately needed it.

The occupation MacArthur headed, though termed Allied, was entirely American except for some Australian soldiers and an occasional non-American in the headquarters staff. The Soviet Union refused to put troops under MacArthur's command, and Chiang Kai-shek was too busy trying to win back control over North China from the Communists to participate. Subsequently, through an agreement announced at Moscow on December 27, 1945, two international bodies were set up to supervise the occupation. The Far Eastern Commission in Washington, made up of the eleven (and subsequently thirteen) countries that had fought in the war against Japan, was to determine major policies. The Allied Council for Japan in Tokyo, made up of the four major powers, was to advise MacArthur in the field. Neither proved meaningful institutions. The Allied Council became merely a forum for angry debate between the Soviet and American representatives before their embarrassed colleagues from China and the British Commonwealth. Since the United States had the right to a veto in the deliberations of the Far Eastern Commission and also the right to take steps unilaterally in Japan pending its decisions, the commission could in effect do nothing more than approve American policies, which MacArthur in any case was already carrying out.

Long before the end of the war, the American government had begun preparations to deal with the postwar problems of Japan. In striking contrast to its failure to prepare for new responsibilities in Korea and other parts of East Asia, it trained large numbers of military men in the Japanese language and in the problems of administering Japan, and a United States Initial Postsurrender Policy for Japan was drafted. This was an extraordinarily broad-minded and far-seeing document, which served well as the basic guide for the crucial early stages of the occupation. The American policy for Japan was stern but constructive. It was based on the conditions outlined in the Potsdam Proclamation and on the realization that a policy of revenge would only breed hatred and unrest; that a policy of retribution would reduce the Japanese to desperation without achieving more lasting improvements in their role in the world; and that only through a policy of enlightened reform was Japan likely to be changed from a disturber to a supporter of world peace.

The Americans, realizing the impossibility of administering directly a nation as complex and culturally and linguistically alien as Japan, decided to rule through the Japanese government. They inundated the nation for a short time with American and Australian troops to demonstrate the futility of opposition, but otherwise they only developed a large occupation bureaucracy in Tokyo to supervise the Japanese government and maintained relatively small teams in the prefectures to check on the results. At first entirely military in composition, the occupation bureaucracy gradually became in large part civilian, but it retained a basically military structure until the end.

The first few months of the occupation constituted essentially a period of organization and ground-clearing for the reforms the Americans intended to carry out. The first objective was the negative one of demilitarizing Japan. The surrender had of course brought a speedy end to Japanese control not only over her recent conquests, but over Korea and Taiwan as well, and a start was made on repatriating all Japanese overseas. Over 6 million soldiers and civilians were gathered up and dumped back in Japan by the end of 1947, leaving only a few hundred thousand still in Soviet prison camps in

Siberia. Meanwhile the army and navy ministries had been converted into the First and Second Demobilization Ministries, which oversaw the speedy demobilization of the military forces at home and then went out of existence themselves.

All munitions industries were closed down, and the occupation embarked on an ambitious program of making available as reparations to the countries Japan had despoiled all of Japan's industrial capacity in excess of her bare living needs. But this proved to be an unrealistic attempt. The victors found difficulty in reaching agreement on the division of the spoils; worn-out Japanese industrial equipment was not worth transporting and setting up in other countries, whose economic needs and capacities it might not fit in any case; and it was soon discovered that Japan had no excess industrial capacity, but herself faced a grim fight for economic survival.

On the political side, organizations deemed ultranationalistic or militaristic were disbanded; repressive laws were nullified; Communists and other political prisoners were freed; and the special tie between the Shinto religion and the state was dissolved. As a result of this last measure, many of the great historic shrines, thrown back on their own inadequate economic resources, fell into serious financial difficulties. War criminals were also brought to trial. Large numbers of military men accused of atrocities were speedily handled on the spot, either in Japan or abroad, and twenty-five former government leaders were tried by an international tribunal in Tokyo, in the same manner as the Nazi leaders at Nuremberg, for crimes against peace. There had been, however, no clear-cut leadership group in Japan or any clear plot. By the time the judgments were finally handed down late in 1948 and seven of the men were hung, including Tojo and one civilian, the former prime minister Hirota (Konoe had escaped by committing suicide), the attitude of the Japanese public had turned from anger against these discredited old men to pity.

A more significant move was the so-called purge. All those felt to be in any way responsible for Japanese conquests abroad were banned from government service and from any position of substantial responsibility in society. All former military officers and military police were put in this category, together with most men who had occupied high positions in the civil government, all politicians who had accepted sponsorship by Konoe's Imperial Rule Assistance Association, and large numbers of leading businessmen. The extension of purge proceedings to teachers, combined with the desperate economic plight of this group, resulted in many resignations from schools. Roughly 200,000 persons were involved in the purge, and many others were driven out of office or positions of influence by its threat. The whole purge can be criticized because it was carried out by categories, not on the basis of individual actions, and thus it undermined the democratic concept of individual rights. Still, it did sweep away much of the old leadership, at least temporarily, and made room for new, even if not necessarily better, men.

By February 1946 the occupation was well enough in control to permit the start of a more constructive second phase. The Americans were determined to carry through a drastic political reform on the reasonable assumption that a democratic Japan was more likely to remain a supporter of peace than an autocratic Japan. The political reforms centered around the writing of a new constitution. When the Japanese government came up in February with what MacArthur felt to be unsatisfactory proposals for constitutional reform, he had his own staff quickly draft an entirely new document, originally in English, as the end-product clearly shows. After only slight modifications by the Japanese government, this was presented to the Diet in the form of an amendment by the emperor to the 1889 constitution, was passed by this body, and went into effect on May 3, 1947.

The new constitution made two basic changes in Japan's political structure. One was to bring the theory of the emperor's position into line with the reality, by making absolutely clear that he was merely "the symbol of the State and of the unity of the people," and had no political powers whatsoever. The emperor himself had already prepared the way by announcing to his people on January 1, 1946, that he was in no sense "divine." Many persons abroad had urged that the emperor be prosecuted as a war criminal. This would certainly have been unjust, and it might have produced chaos in Japan. The solution found for the problem of the "imperial will" was vastly preferable.

The other major change in the constitution was the clear and unequivocal establishment of the British parliamentary system that Japan had been developing by evolutionary methods before the thirties. The new constitution made explicit the supremacy of the House of Representatives, which remained essentially unchanged from what it had become by the twenties, and abolished all competing centers of political power, such as the military, the Privy Council, and the House of Peers. The high court officials and the bureaucracy were made clearly subordinate to the prime minister, who was to be elected by the House of Representatives from among the members of the Diet. The House of Peers was replaced by a purely elective 250-man House of Councillors, chosen half at a time every three years for a six-year term, two-fifths by the country as a whole and the other three-fifths by prefecture-wide constituencies. The powers of the upper house were clearly subordinated to those of the House of Representatives. On the budget and the choice of the prime minister, the decision of the lower house was to prevail, and on other matters a two-thirds vote of the lower house could override the upper. The only significant power of the House of Councillors was that amendments to the constitution required a two-thirds vote of both houses.

Among other lesser features of the constitution were its provisions that prefectural governors must be popularly elected, as was already the case with mayors and prefectural and municipal assemblies, and its creation of an independent judiciary under a Supreme Court, which was given powers of judicial review of the constitutionality of legislation, in the American manner. Judicial review, however, was unfamiliar to the Japanese and inconsistent with the British system of parliamentary supremacy. It thus did not develop into an important part of the new system. The constitution spelled out in great detail the "fundamental human rights" of the people, which were declared to be "eternal and inviolate." All people were to be "respected as individuals," and there was to be no discrimination by sex or in any other way. Women thus were assured of the vote, and the sexes were specifically declared to have equal rights in marriage.

The most interesting provision of the constitution was the "renunciation of war," as its second chapter (Article 9) is entitled. This fitted well the American aim to disarm Japan permanently and the revulsion against militarism that had swept Japan. Japan "forever" renounced war and the maintenance of "land, sea, and air forces, as well as other war potential."

The occupation buttressed its constitutional changes with a flood of supporting legislation and lesser reforms. The infamous Home Ministry, which had controlled the police and prefectural governments, was broken up, and its largest surviving part was renamed the Autonomy Ministry, referring to local government. Greater powers for taxation and legislation were given to local governmental bodies, and control over the police and education was dispersed among them. On the whole, decentralization of this sort, however appropriate to America's size and diversity, was not well suited to a relatively small, homogeneous country like Japan. Atomized police and school jurisdictions did not operate well, and in time control over both gravitated in large part back into the hands of the central government.

More important and lasting was the sweeping program of economic and social revolution which the occupation carried out to undergird its political reforms. The American planners were quite right in assuming that a more equitable division of wealth, opportunity, and power would help ensure the stability of Japan as a peaceful, democratic country. Still, the revolutionary zeal the Americans displayed was surprising, in view of their record at home and elsewhere abroad. The usual justification was that Japanese society was so thoroughly evil that only drastic measures could correct it. The concept was in part the product of simple ignorance about Japan, in part the result of Marxist interpretations, which were quite prevalent in American analyses of Japan until the cold war psychology swept them away. But, however wrong the diagnosis, the medicine proved efficacious. MacArthur turned out to be the most radical, one might even say socialistic, leader the United States ever produced, and also one of the most successful. But, of course, revolutionary change is easier to carry out through arbitrary military power in someone else's country than through democratic means at home.

The occupation authorities devoted special efforts to breaking up the great concentrations of wealth in the hands of the zaibatsu both on the dubious grounds that the zaibatsu system had been responsible for Japan's imperialistic aggressions abroad and on the more valid grounds that such great concentrations of wealth were not conducive to the development of a healthy democratic system at home. Members of zaibatsu families and their chief executives were purged, their assets frozen, and the bulk of their holdings taken over by the government in a general capital levy, which was graduated to run from 25 percent on modest holdings of 100,000 yen to 90 percent on fortunes of more than 15 million yen. Steeply graduated income and inheritance taxes were also imposed, making the future accumulation of great wealth much more difficult than it had been in the past. As a consequence, the Mitsui and the other zaibatsu families quickly faded into modest affluence and political irrelevance.

The combines themselves were broken up into the various companies of which they were made, and corporation laws were changed to prevent their reconstitution. At one time it was planned to break up more than 300 of the larger remaining companies in an operation reminiscent of "trust-busting" efforts in the United States, but this program proved both difficult and inadvisable in the face of continuing economic stagnation in Japan, and was scaled down by 1949 to less than a score of companies. In more recent years it has often been asserted that the zaibatsu combines have been restored, but this is not correct. The mergers of some big companies and the cooperation that has developed between others are both a far cry from the centrally owned and controlled combines of prewar days.

The reverse side of the coin was an effort to develop the political consciousness and power of industrial labor and the peasantry. Labor legislation was revised to conform to the most advanced concepts of Europe and the United States, and veteran Japanese labor leaders from the twenties, with the active encouragement of the occupation, built up a rapidly burgeoning and often violently assertive labor movement. By 1949 more than 6 1/2 million workers had been enrolled in labor unions. From the start, the Communists controlled a large share of the unions, and the movement further differed from that of the United States in that a high percentage of the organized workers were government employees— either teachers, white collar workers in government offices, or laborers on the national railways or in other nationalized industries. As a result, the occupation authorities soon discovered to their distress that organized labor often showed less interest in bargaining with management than in political agitation, which seemed a more direct way to affect government wage scales or achieve Communist ends.

The most daring and sweeping of all the occupation reforms was aimed at improving the lot of the tenant farmer and awakening his political consciousness. This was the land reform program, which while slow to get underway was carried out with thoroughness between 1947 and 1949. Some decades earlier, the Japanese government, worried by the rapid increase in tenancy, had managed to stop its further growth, and the figure for tenant-cultivated land had remained under 50 percent. By 1949 it had been rolled back to a mere 10 percent, and subsequently it declined to about half that figure. This was achieved by abolishing absentee land ownership and by limiting members of farm communities to the ownership of the land they themselves cultivated, plus an area roughly equivalent to one average-sized farm. The result was that in most parts of Japan, where an average-sized farm was about 2 1/2 acres, the largest holding could be no more than about 10 acres. Generous credit terms were made available to the former tenants, and since the sale price of the land did not take into consideration the runaway inflation that followed the war, payment was relatively simple. This procedure, however, naturally entailed a sharp reduction in the wealth of the former landowners, who received in real value only about a penny on the dollar. This was scarcely just compensation, but the reform, backed as it was by the unchallengeable authority of the occupation, was accepted and soon produced a permanent change in the social and economic landscape of rural Japan.

The occupation authorities also attempted to carry out a wide range of social and educational reforms in order to implement the respect for the individual and the equality of all citizens called for in the constitution. The nobility was abolished and all titles dropped, except for the emperor himself and his immediate family. Women, who had already been pushed into more independent economic roles during the war years, were now given full legal equality with men in every way, and began to forge ahead toward greater social equality. The authority of the family head over other adult members and over branch families, which was a survival from the feudal past, was eliminated.

Elementary education had from the start been egalitarian, but now an effort was made to reduce the elitist flavor of the higher levels of schooling and to shift the emphasis throughout from rote memory work and indoctrination to training young people to think for themselves as members of a democratic society. Textbooks were entirely revised to eliminate militaristic and nationalistic propaganda, and the old courses on ethics, which were thought to have inculcated these doctrines, were banned in favor of new courses in the social sciences. Compulsory education was extended with no great difficulty from six to nine years, because even before the war most children had sought some further education beyond the required six years. The standing of schools at each level was, at least in theory, equalized, so that the next level of education would be open to all those who had completed the preceding one.

In addition, the levels beyond the initial six years of primary school were made over to conform to those customary in America: the three-year junior high school, three-year senior high school, and four-year college or university, as it is always called in Japan. In the process, most of the old five-year middle schools added another year to encompass both junior and senior high schools, while the various types of three-year higher schools, by dropping their lowest year and adding two higher years and then combining with other higher schools, became multifaculty universities, paralleling in name if not in reality or prestige the old prewar universities.

The shift in school systems from what the Japanese, referring to the number of years at each level, called the

6–5–3–3 system to the American 6–3–3–4 system caused tremendous confusion. The sudden jump in the number of universities and the great increase in students attending the higher levels of education, together with the elimination of one year at the top of the system, also resulted in a substantial lowering of university standards. All this was deeply resented by many Japanese. On the other hand, the new system did widen educational opportunities past the elementary level, and the new emphasis, particularly in the lower grades, produced in time what seemed almost like a new breed of young Japanese —more direct, casual, and undisciplined than their prewar predecessors, but at the same time more independent, spontaneous, and lively.

By the autumn of 1948, a great shift in spirit and emphasis was evident in the occupation. It was now more than three years old, and most of its major reforms had been completed or else were well under way. The focus of interest began to shift from reform to economic recovery, because the success of the reforms now seemed less in doubt than whether the patient would live at all. Industrial production in 1946 had dropped to a seventh of what it had been in 1941, and even agricultural production was down to three-fifths. Meanwhile the population, under the impact of the return of 6 million Japanese from abroad and the postwar baby boom resulting from the joining of long-separated families, had soared to around 80 million. It seemed doubtful that adequate sustenance could ever be found for that many people on so narrow a geographic base. The sweeping reform programs that had forced the government to live beyond its means contributed to a rampant inflation of more than a hundredfold, which made it difficult to stabilize the economy.

Japan had suffered proportionately more from the war than any of the other major combatants and had recovered appreciably less. Her future as an economically viable unit was in serious doubt. The Japanese were living at a bare subsistence level, and at that on American largess—a dole of close to half a billion dollars a year. Democracy or political stability of any sort would be impossible in the long run without economic stability. Political and social reforms, however desirable in themselves, had little chance for eventual success unless there was a sound economic foundation.

The external world situation also contributed to the change in the spirit of the occupation. At the end of the war Japan had been a defeated, isolated nation facing a united, triumphant world. There seemed ample time to try to reform her, and how she progressed economically seemed to be a matter of concern only to the Japanese. But the unity of the outside world had withered in the chill winds of the cold war. By the autumn of 1948 it was clear that the Communists were winning in China. Much of the rest of Asia was in chaos. There was obviously no united world, but a growing division into what seemed at the time to be two hostile camps, with Japan close to the borderline between them, both geographically and politically. She was seen as a potential battlefield in the cold war and, because of her once-considerable industrial power, a possible factor of importance in the worldwide contest.

Economic recovery thus had become a major objective in itself, and reforms which seemed to conflict with it were modified or dropped. It was at this time that the effort to break up the larger industrial firms was scaled down and the attempt to distribute as reparations Japan's supposed excess industrial facilities was abandoned. On the basis of the recommendations made in April 1949 by the Dodge Mission, which was headed by a Detroit banker of that name, the Japanese government embarked on a program of severe fiscal austerity. It also managed to stabilize the yen at 360 to one American dollar, as opposed to the prewar rate of about 3 to 1. Labor union activities that might endanger production were restricted. As early as February 1, 1947, the occupation had stopped a proposed general strike, and in July 1948 it prohibited strikes by civil servants. In 1949 Japanese industrialists took advantage of the retrenchments enforced by the recommendations of the Dodge Mission to carry out a so-called Red purge of troublesome Leftist activists from their payrolls.

All these changes in emphasis convinced the Japanese Left that the occupation had shifted "180 degrees" in direction. They had originally welcomed the occupation reforms with enthusiasm as first steps toward the achievement of their own socialist or communist objectives. Now they felt the occupation had betrayed them. With increasing vigor, they denounced it and sought to undermine it and its policies. Other Japanese too were beginning to become more critical. The despair and confusion of the early postwar years were wearing off, and most Japanese had come to realize that not all that was distinctively Japanese was bad and not all that the Americans were attempting was wise. Obviously, the occupation authorities had in many matters been following American patterns too closely, and thus had often attempted to do either the impossible or the unnecessary. Criticism of American policies grew and was accompanied by increasing resentment of the privileges and luxuries the Americans had arrogated to themselves, often at the expense and inconvenience of the Japanese. Resentment of this sort was inevitable in such a situation, and though it was surprisingly slow to develop, it became an increasingly important factor in the situation.

The occupation too had lost much of its earlier élan. The youthful and somewhat undisciplined draftees who had taken the place of the original war veterans in the army of occupation could not retain the respect of the Japanese public. The civilian employees and professional military officers on routine assignments who succeeded to the posts of many of the original staff officers, while for the most part conscientious and devoted workers, could not recapture the full enthusiasm of the men they replaced. The military organization of the occupation also was increasingly getting in the way of the reforms it was trying to achieve. There was, after all, a basic contradiction between the absolute authority of an external military force and the development of democratic institutions, and this became clearer with each passing year.

The time had obviously come to end the occupation. Its very nature and the opposition it was starting to stir up against itself were beginning to militate against the success of the reforms it had initiated. There was a definite limit to what could be accomplished in the reform of Japan by foreign dictate. What was now needed was for the Japanese themselves through assimilation and adaptation to adjust the new rules to their realities, and to gain experience in living and governing themselves according to the new processes. MacArthur's original estimate of about three years as the desirable duration of the occupation was not far off the mark.

In 1947 the government in Washington had begun

efforts to bring the occupation to an end through a peace treaty, but in a divided world this was not easy to do. The Soviet Union blocked all attempts to hold a peace conference by insisting that peace terms should be decided solely by the great powers and that she must have a veto right in such decisions. Since the Russians had no desire to see the democratic experiment in Japan succeed, they would no doubt have used the veto to sabotage the type of peace settlement the Americans and their allies desired. The resulting impasse prolonged the occupation for several years. Eventually, the United States decided to proceed without Russian participation, if the Soviet Union did not change her stand. In April 1950 Dulles, the later secretary of state, was put in charge of preparations for the peace treaty, and in September the United States announced her intention to push ahead toward its achievement. Dulles started bilateral negotiations with the various countries involved, and in this way worked out the text of the peace treaty in advance of the peace conference. This new departure in diplomatic procedures was made possible by the increased facilities for rapid communication among the various capitals of the world.

The occupation was obviously entering a new and final phase. The terms for its liquidation were already being drafted, and Japanese and Americans alike began to look forward to the imminent restoration of Japanese sovereignty. Earlier plans for the peace treaty had envisaged certain formal Allied controls over Japan lasting for many years. The long delay in the treaty, however, had made such controls seem undesirable. Japan was to be restored to full sovereignty and would soon be in a position to revise the postwar reforms as she saw fit. The remaining days of the occupation gradually turned into a period of transition, in which the Japanese could begin to reassume responsibility for their own affairs and start the inevitable process of adaptation and revision of the work of the occupation.

This transfer of authority was accelerated by two external developments. One was the invasion of South Korea by the Communist regime of North Korea on June 25, 1950, and the heavy involvement of the United States in the war which resulted. The attention of the American authorities in Japan and of the government in Washington became focused primarily on military developments in Korea rather than on civil reform in Japan. At the same time the Korean War brought a sharp increase in American purchases of goods and services in Japan, and produced a marked improvement in the economic situation there. Thus Japanese self-confidence and economic strength both grew just when American interest in domestic Japanese affairs declined.

And then, as a byproduct of the Korean War, MacArthur was dismissed on April 11, 1951. The Japanese at first were shocked and apprehensive lest this meant a sudden change in American policies toward Japan. When they saw this was not the case, they were not only greatly relieved, but also began to look upon the dismissal as a valuable object lesson in democracy. For all the American preaching about democracy during the earlier occupation years, the Japanese were amazed and deeply impressed to see that a single message from the American civil government could in actuality end the authority of a great military pro-consul, who to them had seemed all-powerful. MacArthur's involuntary last lesson in democracy for the Japanese was by no means his least.

General Ridgway was appointed to succeed MacArthur

as SCAP as well as in his military command in the area, but he could not really take his predecessor's place in Japan. MacArthur's role had been unique, and no one could replace him as the great reformer of postwar Japan. Ridgway wisely made no attempt to do so. Instead, he encouraged the Japanese to assume leadership with only a minimum of assistance and direction from the occupation authorities. The transition from occupation to independence was now fully under way. Already the Japanese were being allowed to resume normal relations with the outside world. At home, the process of revision had started and was to be seen most clearly in the growing numbers of persons and groups removed from the purge classification. When the peace treaty was signed in San Francisco on September 8, 1951, it was only an incident in the process of transition—a clarification of the rules for the formal transfer of authority, which finally took place when the treaty went into effect on April 28, 1952.

Forty-eight nations signed the peace treaty with Japan, but not her two giant neighbors, Communist China and the Soviet Union. The latter, to everyone's surprise, had come to San Francisco, but only to refuse to join in the treaty. Since the United States recognized the Nationalist Chinese government, now on Taiwan, while several of the signatory nations recognized the Communist government in control of the Chinese mainland, it had proved impossible to decide which Chinese government should be invited to San Francisco. The next most populous Asian country, India, had also abstained from the conference, largely as a protest against the exclusion of China. Subsequently, however, both India and Nationalist China signed treaties of peace with Japan.

The peace treaty specified Japan's acquiescence to the

dismemberment of her empire, which had already taken place in conformity with the Potsdam Proclamation and the terms of surrender. Korea once again had become an independent though tragically divided nation. Taiwan and the Pescadores Islands had reverted to China and had become the sole remaining refuge of the Chinese Nationalists. The North Pacific islands, which the Japanese had held under a mandate from the League of Nations, had been formally transferred to the United States in 1947 as a trusteeship territory under the United Nations. The Soviet Union, in accordance with the Yalta Agreement of February 1945, had occupied southern Sakhalin and the Kurile Islands north of Hokkaido. The United States similarly had occupied the Ryukyu and Bonin islands, and administered them as areas separate from Japan. In the peace treaty Japan renounced her claims to all these territories. Thus the treaty confirmed the limitation of Japan to the four main islands of Honshu, Kyushu, Shikoku, and Hokkaido and the smaller islands which adjoined them.

The treaty, however, did not specify the ultimate disposal of some of the areas Japan had given up. Nor did it resolve certain other basic problems. Reparations, while referred to, were left in an uncertain state. Because imports still exceeded exports, the Japanese economy remained dependent on American aid, and in the economic field no sharp line could be drawn between the occupation and postoccupation periods. Japan also remained heavily dependent on the United States in the field of defense. The removal from Japan of most American ground forces following the outbreak of the Korean War had led to the establishment of a National Police Reserve, a sort of embryonic army of 75,000 men, to replace the American soldiers, but this was only slight military power for a country of Japan's size, and the people as a whole remained violently opposed to any substantial rearmament. Thus the only solution to Japan's defense problems in a perilously unstable part of the world was a bilateral security pact with the United States, signed on the same day as the treaty and providing for the continuation of American bases and forces in Japan.

Japan had regained formal independence, but she was still far from able to stand fully on her own feet. Her economic future seemed precarious. She was surrounded by turmoil throughout East Asia and by the hostility of the peoples she had conquered. American military forces remained stationed throughout the land. And yet to the Japanese people the prospects looked far more hopeful than had seemed possible in the early postwar years. Americans too could look back with satisfaction on the occupation. More had been achieved in reforming Japan than had been expected. United States policy toward Japan, probably just because of its revolutionary nature, had proved by far the most successful aspect of postwar American policy in Asia.

12 ✸ RECOVERY

The Americans gave themselves full credit for the remarkable transformation of Japan during the occupation,
but little of this would have been possible without the
firm foundations for democracy that the Japanese already possessed: universal literacy, high levels of governmental efficiency, strong habits of hard work and cooperation, and more than a half century of experience
with democratic electoral and parliamentary institutions.
The supposed lack of democratic foundations made the
American reform program radical; their actual presence
made it successful. Nor would the reforms have succeeded as well as they did except for the extraordinary
postwar situation in Japan, in which the Americans were
in unchallenged control of the nation and able to act
as a benevolent *force majeure*, and the Japanese, thoroughly disillusioned with their own recent past, were
eager for change and ready to accept guidance. When
the Americans subsequently attempted to help build
democracies in less-developed countries which lacked
these foundations and the special postwar Japanese psy-

chology, but were instead in the grip of an assertive new nationalism, they discovered that they had lost their supposed magic touch. The Americans do deserve credit for formulating and guiding the democratic reforms of the occupation period, but the Japanese deserve most of the credit for their success.

Exhausted, dispirited, and bewildered at the end of the war, the Japanese fell back on a fatalistic acceptance of adversity and put their faith in dogged, hard work. Long accustomed to restoring the natural devastations of typhoons and earthquakes, they threw themselves with characteristic determination and surprising vigor into the work of restoring the country from the man-made holocaust of war. A scum of shacks began to cover the burned-out wastes of the cities, and these were replaced in time with progressively sturdier buildings. Efforts were made to replace destroyed industries with makeshift new ones by utilizing the wreckage of the war as raw materials.

Japan's farms, despite a lack of fertilizer and new investment, had maintained themselves better than her factories, but it had been a long time since domestic agriculture, even under the best of circumstances, had been able to feed Japan's rapidly expanding population. Naturally it was the city dweller who suffered most. His caloric intake fell to the semistarvation level of 1,500 calories. Those whose homes had not been burned out made exhausting trips to the countryside to seek food from the farmers in exchange for their remaining family possessions. This peeling off of successive layers of their goods they wryly called an "onion existence." Others attempted to supplement their diet with pathetic crops grown on whatever scrap of land they could find—an unused roadway or the burned-out site of their former home. Runaway inflation further plagued the wage- or salary-earner.

All this produced a drastic reversal in relative economic status between rural and city people. In the countryside, the peasant still had his old home and produced ample food for himself. But urban residents had been for the most part burned out, had seen their means of livelihood destroyed, and were inadequately fed. Many were kept alive only by American food shipments, often of unfamiliar and to Japanese unappetizing substitutes for their normal rice diet. Only the black market prospered in the cities—but it was dominated by gangsters and Koreans. The latter had been brought to Japan during the war to work in the mines and factories vacated by Japanese draftees, and after Japan's defeat some 600,000 of them elected to stay on in Japan, where the occupation accorded them a special status as semivictors, and they, with their deep resentment against Japan, chose to regard themselves as above its laws. No city dweller could live without recourse to the black market. This was not only costly but psychologically damaging to Japanese, with their punctiliousness about observing both law and custom. The squalor and dirtiness of postwar Japan was also damaging to a people who tended to be meticulously neat and made almost a fetish of bathing.

These conditions of dire want and demoralization improved only very slowly. Per capita income, which had sunk to the almost incredible figure of $17 in 1946, had climbed back by 1950 only to $132, an extremely low level for an industrialized nation. But then economic recovery began to pick up speed. The reforms recommended by the Dodge Mission in the spring of 1949 did result in the balancing of the budget, a check on the inflationary spiral, and the virtual elimination of the black market, and thus created a stable foundation for further recovery. The outbreak of the Korean War in 1950 produced a big American demand for Japanese goods and services, and a sudden spurt in the whole economy resulted.

Once started in motion, Japanese industry rolled ahead with increasing speed. The hard-work ethics of the Japanese, their high levels of education and technical skills, and the widespread drive for higher education gave Japan capacities for economic growth not found in most less-developed countries or in many industrialized ones. Wrecked or worn-out machinery was gradually replaced with the latest equipment, which sometimes gave Japanese factories an advantage over less recently modernized competitors in the West. New technology developed in the West since 1937, when the war had cut Japan off from industrial advances abroad, was introduced at an increasing speed, accelerating industrial growth. In particular, technical knowhow from the United States, embodied in hundreds of agreements on patents and affiliations between American and Japanese firms, made a huge contribution to the reviving economy. So also did an immense flow of American credit to capital-hungry Japan, largely in the form of bank loans, but increasingly as investments in Japanese securities. A veritable revolution in power resources also started as oil from the Persian Gulf, transported to Japan at declining costs by mammoth tankers, began to overshadow limited hydroelectric power and the relatively costly coal of Japanese mines.

Hand in hand with industrial recovery went the restoration of foreign trade, which was both necessary for any substantial recovery and a natural product of it. Old foreign markets in Asia for cheap Japanese manufactures were slowly recaptured, and new ones were developed in the United States and throughout the world. The first industrial and trade successes were in textiles and the other light industries the Japanese had mastered long before the war, but then they forged into more advanced and complex new fields, such as cameras, motorcycles, shipbuilding, and electronics. These required a great deal of highly skilled labor, and the Japanese, with their combination of advanced industrial skills and relatively low wages, consequently had an advantage over less skilled or more highly paid competitors. Bit by bit the worldwide image of Japan as a producer of cheap and shoddy goods changed to that of a producer of quality manufactures.

Meanwhile, Japanese agriculture was growing rapidly in productivity. This was not the result of any expansion of area, because this was impossible. Nor was it the product of land reform. The increased incentives of a system in which 90 percent of the land was owned by the people who farmed it was probably more than offset by the inefficiencies of an even further atomization of land holdings. What had happened was that a great new surge in technology and investment had taken place. There had been a decade of scientific advances in the world that the farms of Japan had lost out on. There were new insecticides and improved chemical fertilizers, which the Japanese came to use lavishly, and new machinery, such as small motorized threshers. In time, miniature tractors, called by the Japanese "bean tractors," which were well adapted to their tiny fields, came into common use. The Japanese farmer, moreover, being relatively well off in the postwar years, had the capital to invest in these improvements. The net result was that by the mid-fifties bumper crops had become the rule, and the Japanese suddenly realized that they were not just being blessed by favorable weather conditions year after year but had achieved an entirely new level of agricultural production.

Not all the economic growth was healthy. At first much of it went into a rash of pinball establishments— a postwar craze—and other tawdry amusements. There was also a disconcerting tendency for the economy to go too fast, "overheat," and threaten a dangerous return to inflation. This happened in 1953, 1957, and again in 1961. Each time it proved necessary for the government to take measures to slow the economy down. The very success of industry also accentuated the old problem of the dual economic structure. The farmers had become more productive, but at nothing like the rate of workers in the newer industries, and service workers and the old handicraft or less-mechanized industries lagged even further behind. In trying to expand its markets abroad, Japan also inherited problems from the war. In nearby Asian countries there was fear and distrust even of Japanese economic expansion, and in Europe and to some degree in the United States, discriminatory limitations were put on Japanese imports.

Moreover, a relatively short period of industrial modernization together with terrible wartime destruction had left Japan a capital-poor country not just in the financial sense, but also in terms of basic capital improvements. Schools, hospitals, and other public buildings were inadequate for a country of Japan's standing. Sewage and some other modern facilities were largely lacking. The road system was still almost primitive. Traditional wooden architecture, which was more sensible than stone in a forested, earthquake-prone country, left it without a backlog of more permanent structures surviving from earlier centuries, such as existed in Europe and many other regions. There was, in fact, a woeful shortage of housing, especially in the cities.

Still, the overall surge of the economy was impressive. In the mid-fifties Japan not only went racing past the productive levels of the thirties, but past its old per capita income levels. The gross national product grew on an average at about 10 percent per year, even after subtracting some inflationary up-creep. It has maintained this level ever since, a far higher rate of growth than any other country has ever enjoyed over a comparable period of time.

On the other hand, population growth, following the subsidence of the postwar baby boom, declined to about 1 percent a year, one of the lowest rates in the world. This was the result of liberal abortion laws, very laxly enforced, and a great enthusiasm for birth control. There were few religious or social obstacles to birth control in Japan, and it was vigorously advocated by both government and industry, but the chief motive power was probably the desire of most parents to see their children well educated and given a chance to succeed. This seemed more possible with two or three children than with the traditional large family.

A 1 percent rate of population increase subtracted very little from a 10 percent rate of economic growth, leaving much room for per capita advances. Of course, this sort of industrial growth required an even higher level of investment, but this the Japanese, with their traditional saving propensities, achieved, even though the great concentrations of wealth of the prewar period were now gone. At the same time, enough remained to give workers in the newer industries close to a 10 percent annual increase in wages, and this helped pull up other wage levels and living standards generally. By the mid-fifties the Japanese public was happily talking of a "Jimmu boom," meaning the greatest economic boom since the mythical founding of Japan by Jimmu in 660 B.C.

The economic "miracle" of Japan, as it came to be called, naturally influenced society and attitudes. The destruction of the war and the upheavals of the occupation were themselves enough to set off vast sociological changes, but these were accelerated and heightened by the breakneck economic pace and the unaccustomed affluence it began to produce. The disaster of defeat had discredited all traditional authority and values. The dispersal of population caused by imperialist expansion and wartime air raids and the grinding poverty of the early postwar years had disrupted the traditional patterns of life. And then, when recovery did come, it brought broad new adjustments; a vast further urbanization of the population; dislocations resulting from increasing automation; the blighting of mining areas, as imported oil replaced domestic coal; and changing patterns of relationships and an accelerating pace of life, as prosperity introduced an intense, almost frenetic, new tempo of activity.

The Japanese family was deeply affected by all this. Prewar tendencies for the typical family to shrink to the conjugal pair and their pre-adult children and for women and youths to free themselves from the authority of the *paterfamilias* were greatly strengthened by the occupation reforms and the new affluence. Increasing numbers of young Japanese also went on beyond the compulsory nine years of education to the senior high school and university level, greatly changing the educational make-up of society.

The decline of respect for governmental and family authority made the organs of public information all the more important. The Japanese had for long been a reading people, but with the new affluence there was a great increase in the publication of books and circulation of magazines. Monthly magazines had been important for decades, but now there was a flood of new weeklies, and newspapers became even bigger and more influential than before. The three largest, the *Asahi, Mainichi,* and *Yomiuri,* which were published and distributed throughout the nation, came to have a combined morning circulation of over 10 million and an evening circulation only somewhat smaller. A middle-sized national or regional paper would exceed the 1 million mark. Taken as a whole, the quality of newspapers was excellent and their influence enormous, probably greater than in any other nation. During the fifties they were joined in importance by television, which in Japan became known not as TV or the "telly," but as *terebi.* The competition resulting from the division of Japanese television between two government networks, one of them purely educational, and five private networks, produced a diversity and a balance between amusement and education as good as in any country in the world.

Nothing was more strikingly evident in the fifties than the rapid rate of urbanization. While every prefecture with a predominantly rural make-up started to lose population, all the cities grew fast, and the larger they were, the more rapid was the pace. Tokyo in the sixties passed the 11 million mark in population, becoming the largest municipality in the world. Yokohama and a large number of other satellite cities and towns increased the Tokyo population node by several million more. All the major cities witnessed a feverish building boom of steel-boned structures in their downtown areas, and they became ringed in their farther suburbs by so-called *danchi*, or developments, which consisted of serried rows of drab, four- to six-story concrete apartment houses containing amazingly small apartments. Department stores, already well established before the war, proliferated and became fabulous institutions, crowded with goods and people and offering such side attractions as art exhibits and children's amusement parks on the roof.

Japan was producing its own version of the affluent society, decidedly less fat than that of the West but perhaps for that very reason more lively. The chief impression given by the cities of Japan became one of vitality, gaiety, and unbounding vigor. All the arts, both native and Western, flourished exuberantly. Intellectual life became more vigorous and prolific than ever. Literature and films bubbled with creativity. The pleasure districts of Tokyo, with their night clubs, cabarets, bars, and fantastically variegated neon lights, became probably the biggest, gaudiest, and gayest in the world.

Almost all Japanese homes, rural as well as urban, came to possess a television set. Virtually everyone had a good camera. Small washing machines and electric refrigerators became commonplace. Electric rice cookers and numerous other mechanical conveniences eased the life of the housewife, and many homes and apartments came to have electric air conditioners. Even the family car began to make its appearance, though with disastrous consequences for Japan's inadequate road system. The English word "leisure" became the catchword of the day, and everyone spoke of the "leisure boom." Professional baseball games, skiing resorts, and summer beaches all were inundated with people. The dark mood of the early postwar years had been largely dispelled, and *akarui*, meaning "bright," became the favorite adjective to describe "life," "society," and almost anything to which it could be logically affixed. Even rural Japan shared in the new life. A television set bringing its citified fare into the farm household, a motorcycle and later a small truck, a party phone operated by the local agricultural cooperative—such things deeply affected the life of the farmer. The gulf produced between rural and urban Japan by an earlier stage of Japan's modernization began to close.

Many of these changes, of course, had their seamy side. The cities of Japan became hopelessly overcrowded; water and air became seriously polluted; water supplies in Tokyo at times fell to dangerously low levels; inadequate roadways became the scene of the world's worst traffic snarls; the death toll on streets and highways rose alarmingly; the superb rail network and vast urban commuting systems became absurdly overcrowded. More disturbing was the appearance of the spiritual ills of an industrialized, urban society, such as the sense of alienation and confusion on the part of many people adrift in the human sea of the modern city. Crime and juvenile delinquency, though minor by American standards, became a serious worry to a people accustomed to strict obedience and strong family bonds.

Japan's record-breaking economic pace and the apparent ease with which she took great sociological changes in stride are in themselves remarkable, but become all the more surprising when one considers that, even after the end of the occupation, Japan remained an intellectually confused and politically divided nation. The war, defeat, and subsequent occupation were all great shocks leaving deep wounds on the Japanese psyche, which healed only slowly. All old values were cast into doubt, and new ones remained bitterly disputed in a rapidly changing situation. All that was clear was change itself, but toward what ultimate end and for what purpose remained the question. Imagine the innovations that have swept the United States since the 1920s and multiply these by a factor of three or four, and you will have some idea of what the Japanese have been through.

There were two things, however, on which most postwar Japanese were agreed. They had little confidence in Japan as a nation, and they were determined never to become embroiled in war again. Their loss of national self-esteem manifested itself in an avoidance of all nationalistic expressions, verbal or visual. Even the national flag was used sparingly, and the national anthem was played so seldom that children who heard it over television at the opening of the professional wrestling bouts known as *sumo* thought of it as the "*sumo* song." Anything international was automatically viewed with favor, anything strictly national with a certain degree of suspicion, at least by younger Japanese. Despite their remarkable postwar accomplishments, the Japanese tended to underrate themselves. In part, this was because, with unconscious snobbery, they compared themselves not with other non-Western countries, but only with the most advanced countries of Western Europe and North America, which, with their head start in modernization and richer geographic bases, were quite understandably ahead of Japan in many ways.

The deep longing for peace and the resultant idealistic pacifism were natural reactions to the disasters of the war. However bewildering the postwar world might be, certain things were crystal clear to most Japanese. It seemed self-evident that the militarists were tragically wrong, that war does not pay, that Japan must at all costs avoid any involvement in future wars, and that she should try to maintain a neutral position outside the conflicts that embroiled other countries. As the only people who had ever suffered nuclear attack, the Japanese showed particular sensitivity to nuclear weapons. They were adamantly against any thought of the introduction of such weapons into Japan, even for defense purposes, and passionately protested their development and testing by other nations, particularly by the United States. The renunciation of war in the new constitution had overwhelming support. Even after the economy had been fully restored, the Japanese preferred to speak softly in international matters and carry no stick at all. Realizing the deep animosities their wartime conquests had stirred in neighboring lands, they held back from taking leadership even among those countries which obviously needed their help and had much to learn from them.

Although Japanese were in general agreement on these matters, in many other ways postwar Japan was a dangerously divided country. Differences of attitude by generation are marked enough in the West, but they became vastly greater in Japan. A youth who received the bulk of his education after the end of the war, his father who reached maturity in the 1920s, and his grandfather who was educated in the Meiji period were the products not just of different generations, but of different worlds. Their experiences and the outlooks these produced were so dissimilar that the different generations hardly spoke the same language. While this situation did not result in

serious frictions within family life, it did produce dangerous gaps in understanding between the generations in
universities and in society in general.

The gulf between occupational groups was sometimes
almost as wide, and certainly greater than in the profes-
sionally more fluid society of the United States. The
government official or big businessman lived in a different world from the so-called intellectual, or *interi*.
The latter became a term of pride in Japan, used for a
wide variety of people, particularly university professors,
writers, and the like, yet including almost anyone who
had received a higher education but was not a big businessman or government official. The latter two groups
were largely the products of the same universities as the
intellectuals, receiving there the same Germanic sort of
theoretical, idealistic education, but their professions
had forced them to become more pragmatic men of affairs, while the intellectuals tended to cling to their
bookish theories, unsullied by any compromise with supposedly sordid reality. Such differences are not unknown
in the West, but the gap was on the whole much greater
in Japan.

A similar intellectual gap developed between residents
of rural and small town Japan and city intellectuals and
their younger cohorts among university students. Rural
and small town Japan, the traditional stronghold of the
old political parties, had its own well-established patterns of pragmatic democratic politics based on personal
associations, patronage, and other local considerations—
a pattern not unlike that of much of the United States.
City intellectuals tended to reject all this as "feudalistic,"
insisting intolerantly on their own more theoretical concepts of democracy, socialism, or communism.

Industrial labor and management also viewed each

other with a degree of suspicion and hostility that was not uncommon in the United States a few decades ago but has largely faded since then. In a sense, these labor-management attitudes in Japan were surprising, because employment practices there still retained some of the desirable humane qualities of the pre-industrial past. Employers tended to feel a lifetime obligation to employees and normally did not consider lack of work or profits as sufficient reason for dismissal. As a result, Japan by the late fifties had virtually no unemployment problem, though there was still a great deal of underemployment. Wages, which were much more heavily in the form of fringe benefits than in the West, tended to be paternalistic, based more on length of service and family need than on the value of services performed. Yet, despite these more personalized characteristics of the employer-employee relationship, organized industrial labor and big business regarded each other quite openly as "the enemy," and the unions engaged not in bargaining, but in an annual "spring struggle" over wages.

In all these ways, postwar Japan was inevitably a divided, disrupted society, but this situation was greatly exacerbated by disagreement and confusion over national goals. The American occupation had carried through a remarkable program of political, economic, and social reforms based on a coherent American political philosophy, but it had made only half-hearted attempts to inculcate the philosophy itself. This was probably because Americans do not tend to approach problems through theory, and perhaps it was just as well that a basically military organization left it alone. In any case, the Japanese, who had been isolated from the rest of the world first by the war and then by the occupation, were left to interpret the American reforms in their own terms.

For most small town and rural people, this meant in terms of how these reforms affected their own private lives, and the reaction was overwhelmingly favorable. For intellectuals and many other urban groups, it was largely in terms of the theories they knew, and these were largely Marxist.

Marxist doctrines, which had appealed to university students and other intellectuals at the end of World War I, had spread despite the militaristic reaction of the thirties. Conservative thought at that time was retreating behind the mystical concept of the "imperial will," and liberal, democratic thinkers found themselves ground between this obscurantist doctrine and the emerging reality of totalitarian controls. In any case, they never developed a true philosophy for themselves, and their adherents in the parties, following their usual practice of pragmatic compromise, discredited themselves by cooperating with the military. Only the extreme Left had withstood compromise and had thereby preserved its doctrines intact as an appealing alternative to military dictatorship. When the militarists and emperor-centered conservatives went down in ignominious defeat, the Japanese public assumed that their socialist and communist critics had been proved right. The American occupation left the intellectual field open to them, and they came to dominate the magazines, newspapers, university faculties, and, naturally, their student bodies. The powerful Teachers Union of primary and secondary school teachers also came under the control of extreme Leftists. Though the reforms of the occupation and the Japanese institutions these helped produce were grounded in a liberal, democratic tradition, Japanese thought took on a heavily Marxist flavor.

Japanese Marxism remained much truer in doctrine to

the classical Marxism of the nineteenth century than did most postwar derivatives in the rest of the industrialized world, whether in communist, socialist, or so-called capitalist countries. According to this doctrine, it is a truism that a stage in history known as "capitalism," which is Marx's analysis of the early industrial societies of Western Europe and what he assumed would happen to them, would inevitably be followed by a historical stage called "socialism," which is his utopian dream of the future. In this stage all persons would work according to their capacities and receive according to their needs. Since capitalism is said to be the breeder of imperialism and the latter the cause of war, all international tension is to be laid at capitalism's door. Japanese Marxism proved an extremely hardy plant in postwar Japan. Its failure to correspond to the facts of twentieth-century history, even as these unfolded within Japan itself, did not seem to blight its popularity. The true believers and even many conservative Japanese, who were unaware of how much they remained influenced by their Marxist education, seemed hardly to notice that so-called capitalism had turned into something far different from what Marx assumed it would become and that the supposedly socialist societies approximated Marx's dream very little.

Marxism flourished despite a most infertile emotional soil. Rural and small town Japan remained basically conservative in disposition, and the Japanese as a whole were still an extremely pragmatic people. Moreover, there were deeply ingrained prejudices against the major so-called socialist countries and in favor of the principal so-called capitalist countries. No people were more suspected and feared in Japan than the Russians, and the attitude toward the Chinese was more that of condescension than real respect. By contrast, there was much admiration for the United States and the democracies of Western Europe. Most Japanese realized the tremendous importance to Japan of friendly relations with the United States, and there was also an amazingly strong grass-roots admiration and affection for America expressed in the most sincere of all ways—wholesale imitation.

From the beginning, the postwar Japanese thus moved down two diverging roads. The practical reforms of the occupation and the close connections with and admiration for the United States led in one direction. The Marxist thinking of the intellectuals and of many other urban Japanese led in another. The inevitable tension between these two pulls was heightened by the cold war. The nation which was trying to reform Japan appeared to have become the chief enemy of the system that many Japanese believed in. Large sectors of the Japanese public began to debate with utter seriousness whether it was "American imperialism" or "Japanese monopoly capitalism," a term used rather loosely to embrace all big business, that was the chief enemy of the Japanese people.

This situation aggravated what might be called the "American fixation," which was a hardly surprising characteristic of postwar Japan. The great economic and military power of the United States has produced a sort of "hang-up" over America in most countries, but it was particularly strong in postwar Japan, where there was a severe clash between feelings of dependence on the United States and resentment against her. Almost all the most divisive issues in postwar Japanese politics seemed in one way or another to involve attitudes toward the United States and the Japanese relationship with her. It was after all the United States that almost single-handed had crushed Japan and then occupied the country for close to seven years. Even after the end of the occupation, a virtually unarmed Japan remained dependent for her defense on American military bases. Cultural and educational ties abroad were overwhelmingly with the United States, and parts of Japan itself seemed to be overrun by Americans. It is not surprising that adult Japanese tended to assume that any Occidental in Japan was an American unless there was clear proof to the contrary, and children quite simply called them all Americans, instead of *gaijin*, or "foreigners," the usual term for Westerners.

Japan by the late fifties was on the surface a resounding economic success, but Japanese continued to feel economically dependent on the United States. Some of them realized that one reason for Japan's rapid economic surge forward was the very low level of her defense expenditures, made possible by the Security Treaty with the United States. Unlike most European countries, which spent around 4 or 5 percent of their gross national product for defense purposes, or the United States herself, which spent around 9 percent, Japanese defense expenditures remained around 1 percent. The United States had also provided the bulk of the new technology for the restoration of Japan's economy and much of the capital. She supplied close to 30 percent of the imported raw materials on which Japan lived and a comparable share of Japan's crucial foreign markets. These figures were not out of line with America's position of having roughly a third of the world economy, but they underlined Japan's great dependence on the economic link with the United States. Japanese who feared external economic domination over Japan naturally thought primarily about American corporations and banks. Those who worried about foreign protectionist measures against Japanese goods thought primarily about what the American Congress might do.

Almost anything that Japanese objected to in postwar Japan could also be blamed at least in part on the United States. This, of course, was true of all the occupation reforms and what had developed from them. All Japanese, and particularly conservative ones, found much to criticize there. Those who longed for neutrality toward strife elsewhere in the world, to say nothing of those who advocated a communist alignment for Japan, found in the American military alliance and bases a natural target of attack. Those who embraced Marxist theories saw in the United States, as the "leader of the capitalist camp," the obvious enemy. Almost all Japanese found the continued presence of American troops and bases in Japan disturbing, and disappointment over growing world tensions tended to be directed against "American Far Eastern policy," rather than toward the policies and activities of countries more removed from everyday Japanese life.

The unusual absence of nationalistic attitudes in postwar Japan also left most Japanese with a great uneasiness about what Japan was and would become, and this malaise too became directed largely against the United States. Those who feared that Japan was losing her cultural identity or soul thought primarily in terms of "Americanization." It was easy to blame all the ills of modern industrial society on the United States, where many of them were indeed very apparent. If even the French could fear American "coca-colonization" and the inroads of "Franglais," it is small wonder that the Japanese worried about "Americanization." It should be noted, however, that, protected as they were by much higher bulwarks of linguistic distinctiveness, they showed little concern about the huge new influx of English words, and instead made full use of them in amusing abbreviations and imaginative new specialized meanings and compounds.

The deep social and intellectual cleavages in postwar Japan and the uneasiness about the relationship with the United States produced a turbulent situation on the surface of Japanese politics, but at a lower level the main political flow remained remarkably steady. Despite common American and Japanese assumptions that Japan had made an entirely new political start after the war, this flow was basically the continuation of prewar trends, especially those of the twenties. The old parties, strongly based on the electorate of rural and small town Japan, reemerged into a leadership role, and they were joined by the business community and the bureaucracy in what became, in postwar terms, a fundamentally conservative political and economic "establishment." This conservative "establishment" disapproved of many of the occupation's economic and social reforms and sought to modify or ameliorate them, but the political reforms were basically a fulfillment of the evolutionary tendencies of the twenties and were therefore easier to accept.

Intellectuals, urban labor, and other dissident elements were on the whole more enthusiastic about the occupation reforms than were the conservatives, but they became progressively more disenchanted with American policies both within Japan and elsewhere in the world. Finding themselves unable to win a majority in the Diet or even in many local elections, they turned increasingly to confrontation politics—disruption in the Diet, political strikes in industry, and mass demonstrations in the street. Many of the Leftists, after all, had no particular faith in parliamentary democracy and looked upon it as merely one of the possible ways to establish a socialist state. It is a sad commentary on the American occupation that *demo*, one of the most used of all postwar Japanese words, was derived not from "democracy," but from "demonstration." These confrontation policies, together with the inflamed rhetoric of the newspapers and magazines, which tended to lean toward the Left, gave an appearance of wild confusion to Japanese politics even when electoral results remained steady and predictable and the "establishment" continued a fairly efficient and firm rule.

The occupation while it lasted also gave considerable political stability to Japan. The Americans had assumed at first that a popular revolution might sweep away the Japanese government, but none materialized, and when it became evident that the only pressures for revolution were from the extreme Left, the occupation began to stand in the way of any political change through violence. But its greatest contribution to stability was the sweeping program of reforms, which, being carried out by an unchallengeable external force, were executed far more easily and smoothly than if they had been attempted by a domestic leadership dependent on the polls. Once put into effect, these reforms greatly reduced the pressures for change.

In early November 1945, only two months after the start of the occupation, the old parties that had disappeared into the Imperial Rule Assistance Association in 1940 all reemerged from its dead shell. The old Minseito was reborn as the Progressive party (Shinpoto) and chose as its president Shidehara, the liberal foreign minister of the Kenseikai-Minseito cabinets of the twenties. Shidehara had on October 9 become prime minister in place of the imperial prince who had been chosen to ensure the surrender of the armed forces. The Seiyukai reappeared under its nineteenth-century name of Liberal party (Jiyuto). The former Social Mass party made a fresh start under the less ambiguous name of Socialist party (Shakaito). Even the Communist party (Kyosanto), which had not been a legal entity since 1924, was reborn on December 1. It was organized by old leaders who had emerged from prison, and was soon joined by other old leaders returning to Japan after long sojourns with the Chinese Communists.

The first postwar general election was held on April 10, 1946. The confused political situation was revealed by the fact that more than a third of the votes for members of the lower house went to independents (20.4 percent) and a mass of 60 minor parties (14.9 percent). The Socialists almost doubled their 1937 share of the vote (9.1 percent) to 17.8 percent. The Communists, despite great publicity, won only 3.8 percent of the vote. The remaining 43 percent went to the Liberals and Progressives, far less than their 71 percent in 1937, but still an impressive demonstration of political continuity. This was all the more remarkable because of the purge of most former Dietmen as members of the Imperial Rule Assistance Association. As a consequence, there was a turnover of 81 percent of the membership of the lower house.

The Liberal party won a plurality in the House of Representatives with 140 of the 466 seats. Its leader since its reconstitution had been an old politician, Hatoyama, but the occupation purged him on the eve of the election because of his dismissal of university professors on political grounds when he had been education minister in the early thirties. His successor, Yoshida, a former foreign ministry bureaucrat and ambassador to London, who had taken a clearly antiwar stand, was made prime minister on May 22.

Yoshida served as prime minister for seven of the next eight and a half years. He personally illustrated several of the characteristics of the politics of the times. He was one of many former bureaucrats who, seeing the new locus of political power, joined the parties and ran for election to the Diet. Such former bureaucrats were often the cream of the Japanese educational system, and they had had broad experience in governmental matters. As a result, they often dominated the conservative parties, and they occupied the prime ministership for all but two of the first twenty-five postwar years. Yoshida also illustrated the peculiar status of the Japanese government as the executor of the policies of the American occupation. He could survive as prime minister with only minority support in the Diet, and the most important function of his government was to deal with the Americans and try to influence them. For this task, a good knowledge of English was valuable, and it is no accident that Shidehara, Yoshida, and Ashida, one of the two other prime ministers under the occupation, were all products of the foreign ministry. The peculiar relationship with the occupation also meant that Yoshida, when he had occupation support, could run things in a more heavy-handed manner than proved feasible after the occupation ended. He was the only strong political leader to emerge in postwar Japan and won for himself the English sobriquet of "one-man" Yoshida.

In April 1947 a series of elections were held to prepare for the inauguration of the new constitution the next month. The prewar tendency to avoid party labels in local elections reasserted itself when virtually two-thirds of the 46 prefectural governors, more than two-thirds of the city mayors, and nine-tenths of the town and village mayors were elected as independents. Even in the first election for the House of Councillors, close to half the members elected were also independents. At the same time, the overwhelming majority of all these independents were clearly conservatives, close in their political views to the policies of the traditional parties and often intimately allied with them. Despite the great changes of the occupation, or perhaps because of them, Japan remained essentially a conservative country.

The second postwar general election for the lower house on April 20, 1947, revealed a considerable shaking down of the situation in national politics since the election a year earlier. One minor political group, the Co-operative party (Kyodoto), won 7 percent of the vote, but the other minor parties and independents dropped to a mere 11 percent of the total. The Communist vote stayed almost constant at 3.7 percent, and the remaining 78 percent was divided almost equally among the three major parties, the Socialists, Liberals, and the Democrats (Minshuto), as the Progressive party had been renamed.

The election also illustrated another significant point. In prewar elections the party in power, being able to distribute rewards, usually gained seats. The Liberals, though ostensibly "in power," were not in a position under the occupation to provide such rewards, and they had to accept criticisms directed against occupation policies. They lost nine seats, and the Socialists, though a hairline below the Liberals in popular votes, emerged as the plurality party with 143 seats. On May 24 they formed a coalition cabinet with the Democrats and the

Cooperative party, under the leadership of the veteran Christian Socialist, Katayama.

The Socialist-led government was a strange amalgam of divisive forces, and the Socialists in any case were in no position under the occupation to carry out a Socialist policy. Indeed, it was they who were now vulnerable to criticisms directed against occupation policies. Old pre-war divisions within the Socialist movement also reasserted themselves, and Katayama, in the face of a revolt of the left wing of his own party, resigned and was succeeded on March 10, 1948, by the former diplomat Ashida as head of the Democratic party and the leader of a coalition cabinet made up of the same three parties. This second coalition had an even less happy history, and Ashida was forced to resign only seven months later by the defection of the Socialists amid widespread charges of corruption.

Yoshida came back as prime minister on October 15, 1948, again with only minority support in the Diet, but he dissolved the lower house and held a general election on January 23, 1949. The Democratic, Socialist, and Cooperative parties, as the government parties of the two previous cabinets, stood seriously discredited in the eyes of the public, and their popular vote fell drastically, to 15.7, 13.5, and 3.4 percent, respectively. Independents and minor parties picked up only a small part of the vote the three parties lost, and it went instead largely to the two parties in opposition at the two extremes of the political spectrum. The Communists more than doubled their vote to 9.7 percent, and the Liberals, with about 44 percent of the vote, won 264 seats, the first one-party majority in the postwar Diet. Yoshida and his cabinet of Liberals continued vigorously on through the rest of the occupation period, thus becoming the Japanese government in power at the time the peace treaty went into effect.

Yoshida's return as prime minister coincided with the occupation's shift in emphasis from reform to economic recovery, and the next year it began to relinquish controls to the Japanese government in preparation for the return of full sovereignty. The purge was lifted from many categories of people in the course of 1951, and all were freed from its limitations after the peace treaty went into effect on March 28, 1952. The shift in authority had come just in time. The Japanese public had been getting increasingly restive under foreign rule. The explosiveness of the situation was revealed by widespread rioting and damage to American property on the occasion of the first post-occupation May Day, the great Leftist holiday, which came only a month after Japan had recovered her independence.

With Japan finally out from under the occupation, the time had come for new elections, which Yoshida held on October 1, 1952. His Liberals increased their popular support a little, though poorer distribution of the vote resulted in a loss of seats to 240, still a clear majority. The Progressives (Kaishinto, the historic name of the 1880s), as the Democrats had renamed themselves, had absorbed the small Cooperative party following the previous election and showed some recovery from their 1949 electoral disaster, but the parties of the Left were in serious trouble.

The Communists had been discredited in the eyes of the public during the summer of 1949 by several acts of violence generally attributed to them. Ever since the war, the Japanese public has reacted sharply against any violence that took human lives. The Communists fell into even worse trouble after Moscow openly censured them in January 1950 for their realistic but soft line, according to which they even tolerated the imperial institution and called for a "lovable Communist party." The consequent return to intransigence lost them support and led to a suppression of their newspaper and a purge of their leaders by the occupation. The Communist leaders for the most part went underground, and the decline of the party became evident when it won only 2.6 percent of the vote in 1952 and not a single seat.

The problem of the Socialists was of a different nature. Ideological divisions revived from prewar days had helped wreck the Katayama cabinet, and disagreement over the peace treaty produced a complete split of the party into left- and right-wing factions in October 1951, with the left wing refusing to support the peace treaty because of the exclusion from it of the two great Communist countries, the Soviet Union and Communist China. These two wings entered the 1952 election presenting separate slates, and though they together won 21 percent of the vote and 111 seats, with the right wing in a slight lead over its rival, they undoubtedly did less well than if they had been unified.

Beneath the split of the Socialist party was an equally sharp division among the labor unions. Since these provided the bulk of the grass-roots organization for the party, about half its Diet membership, and a large part of its vote, they exercised a disproportionately large influence in party decisions. From the early days of the occupation there had been violent struggles between the Communists and Socialists for control of the labor movement. The Communists, being better organized and disciplined, were skillful at winning control over unions, but repeated rank-and-file "democratization" or "anti-Communist" movements brought most unions back under Socialist control. Even the Socialist-controlled unions, however, began to divide into two types. Those of blue collar workers in private industry increasingly came to emphasize strikes and bargaining aimed at increasing their own wages, while unions of white collar workers and government employees tended to remain focused on direct political action against the government and on global issues. Unions, particularly those of this second type, formed a national federation called Sohyo, which had started in 1950 as an "anti-Communist" movement, and this became the main labor group supporting the left wing. A considerably smaller grouping, made up largely of the more moderate, economically oriented type of union, became the chief support of the right wing. It took the name Zenro in 1954 and shifted to Domei in the early sixties. Some unions remained under Communist control, and many others chose to be independent of national organizations or joined a loose grouping of "Neutrals."

The conservative parties, too, had their problems of unity. They had always been basically clubs of Diet members grouped together for more effective action in the Diet, but their grass-roots organizations were weak, as the overwhelming success of independents in local elections showed. The real local foundations for the conservative parties consisted of the personal, local power bases (*jiban*) of the individual Dietmen and increasingly the personal support organizations (*koenkai*) they developed. The essential ingredient for both was the support of local politicians and power groups, and this tended to depend on local rather than national issues.

The conservative parliamentarian thus was more the product of his own local political connections, as in the United States, than the product of a centrally controlled national party, as in England. This independence of the Dietman from the national party was heightened by two other factors. One was the weakness of the central finances of the party. The other was the peculiar electoral system, in which three to five persons were elected from a single electoral district, thus putting candidates from the same party into more serious competition with one another for the local vote than with candidates from the Leftist parties, whose electoral support was less easily appealed to. The Dietman's chief political rivals in elections were other members of his own party, just as they were his chief rivals, when the party was in power, for appointment to a high government post, such as cabinet minister, parliamentary vice-minister, or committee chairman in the Diet.

Such a situation might have led to a highly undisciplined party vote in the Diet, as in the American Congress. That it did not perhaps illustrates the greater Japanese tendency toward cooperation and the survival of premodern patterns of social relationships. The conservative Dietman tended to attach himself in a "feudalistic" follower-leader relationship to some very powerful man in the party, who could channel him funds for elections and help him win an appropriate post in the government. The result was a rampant factionalism that dominated intraparty politics and always threatened the parties with desertions, not of individuals, but of groups. The factions, while naturally dividing on policy grounds too, were much more personal than ideological. This had been the prewar pattern, and it showed up strongly not only in the postwar conservative parties, but in the

Socialist party too, despite its labor union base and strong ideological cleavages. Among the conservatives, factions switched freely between the Democrat-Progressives and the Liberals, accounting in part for the rise and fall in the number of their votes.

Yoshida faced a particularly severe factional problem in his Liberal party when the original party leader, Hatoyama, who had been purged by the occupation, re-emerged from the purge after the end of the occupation and tried to reclaim his former position. When Yoshida refused to yield, Hatoyama and his following split off from the party in March 1953. Yoshida, now lacking a parliamentary majority, dissolved the Diet and held an election on April 19. His wing of the Liberal party won 39 percent of the vote and obtained 199 seats, well short of a majority but far ahead of the next largest party, the Progressives, with 76 seats. Yoshida continued precariously in power with minority support for another year and a half.

Hatoyama returned to the attack in the autumn of 1954. In November he joined the Progressives and re-organized them under their old name of Democrats. Meanwhile, another veteran politician, Ogata, was trying to unite the two conservative parties under his own leadership. When his efforts failed, he threatened to desert Yoshida, who in December 1954 finally relinquished his weakening grasp on the prime ministership, and passed it on to Hatoyama. To consolidate his position, Hatoyama held elections on February 25, 1955. The Liberals declined sharply (26.6 percent of the vote), and the Democrats emerged as the plurality party with 36.6 percent of the vote and 185 seats.

The independents, Communists, and other small parties had by this time a mere 7.6 percent of the total vote, and Japanese national politics had settled into a four-way split among two conservative and two socialist parties. There were obvious advantages in unification for both sides, and it was a foregone conclusion that if one succeeded in unifying, the other would be forced to follow suit. The Socialists, on October 13, 1955, were the first to achieve this goal, and a month later, on November 15, the conservatives coalesced under the obvious name of the Liberal Democratic party (Jiyu-min-shuto, usually abbreviated to Jiminto). The two-party system of the twenties had at last been reconstituted. Hatoyama continued on as prime minister and was elected the first president of the unified conservative party the next spring.

The prewar politicians were mostly old men by now. Ogata, one of the contenders for leadership, died in 1956, and failing health forced Hatoyama to resign the prime ministership that December. He was succeeded by Ishibashi, another old politician, but Ishibashi almost immediately fell ill and was succeeded on February 25, 1957, by his chief rival, Kishi, an ex-bureaucrat, who had been purged during the occupation because he had been in General Tojo's wartime cabinet. When Kishi held a general election on May 22, 1958, his Liberal Democrats won a clear majority of 57 percent of the popular vote and 287 seats to 166 for the Socialists.

Beginning with Yoshida's return to the prime ministership in October 1948, the conservatives had established a firm grip on the Japanese Diet and government, and after the spring of 1952 they were free of all direct control by the United States. They naturally attempted to reshape the situation in Japan in accordance with their ideas. Many old-fashioned Japanese hoped, and still larger numbers of Japanese feared, that this would mean a wholesale scrapping or modification of the occupation reforms. But in actuality not much of a swing back to older patterns occurred. Many of the reforms, such as the new school system, had already created such entrenched interests that they had become irreversible. Japanese leaders could scoff at the weak new provincial universities, but locally based politicians could not vote to abolish or downgrade them when the local pride of the electorate was involved.

The general revulsion against the past also made the public at large sensitive to any hint of a return to the old order. The Socialists and Communists in particular, fearful that any change in the new system might start an avalanche of legislation that would sweep Japan back to prewar conditions, fought with fury and desperation all proposals for change, however reasonable and innocuous they might individually appear to be. For example, a nationwide system of testing the achievement of schoolchildren was bitterly fought as a way of evaluating teachers who might then be dismissed, ostensibly for inefficiency, but really on political grounds, thus opening the door to the use of schools, as before the war, for indoctrination by the government.

The conservative leaders, all older men with prewar educations, were particularly eager to revise the constitution. To them, it seemed important to restore the theory that the emperor was a sovereign ruler, and not just a symbol. The renunciation of the right to maintain military defenses seemed to them folly in the world as it existed. The obvious American origin and strange sound of much of the constitution was a constant irritant. While friendly toward the United States and eager to maintain the defense relationship, the conservatives argued that the American hand in the constitution necessitated its revision. In contrast, the Socialists and Communists, who by this time were violently anti-American, argued that the constitution was a good document, despite its American taint, and must not be changed a jot. Even an amendment which clearly improved the constitution, they feared, would open the door to other dangerous modifications.

The conservatives started a movement to amend the constitution in 1954 and in 1956 set up a commission to study the problem. However, when it reported back some years later with recommendations for changes, the issue was obviously a fading one. Since 1955 the Leftists had had more than a third of the votes in both houses of the Diet, enough to block any amendment. Younger people, moreover, showed no interest in the question of the emperor's status, and the defense problem was being approached more successfully through reinterpretation of the constitution than it could ever have been through amendment.

As has been mentioned, a National Police Reserve of 75,000 men had been organized in the summer of 1950 to replace American troops sent to the Korean War, and in August 1952, shortly after the peace treaty went into effect, Yoshida added to it a National Safety Force that included a small naval component. In February 1954 he further expanded these units, renaming them the Ground Self-Defense Force and Maritime Self-Defense Force, and added a small Air Self-Defense Force. All three were put under a Self-Defense Agency. The theory behind all this was that the constitution, in renouncing war, had not renounced self-defense. The head of the Self-Defense Agency, while occupying a subcabinet post, normally had cabinet status as a minister without portfolio, as was the case with several other subcabinet agencies. In 1954 the atomization of the police force was corrected, and some central controls were reinstituted. Two years later school boards were made appointive rather than elective, and a partial return to guidance, if not always control, by the Ministry of Education was begun.

The Self-Defense Forces, the police, and the administration of the school system were the three chief areas in which there was a significant recession from the high-water marks of the occupation reforms, but there were a number of other lesser modifications that could at the time be interpreted, depending on one's view, as sensible adjustments to reality or as harbingers of a catastrophic return to prewar patterns. All these changes were bitterly opposed by the Left in the Diet and through public demonstrations and other confrontations with government authority. In retrospect, however, they appear to have constituted not so much a swing back toward pre-war Japan, as a sensible shaking down of some of the less successful of the occupation reforms.

Japan also started to settle her accounts and reestablish relations with her neighbors. Yoshida had followed the general peace treaty by concluding a similar one with the Chinese Nationalist government on Taiwan, showing clearly that Japan would conform with the American position on the two Chinese regimes. The reparations issue had been left dangling by the peace treaty, but in November 1954 Japan signed a reparations agreement with Burma and followed this during the next five years with similar agreements with the Philippines, Indonesia, and South Vietnam.

The Japanese were also eager to win their way back into the international community, and particularly into the United Nations, which most Japanese, in their admiration for all things international, regarded with unbounded enthusiasm. Unfortunately, the Soviet Union, which had not joined in the 1952 peace treaty and was therefore technically still at war with Japan, kept vetoing the application, though Japan in 1955 did gain entrance to the GATT (the General Agreement on Tariffs and Trade). Hatoyama was determined to settle matters with the Soviet Union and thus open the way to Japanese membership in the United Nations. But this was not easy, because there were real bones of contention between the two countries, and Japanese resentment against the Russians ran high. For one thing, large numbers of war prisoners had never returned from Siberia and had to be considered the victims of conditions in Soviet prison camps. Another problem was that, while in the peace treaty Japan had renounced her claims to the Kurile Islands, the Japanese insisted that certain small islands the Soviets had seized belonged to Hokkaido rather than to the Kuriles, and they also maintained, with complete validity, that the southern Kuriles, at least, were indisputably Japanese by all rights of discovery and development and should therefore be returned. These claims, met by an uncompromising Soviet stand on territorial matters, made a full peace treaty impossible, but Hatoyama was able to achieve a "normalization" of relations with the Soviet Union in October 1956; as a consequence, Japan finally won acceptance into the United Nations two months later.

The conservatives were clearly in command of the ship of state and steering it successfully. The respective unifications of the conservative and Socialist parties, however, accentuated the division between Left and Right in Japan, and her reemergence into international society heightened clashes over foreign policies. As the years after the peace treaty lengthened and Japan began to emerge from the American political shadow, the advocates of neutrality or of a Communist alignment became increasingly insistent that Japan establish close relations not just with the so-called free world, but with the Communist powers as well. Hatoyama's settlement with the Soviet Union had been designed in part to meet these demands, but Communist China remained the real problem.

Whatever the regime might be that ruled China's vast continental mass, the Japanese people as a whole tended to look on China herself with romanticism and warmth as the source of their civilization—as their Greece and Rome. This attitude was compounded by a sense of guilt over their wartime misdeeds in China, plus a condescending tendency to overlook the unpleasant in China and lavish praise on accomplishments which in Japan would have been considered substandard. Another factor was the lure of the hundreds of millions of potential customers next door—a lure once felt by much more distant Americans. Japanese businessmen, particularly those in the less prosperous fields, kept hoping that deft political maneuvering might somehow open these supposedly lush new pastures.

The Japanese government, too, still worrying about Japan's economic future, was eager for trade with any country and devised the slogan "the separation of politics and economics" to justify Japanese recognition of the Nationalists on Taiwan and trade with both Chinese regimes. Peking, however, was not very cooperative, for the Communists hoped to put pressure on Japanese politics by manipulating the Japanese desire for trade. Seizing on a minor incident, in which a Rightist youth tore down a Chinese Communist flag in Nagasaki in May 1958, Peking cut off all trade with Japan, and it was some years before it was restored to significant levels. Nevertheless, most Japanese continued to hope ardently for better relations with their great neighbor and were deeply dissatisfied with the existing situation, which they tended to blame on America's intransigent China policy. Socialist and Communist leaders beat a path to Peking, where some of them joined the Chinese authorities in public statements that "American imperialism" was the "common enemy" of the Chinese and Japanese people. A famous example of such a statement was made in 1959 by Asanuma, the flamboyant secretary-general of the Socialist party.

The Leftists were becoming increasingly exercised too by the continuing defense relationship with the United States, and many Japanese felt mounting concern and indignation over the presence of American bases and soldiers. To such people, it seemed that greater safety for Japan lay in complete, unarmed neutrality, rather than in a military alliance with the great "capitalist" nation, which by its very nature, according to Marxist theory, was an inevitable warmonger. These attitudes made the frictions and unhappy incidents that always accompany the presence of large numbers of alien soldiers all the more intolerable, and Japan was repeatedly swept by waves of popular indignation. There were constant anti-American demonstrations occasioned by military accidents, traffic mishaps, crimes committed by American military men, and labor disputes between Japanese workers and the authorities at American bases, but the most severe clashes resulted from disputes over land, as was natural in land-poor Japan. Embattled farmers and their Leftist urban supporters clashed with the Americans over maneuver or bombing practice areas and over the extension of runways to accommodate larger planes. The most protracted struggle of this sort started in 1955 at the Tachikawa Air Base in the western suburbs of Tokyo.

The Japanese public, as we have seen, was particularly sensitive to anything involving nuclear weapons. An incident that seriously exacerbated anti-American feelings occurred on March 1, 1954, when fallout from an American nuclear test at Bikini, a mid-Pacific atoll, apparently brought injury and subsequent death to a crew member of a Japanese fishing vessel, the *No. 5 Fukuryu-maru*. The Japanese public reacted with outrage and, with some lack of proportion, linked the incident with the wartime bombings of Hiroshima and Nagasaki as the third nuclear attack on mankind. Annual meetings held at Hiroshima on August 6, the anniversary of the dropping of the first atom bomb, grew in these years into mammoth protests against nuclear testing by the United States (the activities of the Soviet Union in this regard were largely overlooked) and were expanded into general attacks on the United States and Japan's ties with her.

The restoration of the Japanese economy, the development of the Self-Defense Forces, and the public hostility in Japan to American bases made it clear to both the Japanese and American governments that some modification of the original Security Treaty of 1952 between the two countries was advisable. Reflecting the conditions of that time, this treaty had left the United States free to use her bases in Japan to contribute, pretty much as she saw fit, "to the maintenance of international peace and security in the Far East and to the security of Japan." Her forces could also be used, if requested by the Japanese government, "to put down large-scale internal riots and disturbances in Japan." These features, together with the lack of any terminal date for the agreement, made the relationship seem unequal to the Japanese—too much like that of a semicolonial American protectorate.

In September 1958, the two governments announced their intention to revise the agreement, and after protracted negotiations they signed a new Treaty of Mutual Security and Cooperation on January 19, 1960. The new agreement, together with its supplementary documents and statements, made clear that the United States would consult with the Japanese government before using its bases in Japan directly for combat elsewhere in Asia, as had happened during the Korean War, or before introducing nuclear weapons into Japan. It also put a limit of ten years on the treaty, after which either party could terminate it on one year's notice. It might be thought that Japanese Leftists would have welcomed these substantial limitations on the Japanese-American defense relationship, but instead they argued that it was worse than the previous treaty because this time the Japanese government and people shared in responsibility for it, whereas the earlier treaty had been "forced" on Japan before she had regained her independence. The Left therefore prepared for an all-out battle to prevent ratification.

Since the Liberal Democrats held a solid majority in the Diet, the Leftist challenge over the security treaty might have amounted to only one of the many turbulent but minor incidents in Japan's postwar history, had it not been for several other coincidental factors. On May 1, 1960, an American U-2 plane was downed deep in Soviet territory, and the Kremlin indignantly responded by calling off a planned summit meeting between President Eisenhower and Premier Khrushchev. The Japanese public reacted with sharp disappointment, and the debate over the defense alignment with the United States became all the more bitter. Still more unfortunate was the proposed visit of President Eisenhower to Japan scheduled for June 19, 1960. Probably wishing to have the treaty ratified by that date, Prime Minister Kishi decided to hold a sudden surprise vote on ratification in the House of Representatives in the early morning hours of May 20, so that the treaty would go into effect 30 days later in time for the President's visit, even if the House of Councillors failed to act. Since the Socialists had been trying every possible delaying tactic in the Diet, including the boycotting of sessions and the demanding of more time to debate the issue, both the opposition and the public decided that Kishi had "rammed through" the treaty by unconstitutional or at least "undemocratic" methods. Even some of his own party deserted him. Two of the faction leaders, who were both eager to replace Kishi as party president and prime minister, had not been consulted on the decision to hold the vote and as a consequence refused to support his action.

Although Kishi did succeed in clearing the chief legal hurdle to ratification on the night of May 19–20, he had in the process aroused popular indignation to an explosive point. To the antitreaty clamor was added an even louder din against Kishi himself and a rising crescendo against the visit of President Eisenhower. Many sincere believers in democracy felt that they must come out into the streets to oppose Kishi for what they believed was "undemocratic" conduct in not permitting the opposition to air its views fully on an important controversial issue. And many people essentially friendly to the United States voiced opposition to the American President's visit, since in their minds it had become entangled with the debate over ratification and therefore seemed to constitute outside intervention in domestic politics. The powerful press was almost unanimous in its condemnation of Kishi, further fanning the excitement.

The Communists, Socialists, and various radical groups quickly seized the opportunity to make up for past failures. They did their best to build up the combined antitreaty, anti-Kishi, antivisit fervor into a revolutionary upheaval, and large masses of the urban public responded for the first time to the Leftist-led causes. University students played a major role. The Zengakuren, an abbreviation for the "National Federation of Student Self-government Associations," had been organized in 1948 and soon became a grouping of political activists on university campuses. It was under firm Communist control until 1957, but subsequently became an autonomous movement of even more radical student elements, who tended toward Trotskyism or anarchism. The Zengakuren activists now found their normally more apathetic fellow students ready to follow them by the thousands in riotous, snake-dancing demonstrations through the streets of Tokyo. Labor unions, long accustomed to mass demonstrations, mobilized their followings, and housewives, shopkeepers, university professors, and other usually passive groups joined in.

By June the crowds of protesters numbered in the hundreds of thousands, but they remained extraordinarily good-tempered and orderly compared to mobs in most other countries. Individual Americans could move about the streets without fear, little property was destroyed, and injuries, usually occasioned by clashes between Zengakuren zealots and the police, were relatively few and largely superficial. Only one fatality occurred when, on the night of June 15, during the most massive and violent of the demonstrations, a girl student of Tokyo University was trampled to death in the confusion. But the demonstrations were nonetheless effective in intimidating and paralyzing the government. Humiliated and fearful, it requested President Eisenhower on June 16 to cancel his visit, and the American government, recognizing the dangers of the situation, readily complied.

During the rioting of May and June, it seemed to many that Japanese democracy was doomed and that Japan herself was tottering on the brink of chaos. But once the ratification of the treaty went automatically into effect on June 19 and ratifications were exchanged on June 23, the vast disturbance subsided even more rapidly than it had arisen, and it soon became evident that Japan was entering upon a quieter and happier phase in her history than she had seen for some decades.

13 ❁ FULFILLMENT

The security treaty outburst in the spring of 1960 had served as a sort of catharsis, but there were other more basic reasons for the sharp change in popular mood and political climate that followed its subsidence. For one thing, the less urbanized parts of Japan had remained entirely calm throughout the turmoil. The disturbances had been a phenomenon of big cities, mostly Tokyo, where Leftist attitudes were concentrated. More important, the Japanese public as a whole had some serious second thoughts. Many who had bitterly opposed what they felt were "undemocratic" actions by Kishi came to realize that violent public demonstrations were not a safe corrective. Almost all but the extreme Leftists could see that mass rioting was a dangerous way to achieve political decisions.

The newspapers, too, engaged in some serious "self-reflection," as it is called in Japan. Ever since the 1870s, they had played the role of public critics against a usually all-powerful government. Not until 1960 did they realize that, with the termination of the occupation in

1952, the situation had changed completely. The government was relatively weak and easily buffeted about by public opinion, which the newspapers themselves did much to shape. After the 1960 demonstrations, the Japanese press seemed to take a more balanced and constructive tone in its criticism of public policy.

Another factor was that Kishi was soon followed as prime minister by a man who adapted his policies well to the postdemonstration mood and the changing times. Everyone agreed that Kishi could not continue, and the choice went to Ikeda, another ex-bureaucrat, originally from the finance ministry, and the head of a Liberal Democratic faction more to the center than Kishi's far right group. Ikeda, who became prime minister on July 15, 1960, announced that he would take a "low posture," by which he meant he would be more heedful of public opinion and give more respect to opposition views. He apparently hoped that, by avoiding sharp political clashes, he could build a broader national consensus. It was to be the strategy of the tortoise rather than the hare. He also adopted with much fanfare a popular, noncontroversial policy of doubling Japanese incomes within ten years. This was not a plan so much as a realistic prediction, and it was well fitted to Ikeda's own reputation as a highly successful former minister of finance.

The general elections which Ikeda held on November 20, 1960, to demonstrate popular support for his leadership, showed that the uproar the preceding spring had done the Liberal Democratic party no harm. It emerged with 57.5 percent of the vote, almost exactly the same figure as in 1958, and a small increase in the number of Diet seats to 296. The steady conservative undercurrent of Japanese politics was once again demonstrated, but there were other more basic reasons why the social and political tensions of the fifties began to relax in the sixties. Most important was Japan's unparalleled economic success. The economy continued to race ahead at breakneck speed, dazzling the Japanese themselves as well as the rest of the world, and from this new affluence emerged a growing sense of self-esteem and contentment.

Ikeda's plan to double incomes in a decade proved to be a serious underestimate. The gross national product actually doubled in little more than half that time. It continued to rush on at its phenomenal average rate of 10 percent or more in real terms per year, at times rising as high as 14 percent. Before the end of the decade, Japan had shouldered West Germany aside to become the third largest economy in the world, trailing only the two admitted superpowers, the United States and the Soviet Union. The gross national product was approaching $200 billion and per capita incomes had soared well above $1,000. Japan, long a trade-deficit country, was developing a trade surplus, which by the late sixties rose at times to well over a billion dollars. Her productive power was approaching four times that of all Africa and twice that of Latin America, and it was coming close to equaling all the rest of Asia combined, including the human colossi of China and India and the fabulous riches of oil in the Middle East.

Living standards as measured in monetary terms were still only about half those of Northwestern Europe and a quarter those of the United States, but they had shot past the levels of much of Southern and Eastern Europe and were fast closing the gap with the most advanced nations. Some slowing down of the rate of growth in the future seemed probable, but there was reason to believe that Japan would remain for some time the fastest growing major country in the world. Some "futurists" were even predicting that, well before the end of this century, Japan would far surpass the per capita living standards of Northwestern Europe and exceed the total output of the Soviet Union.

This prosperity was largely the result of the tremendous expansion of industry. Japan in some years produced over half the world's shipping tonnage, and she reached third place in steel production, third place in motor vehicles, and second place in electronics. The growth was largely in heavy industry, chemicals, electronics, and sophisticated machinery. Textiles and the other light industries did less well, as newer industrial competitors in Asia pushed into these fields, just as Japan herself had over a half century earlier. In fact, Japanese manufacturers began to transfer some of their more labor-intensive and technically less difficult manufacturing processes to affiliates they set up in countries where wages were lower but industrial labor was reasonably efficient, such as Korea, Taiwan, Hong Kong, and Singapore, all, incidentally, areas that shared with the Japanese the basic East Asian work ethic and orientation toward education.

Much of the great success of Japan's industry was to be attributed to its largely new plant and to its rationalized development since the war. The powerful Ministry of International Trade and Industry (abbreviated as MITI) had exercised careful controls to ensure that Japanese firms imported only the best technology and did so through as advantageous deals as possible. The tradition of cooperation between government and big business also meant that the political and economic leadership could guide the economy with a more delicate hand than was possible in most other industrialized countries, slowing it up when it became "overheated," stimulating it when it became sluggish, and giving special encouragement to the development of future growth industries. Unlike most countries, the problem usually was to prevent more rapid growth than society could adjust to. Commonly, the government set its goals at 7 or 8 percent growth in real terms, only to find the economy had exceeded this by another 2 or 3 percent.

Even the paucity of raw materials in Japan was in some ways an advantage. For example, the steel industry, lacking significant domestic supplies of iron ore or coking coal, could be located entirely at sea level, where it could draw on the cheapest sources of supply throughout the world and benefit from plummeting oceanic transport costs as ships became steadily larger. The result was that Japan's steel industry could bring together Australian or Indian iron ore with American coking coal and produce steel that could be sold in the United States in competition with the products of domestic American iron ore and coal.

Little of Japan's great industrial success could have been achieved, of course, without the great skills in industrial and commercial organization she had built up over many decades, or without her high educational and scientific levels, and her superb working force. Industrial labor shared in the economic advance; in contrast to earlier stages of industrialization, a shortage of labor began to appear. The vast pool of surplus rural population, which at one time had held back the development of a true urban labor force, was drying up. Factories and service industries still continued to use labor more lavishly than in the United States, and relatively early retirement ages also meant that there was still considerable slack in the labor market. But the supply of young new workers began to run short. Japanese employers competed eagerly for college and high school graduates, and most of all, for the graduates of junior high schools, who came to constitute less than a fifth of the new working force. College students and schoolboys were bid for competitively and signed up long in advance of graduation.

The shortage of industrial labor resulted in some amelioration of the problem of the dual structure of the economy. Of course, the great gap in productivity actually widened between workers in the modernized industries and those in agriculture, services, and the more traditional industries. Even within some of the modernized industries, an unfortunate two-class system developed between the regular working force of the big corporations and so-called temporary workers or those employed by the many small subcontracting firms which undertook some of the simpler industrial processes for the major producers. Such peripheral workers did not have the security of life employment of the regular workers in the big companies or many of their fringe benefits. Still, wages and incomes for those working in the lower half of the dual structure were inevitably pulled up a great deal by the insatiable demand for labor in big industry. A complete solution of the problem of the dual structure, however, remained far off. It would require the absorption of a much greater percentage of the total working force into the highly productive industries and a rationalization of the remaining low productivity fields, for example, the substitution of the supermarket for the corner grocery, which was only just beginning.

Japanese agriculture was a special case, because the farmers shared fully in the new prosperity, despite their tiny farms. This was not because of another great surge forward in agricultural technology, as had happened in the first ten postwar years, but because the conservative politicians, realizing where their voting support lay, took good care of their rural clientele. Steadily rising price supports for rice, the chief crop, resulted in bumper rice crops which became twice as costly as rice on the world market, but brought wealth to rural Japan. Another reason for rural prosperity was the drastic drop in the agricultural population. Farm boys and girls, on completing their educations, deserted the countryside en masse, attracted by the glitter and excitement of the cities and the less arduous work in factories. In places the flow reached 90 percent of the graduating classes from the schools, and some eldest sons who remained at home to take over the family farm found difficulty in locating wives. Many adult farmers too were drawn to higher-paying factory jobs in nearby towns or work in the cities on a seasonal basis, if they lived in more remote areas. Farming became increasingly an activity, as the Japanese put it, of "mummy, grandpa, and grandma," and as the last two died off, of "mummy" alone. Agriculture, which had absorbed around half the labor force as late as World War II, now used less than 20 percent.

High agricultural prices, supplementary factory work, and fewer mouths to feed made Japanese farmers quite affluent, at least by Asian standards. Many came to own cars, and some could afford vacation trips to Hong Kong, Hawaii, or even Europe, where the higher fares paid off psychologically with the greater number of different countries that could be visited on a brief tour. But there were also difficulties. The dearth of males in rural areas raised social problems, and long city sojourns for farm fathers resulted in disruptive liaisons with city girls. The long-range problem was even more serious. An agricultural system that was made basically inefficient by its miniscule size could not be supported forever by constantly raising rice prices at the expense of city consumers and the taxpayer. Two and a half acre farms, tiny patches of agriculture in remote valleys, and terraced fields on steep mountainsides hardly went with the type of economy Japan was developing. The only real solution to the agricultural problem in the long run would be to consolidate farms into much bigger units and abandon less productive fields. Some remote farming areas, in fact, were beginning to go out of use, but farm consolidation had as yet hardly begun.

Continued rapid economic growth thus did not solve all Japan's economic problems, and it in fact worsened some. Increases in wages for workers who did not increase their productivity led inevitably to a steady rise in prices, and the speed of economic growth naturally generated other inflationary pressures. Tokyo real estate prices came to be matched only by those of midtown Manhattan. While the war and the occupation had done much to level Japanese incomes, rapid economic growth increased the spread again. The lowest economic bracket in the population slipped somewhat in relative economic standing, and the highest gained a bit, though the homogeneous nature of the Japanese population and the virtual elimination of all prewar wealth meant that the extremes of poverty and wealth were much less pronounced than in the United States.

The prewar strategy of "guns instead of butter" was supplanted after the war by a "factories instead of butter" policy, which probably deprived the Japanese consumer too much in favor of a rate of industrial growth that was so fast it created dangerous social strains. In any case, the investment in social overhead was for long too small as compared with industrial investment. Japan became a country of some of the finest factories in the world and some of the worst housing, roads, and schoolhouses. Social services lagged behind those of most Western European countries, though the surviving paternalism of Japanese business ameliorated the situation somewhat. The huge expansion of higher education that had taken place was dangerously underfinanced. Pollution of air and water grew steadily worse. Urban housing remained extremely cramped, city parks few, and roads unbelievably narrow and congested. Fine new prefectural offices, city halls, and "people's auditoriums" did blossom in most cities, and in the larger ones the construction of great office buildings went on apace. The withdrawal of the old earthquake-inspired limit on the height of buildings permitted 40-story skyscrapers to appear in Tokyo. But a large proportion of the public buildings, such as hospitals and schools, remained antiquated and often dilapidated.

The congestion in transportation at times threatened to suffocate Japan with her own prosperity. This was particularly true in the early sixties, when there was at last a big effort to expand communication facilities in time for the 1964 Olympic Games in Tokyo, and the resulting construction activities added to the general chaos. But eventually these new facilities were completed and began to ease the situation. Elevated highways appeared in Tokyo and Osaka, along with extensive subway systems to share the commuting load with the already highly developed surface railways. High-speed superhighways linked Tokyo, Nagoya, Kyoto, and Osaka, and the new Tokaido Railway, running at speeds well over 100 miles an hour, provided rapid, efficient, and incredibly punctual communication between these cities.

Japan's economic growth made her increasingly dependent on a global pattern of trade. One of the reasons for her industrial success was the size of her own internal market of 100 million people, exceeded only by the United States and the Soviet Union among industrialized countries, but the tenth of the economy which was geared to foreign trade was absolutely essential to her existence. Well over half Japan's power resources (oil and coal), practically all her industrial raw materials (minerals, cotton, wool, lumber, and pulp), and a large part of her food had to be imported and therefore paid for by exports. Much of Japanese needs for protein were met by a huge worldwide fishing industry, which in catch ranked second only to Peru. After many decades, Japan also became self-sufficient again in her chief staple, rice, but this was the result of artificially high prices for domestic rice and declining consumption, as the Japanese switched to more bread and a greatly increased intake of meat and dairy products. The change in diet helped bring a marked increase in height and weight in the younger generation, sometimes producing almost ludicrous contrasts between parents and children. But it did not solve Japan's overall food deficit. Japan remained heavily dependent on wheat from North America or Australia, meat from Australia and New Zealand, and on feed grains (for meat production in Japan), oil-producing soybeans, and many other foodstuffs from the United States. More than 20 percent of her food had to be imported.

The bulk of her foreign markets and sources for vital imported raw materials and food were located far from Japan. North and South America, Western Europe, Australia, Africa, and the Middle East provided more than three-fourths of the imports and took a good two-thirds of the exports, but none of these regions was within 2,000 miles of Japan. In this sense, Japan's economy had become truly global. To have tried to subsist on trade with nearby areas, which her military leaders once thought could be shaped into an economic base for Japan as the "Greater East Asia Co-Prosperity Sphere," would have spelled economic disaster for Japan as she had developed by the sixties.

Prosperity together with the passage of time gradually freed the Japanese from many of the anxieties of the early postwar period. Prosperity undercut Leftist predictions of economic catastrophe, diverted popular attention from the promised panacea of revolution to the enjoyment of immediate pleasures, and poured soothing oil on strife between labor and management. Japan's worst postwar labor dispute at the Miike coal mines in Kyushu was settled on November 1, 1960, when the striking miners were forced to bow to the inevitable rationalization and cutback of coal mining in the face of cheap fuel oil from the Middle East. Increasingly, unions discovered that there was much more to be gained from peaceful bargaining over wage increases, made possible by a burgeoning economy, than from demonstrating in the streets for remote and theoretical political objectives. Labor-management relations of the sixties, while not friendly, became decidedly less turbulent. The annual "spring struggle" over wages became basically a series of lackluster parades and wage negotiations. May Day, labor's day for demonstrating solidarity, became a festive occasion to which workers brought the kiddies.

Japanese became decidedly more satisfied with their lives and more confident in their country. The national flag came more into evidence and the national anthem was heard more often. The word "patriotism" still was used only by extreme Rightists, but "nationalism" as a concept became respectable. Since the old Japanese word for it had been discredited by past usage, the Japanese, as usual, borrowed from English and spoke of *nashonarizumu*. The new mood had become quite apparent by the early autumn of 1964 when the Olympic Games were held in Tokyo. The Japanese had been determined to make this the finest and best-organized Olympic Games in history, and when with their characteristic energy and organizing skill they did exactly this, a glow of national pride and euphoria spread over the nation.

As Japanese, and particularly those of the postwar generation, looked around their country and at the rest of the world, they began to feel proud of Japan. It was good to be a Japanese. Conditions in the rest of Asia seemed pathetic by contrast—and even the West appeared a little stodgy and slow-moving. The floods of businessmen and then of tourists who roamed the world came home content with what they found there. It was intellectually stimulating for the graduate student to spend a year at an American university, but unless he was in New York City he felt as if he had gone to "the sticks." No place seemed to hum with life and cultural activity quite like Tokyo.

A subtle intellectual change began to take place in Japan. Younger persons, perhaps because of the more liberal new education and certainly because they were freer of the psychological scars of the past, were beginning to approach problems in a more relaxed and open-minded way than their elders had. Beginning with economics, Japanese scholarship began to free itself from its Marxist strait jacket. Young scholars led in developing less doctrinaire, more pragmatic lines of reasoning about internal politics and world affairs. They discussed problems of defense and international tension without embarrassment. The tone of the newspapers followed suit.

The Self-Defense Forces, developed in the fifties against violent Leftist opposition, began to win general acceptance by the public. By this time they consisted of about 250,000 mén, with more than 500 small ships and over 1,000 jet planes, a relatively small military for a country of Japan's size and wealth, but a sizable and very efficient force nonetheless. Most Japanese remained proud that Japan had "renounced" war and were strongly opposed to "rearmament," but they came to feel that Japan had the right of self-defense and that the Self-Defense Forces were of appropriate size for this purpose.

There could be no doubt about Japan's cultural vigor. All fields in the arts and literature throbbed with activity. In 1968 Kawabata was awarded the Nobel Prize in Literature, the first man writing in a non-Western language to be so recognized. Japanese architects became world famous. Japanese scientists and scholars were winning recognition throughout the world. Countless big international conventions were held in Japan. Traditional music found greater support than for many decades, but at the same time Tokyo boasted five professional symphony orchestras. It also offered an unsurpassed variety of cafés, each with its own musical specialty, and its restaurants were as varied as those of any city in the world. Not only had it become the biggest metropolis in the world; it had perhaps the highest concentration of university students, close to half of Japan's total of a million and a half.

Older Japanese remained worried that Japan was losing her identity in a sea of Western technology and culture, but not the younger Japanese, who were as much the products of a modern industrialized society as were young

Americans. While they could be distressed about the quality of modern life, they were no more worried than Americans about a loss of national identity. They could see no reason why a modernized Japan was not still fully Japanese. And they were quite right. Japan was reaching the forefront in economic and technological progress in the world, but she remained very distinctively Japanese.

This fact is significant not just for the Japanese themselves, but for all non-Western peoples. Most of them have shared the fears of the Japanese that industrialization and other aspects of modernization would blot out their traditional cultures. And in the early stages of industrialization, this often appeared to be the case. But Japan, which has gone much further in modernization than any other non-Western country, seems to prove the contrary. To be sure, much of Japan's premodern culture has been sloughed off or drastically changed, but probably no more so than has that of the advanced countries of the West, though over a somewhat longer period of time. Japan, while vastly enriching her culture by borrowing from the outside world, has found new vitality in traditional traits. An industrialized and modernized Japan shows every promise of remaining a highly distinctive cultural unit, and at the same time seems to be making an almost disproportionately large contribution, particularly in the field of art, to the common world culture of the second half of the twentieth century.

Japanese in the sixties began to take pride in the obvious impact Japanese culture was having on the outside world and particularly on the United States. Modern concepts of design seemed to derive more from traditional Japanese esthetic principles than from those of the West. All pottery makers in the United States appeared to be disciples of Japanese masters. Japanese landscape gardening enjoyed a worldwide vogue, and Japanese flower arrangement had a wide impact. Japanese movies had their following everywhere, and devotees appeared for a wide range of Japanese disciplines, from Zen at one extreme to *judo* and its modern offshoot, *karate*, at the other.

Japanese culture had obviously survived the transition to a modern, industrialized society; in fact, Japan's chief problem in a rapidly shrinking world in which she had global economic interests had instead become that she was perhaps still too distinctive and in a sense isolated. She was separated from the rest of the world by higher language barriers than any other major nation—with the possible exception of China. This situation was perhaps a blessing in helping to preserve Japan's cultural distinctiveness at an earlier stage of modernization, but it increasingly became a serious national handicap. Few foreigners learn to speak or read Japanese, so the Japanese must learn foreign languages, but because of the distinctiveness of their tongue and the simplicity of its phonetic system, this is no easy task. Since the Meiji period, English has been the chief medium for communication with the outside world, but despite prodigious efforts on the part of virtually all students from the seventh grade through high school and the hard work of about 60,000 full-time English teachers, the results have been meager. Teaching methods have remained antiquated and inefficient, and not many of the teachers themselves can really speak English.

Extremely few Japanese, with the exception of scientists, businessmen engaged in foreign trade, and people involved in the tourist industry, can attempt even a simple conversation in English, though many more make a stab at reading it. As a consequence, the Japanese are handicapped in almost all their foreign contacts. The voice of the nation is much smaller in the councils of the world than it otherwise would be; Japan's potential contribution of skill and knowhow to the less developed countries is inhibited; businessmen find themselves at a disadvantage abroad; the outside world learns far less about Japan than it should; Japanese thought and scholarship, except for the natural sciences, remains somewhat isolated from trends elsewhere in the world; and most intellectual communication with the outside world must pass through so opaque a linguistic screen that understanding is often seriously distorted.

Despite this language handicap and the other problems Japan still faced, however, the internal situation in the early sixties was obviously more stable and better from most points of view than it had been before, and conditions abroad also helped quiet political controversy within Japan. President Kennedy had a tremendous appeal to Japanese, particularly young ones, just as he had to young people everywhere. This together with very successful visits to Japan by Robert Kennedy in January 1962 and again in January 1964 greatly improved the popular image of the United States.

The two governments, concerned by the upheaval over the security treaty, also made efforts to emphasize the nonmilitary aspects of their relationship and to create a greater sense of equality and "partnership." A Committee on Trade and Economic Affairs, made up of members of the two cabinets, was set up and held its first annual meeting in Japan in November 1962. A greater degree of self-government was given by the United States to the Japanese in Okinawa. Largely through American efforts, Japan finally won admission in July 1963 to the OECD (Organization for Economic Cooperation and

Development), as the one non-Atlantic member of this important economic organ of the advanced nations. A side product of this period of good will was the financial settlement in June 1961 of the debt owed the United States for relief supplies provided Japan during the occupation (the so-called GARIOA, or Government and Relief in Occupied Areas). Japan agreed to repay $490 million, which, as in an earlier settlement of a similar debt by the Germans, was about a third of the original sum. While this debt settlement itself was scarcely popular, there was a pronounced relaxation during these years of Japanese resentment against the United States. Problems involving American bases and servicemen became less tense, and Japanese became more content with their relationship with their huge trans-Pacific partner.

Meanwhile developments in the Communist countries had thrown Japanese Leftists into ideological disarray. The rift between the Soviet Union and Communist China, which became obvious in the early sixties, embarrassed the Socialists and put great strains on the Communists, who since then have tended to swing back and forth between pro-Moscow, pro-Peking, and neutral positions. China's 1962 attack on India, a country which was considered admirable in Leftist circles for its outspoken neutralism, caused further embarrassment. And China's development and testing of nuclear weapons from 1964 on proved even more divisive. Chinese nuclear fallout was brought over Japan by the prevailing winds, whereas American nuclear tests had never had this result. Even before this, the whole anti-nuclear bomb movement, which had been an important "united front" activity in the fifties, had fallen apart. The more moderate Socialists, who had already split off from the party in January 1960, deserted the annual August ceremonies to form their own mild movement in 1961, and two years later the Socialists, who felt there must be some condemnation of the Communist nuclear powers as well as of the United States, broke off from the Communists and founded a bitterly competing movement.

In the first years after Mao Tse-tung's triumph in China in 1949, it had seemed to many Japanese that the Chinese Communists might be charting a better road into the future than the one on which the American occupation had helped start Japan. But by the early sixties, it became clear that the Chinese Communists' "Great Leap Forward" had proved an economic disaster. The confusion caused by the Cultural Revolution in 1965 and the disorders of the Red Guards, which started in the late summer of 1966, were followed by a second economic decline that further dimmed the picture of Communist China as a possible world leader. With Red Guards reminding the Japanese of the excesses of their own "young officers" in the thirties and with Japanese living standards soaring more than ten times higher than those of China, it took a very doctrinaire person indeed to see the Chinese as providing a useful model for Japan.

The advance of the Japanese economy together with the changes in the Japanese mood and in perceptions of the outside world had a slow but steady impact on Japanese politics, disrupting the Leftists and dampening their prospects. The split of the Socialists, which had occurred even before the security treaty riots, was, as in 1951, over attitudes toward the United States. A dissident group of thirty-three Diet members, mostly from the former right wing, refused to go along with the party's all-out opposition to the security treaty, favoring instead a gradual elimination of the defense ties with the United States and insisting that the party's activities, in any case, be limited to strictly parliamentary methods of opposition. In January 1960, these men formed the Democratic Socialist party (Minshu Shakaito, or Minshato for short), under the veteran labor leader Nishio. In the November election that year, they proved to be more a splinter movement than a division of the party. Although supported by the Zenro (later Domei) branch of organized labor, they won only 8.7 percent of the popular vote, less than a third as much as the main Socialist party, and a mere 17 seats in the lower house. But they proved a permanent defection, separated from at least some factions in the Socialist party by insurmountable ideological walls. In the manner of many Socialists of Western Europe, they clearly put parliamentary democracy above socialist economic goals in their scale of values. While they remained relatively small, their existence as a separate party cut decidedly into the strength of the main Socialist party.

The Socialist share fell in the 1960 election from 32.9 percent of the vote to 27.5 percent and 145 seats, a loss of 21. There were also continuing tensions over policy and leadership within the party, even after the withdrawal of some of the dissidents into the Democratic Socialists. Many members of the old right wing, who leaned toward the ideas of the Democratic Socialists, had stayed in the party, and a growing division developed between them and the more radical Socialists, who, in their attitudes toward international relations and extra-parliamentary political activities, leaned toward the position of the Communists. There was also a continual pull between the relatively doctrinaire leadership and the more moderate rank and file voters. The consequence was usually a drift of the party to the left when the professionals gathered at conventions and a drift back toward the center when they faced elections.

A leadership crisis was precipitated in October 1960 when Asanuma, who had been chosen chairman of the party a few months earlier, was stabbed to death by a Rightist youth in full view of television cameras. In an effort to soothe factional strife, Kawakami, a mild Christian from the former right wing, was chosen party chairman in March 1961, but Eda, also from the right wing, proved a more controversial figure as secretary-general. He stirred up bitter opposition from the former left wing by his advocacy of "structural change," by which he meant the achievement of socialism by gradual democratic evolution rather than by revolution, and by his so-called "Eda vision" for the future of Japan, which was a combination of America's high living standards, the Soviet Union's thoroughgoing social security system, Britain's parliamentary democracy, and Japan's own "peace constitution."

Eventually Eda had to be replaced by a more neutral figure, Narita. Kawakami, however, died late in 1965, and when Sasaki, an extreme Leftist, won out in the fight to succeed him, the split within the party was again widened. A revolt by the rank and file Socialist Dietmen against Sasaki's high-handed ways led to his replacement in August 1967 by Katsumata, a moderate of bureaucratic background. But Katsumata was discredited by the loss of eight Socialist seats in the House of Councillors election of July 1968. The seriousness of the split within the party was revealed when the party convention in September broke up without deciding on a new leadership. A second try the next month produced a shaky compromise between Narita, who was felt to lean a little to the Left, as chairman, and Eda again as secretary-general.

More disturbing for the Socialists was the slow fading of their dream that social and political tides would within a few years carry them almost automatically to a parliamentary majority and control over the government. Earlier, the steady erosion of the conservative vote had made this concept seem not at all unrealistic. The Liberal Democrats were an amalgamation of the two traditional parties which, starting with the original electorate, made up in large part of the landowners, had developed strong ties in rural Japan. The Liberal Democrats, like their predecessors, also had the support of most of the business community, but they had little appeal to urban labor, the "intellectuals," and white collar workers. For one thing, their policies strongly favored big business and the farmer at the expense of city dwellers, who as a result paid higher food prices and received fewer benefits in social security programs, housing, transportation, and public conveniences. The prewar tendency of these urban groups to vote for the new Leftist parties was greatly accentuated in the postwar period. But it was precisely these segments of the Japanese population that were growing rapidly as the result of further urbanization and industrialization, while the rural community, the backbone of the Liberal Democratic vote, was shrinking with equal rapidity.

This great economic and sociological change, more than any shift in political opinions, produced a steady decline of the conservative vote and a corresponding rise in the vote of the parties of the Left. Their combined vote, which had been 26.5 percent in the 1952 elections, rose steadily with each election until it reached 39.4 percent in 1960, an average gain of close to 2 percentage points a year. A straight-line projection would bring the Left to a clear majority of the vote well before 1970. The election of 1963, however, showed only a little over a 1 percent increase in the Leftist vote over a three-year period, and in the election of January 1967, there was actually a slight falling off. Japan's urbanization was still continuing at a rapid rate, but a ceiling far short of a majority seemed to be appearing in the Leftist vote. Even more distressing, youth appeared to be starting to turn away. Hitherto the percentage of votes for the Leftist parties was overwhelmingly at the younger end of the age scale, but now the youngest voters began to prove a little less inclined to the Left than those a few years older. Leftist ideologues accused the younger generation of "my home-ism," that is, a greater interest in their own personal lives and happiness, symbolized by the ownership of their own little homes, than in great social and political issues.

The expected decline of the conservatives into an electoral minority, in any case, had never meant that the opposition could get together in a unified majority. Socialist and Communist rivalry had always been intense, and now the Democratic Socialists formed a third element unwilling to cooperate with either of the other two, while the Socialists themselves were badly divided. The existing three-way division might conceivably, though not probably, be reduced to a two-way division between Communists and Communist-leaning Socialists on the one side and moderate Socialists and the Democratic Socialists on the other, but a unified Left was out of the question.

Even the position of the Socialists within the divided Left began to deteriorate as the public became disillusioned with their internal struggles and the continued

devotion of their aging leaders to clearly outmoded ideas and rhetoric. Obsessed with grandiose concepts of world history, wedded to unrealistic notions of
international relations, and talking an anachronistic
language of class struggle to an increasingly affluent
population which regarded itself as middle-class, they
failed to profit from the demographic trends that seemed
so favorable to the Left. The burgeoning urban population was full of resentments against the ruling party, but
it was more concerned over immediate bread-and-butter
issues, such as inflation and rising prices, than with the
global fate of "capitalism" and "socialism." The Socialists
thus let the growing protest vote slip between their
fingers. The 1967 election showed a 4 percent drop in
their popular vote and a loss of 4 seats in the lower house
to a level of 140, the lowest since the mid-fifties. The
Socialist share of support by organized labor also began
to decline. Sohyo, the largest federation, which supported
the Socialists, had grown to a membership of about
4,250,000 by 1965, but thereafter leveled off and at times
actually declined. On the other hand, Domei, the much
smaller federation made up largely of blue collar workers
in private industry, which supported the Democratic
Socialists, continued to grow rapidly, and by the late
sixties was coming close to half Sohyo's size.

Socialist hopes were temporarily raised by the election in 1967 of their candidate for the governorship of
Tokyo, Minobe, who like his father of the famous "organ
theory" before the war, was a professor at Tokyo University. But the election for the Tokyo Assembly in July
1969 dashed their hopes again. In this heartland of Leftist political support, the Liberal Democrats increased
their membership from 38 to 54, the Communists
doubled from 9 to 18, but the Socialists fell drastically

from 45 to 24. Then disaster struck for the Socialists in the general elections of December 27, 1969. Their percentage of the national vote plummeted from 27.9 percent of the vote to 21.44 percent, and their seats from 140 to a mere 90. They slipped from being the prospective second party in a two-party system to being merely the largest of a series of small opposition parties.

Some of the more radical voters who had once supported the Socialists were obviously shifting to the Communists, presumably feeling that the Socialists had lost their revolutionary zeal and that a small but relatively united party was more worth backing than a larger but seriously divided one. The Communists staged a comeback after their poor showing throughout the fifties and greatly increased party membership and subscriptions to the party paper, *Akahata* (*Red Flag*). They also expanded their share of the total popular vote from 2.9 percent in 1963 to 4.76 percent in 1967 and 6.8 percent in 1969, and their seats in the Diet jumped from 5 to 14. This, however, was still far short of their previous high-water mark in 1949, when they had won 9.7 percent of the vote and 35 seats.

There was an even greater erosion of Socialist support toward the center of the political spectrum, though not toward the Democratic Socialists, who were hard put even to maintain their own. Their popular vote fell off from 8.7 to 7.37 percent between 1960 and 1963, and only crept back marginally in 1967, though a more realistic appraisal of the number of candidates they could elect helped them raise their showing in the lower house from 23 to 30 seats. In 1969 they again made only tiny gains—to 7.74 percent of the vote and 31 seats, increased subsequently by one, when an independent joined them.

The voters the Socialists lost went more to a new party,

the Komeito (sometimes translated as the Clean Politics party), which was the political arm of a new religious movement, the Soka Gakkai. Theologically an offshoot of Nichiren Buddhism, Soka Gakkai has been the most successful of the so-called new religions since the war. "New religions," as has been mentioned, have been an important phenomenon in Japan for more than a century, but none of the earlier ones had as great success as Soka Gakkai, which quickly built up an ardent following of several million people. Its appeal, as with many of the new religions, appears to be less religious than social. It seems to have succeeded in answering the need of many ordinary Japanese for a sense of direction in a confusing age, and it offers togetherness for those who feel isolated in modern mass society. Soka Gakkai's simple doctrines of absolute faith and immediate worldly benefits are hardly distinctive in Japan, though its militant proselytizing techniques, which hark back to Nichiren's own intransigence in the thirteenth century, are something new. Its real distinctiveness lies in its firm leadership by a group of able young men and their superb skill at organization and showmanship. Soka Gakkai membership is overwhelmingly urban and lower class or lower middle class, just the groups that might be expected to vote for parties of the Left. Thus its development of a political party has probably cut more into the Leftist vote than the conservative.

The Soka Gakkai ventured only cautiously into the political fray, and its actual political views have remained ambiguous. Being in opposition to the ruling Liberal Democratic party, it has tended to phrase its stand on international questions in terms borrowed from the other opposition parties, which are all Leftist, but behind this rhetoric the leaders of the Soka Gakkai appear to be essentially rather old-fashioned and conservative Japanese, more representative of the lower middle class than of radical intellectuals or militant labor groups.

The Soka Gakkai first ran candidates in local elections in 1955 and for the House of Councillors the next year, winning 6 seats. The well-organized Soka Gakkai was in a good position to estimate the vote of its party correctly and to apportion it evenly among its candidates. This ability was particularly advantageous in elections for the House of Councillors, in which half the candidates are elected by the nation as a whole. Often the Soka Gakkai estimated its vote so accurately that it elected every one of its candidates. In 1962 it won 15 seats in the House of Councillors out of 125 members elected, and after organizing the Komeito party in 1964, it increased this showing to 20 seats in 1965, and 24 in 1968. In this last election it won over 15 percent of the votes in the nation-wide electorate, showing that many people were voting for Komeito candidates as a protest against both the conservatives and the Left. The Komeito won 25 out of the 126 seats in the Tokyo Assembly in July 1969, one more than the Socialists. Its first try in the all-important general elections for the lower house was in 1967, when it won 5.38 percent of the vote, a more accurate indication of its hard core strength, and 25 seats. In the general elections of December 1969, it increased its popular support to 10.9 percent, and it picked up 47 seats, making it the third largest party in the Diet. It had also become the most unpredictable major factor in Japanese politics. Experts kept prophesying a ceiling to its vote, but none had as yet appeared. Its generally Leftist stand on international issues was clear-cut, but it seemed doubtful that its stance as a small opposition party really showed what it might stand for if it ever came to power.

The division of the opposition into four competing parties, together with the intellectual disarray of the Left and its fading appeal to voters, gave the Liberal Democrats a firm grip on the government throughout the sixties. In fact, the return to the two-party system of the twenties, which the unification of the Socialist and conservative parties had heralded in 1955, seemed to have turned into what the Japanese dubbed the "one and a half party system," in which the Liberal Democrats held permanent control over the government.

Prime Minister Ikeda proved a wise and generally popular leader, and his four years in power were a period of relative calm. After being reelected to a second two-year term as president of the Liberal Democratic party, he held a general election on November 21, 1963. The slow erosion of conservative strength was still apparent, but the combined vote of the Liberal Democrats and conservative independents was 59.44 percent, and they won 283 and 12 seats, respectively, a thumping majority in a lower house of 467. Ikeda had become prime minister in the nervous aftermath of the security treaty riots, but when he resigned in the autumn of 1964 because of fatal cancer, the nation was basking in the euphoria created by the great success of the Olympic Games.

Ikeda was succeeded on November 9, 1964, by Sato, another ex-bureaucrat and the brother by birth of Kishi (whose name had been changed by adoption into another family). The relationship with Kishi and the fact that his own faction was next only to Kishi's on the extreme Right did not help Sato's image with the public, and he was never as popular as Ikeda, but the first years of his administration progressed smoothly.

Sato continued Ikeda's efforts to achieve a settlement with Japan's former colony of Korea, or rather with the southern half of it. This was no easy task because of the deep Korean fear and hatred of Japan and the division of the country into two hostile regimes. A settlement involved a number of difficult problems, such as "reparations," controversies over important coastal fisheries, the status of the large Korean minority of 600,000 in Japan, and the relative status of the two Koreas. Eventually, however, a "normalization" of relations was achieved with South Korea in 1965, despite determined opposition by the Socialists and Communists, who favored North Korea. The "normalization" included a Japanese agreement to provide South Korea with $300 million in grants and $200 million in soft loans, as well as other regular commercial loans, but it also left the Japanese free to continue their small trade and fitful contacts with North Korea. While the "normalization" was viewed with misgiving by the public in both Japan and South Korea, it worked out very well. Relations between the two areas began to improve rapidly, and increased trade and huge investments by Japanese in South Korea helped start a surge of rapid economic growth there.

Sato also continued Ikeda's efforts to expand Japan's role in the rest of East Asia. Further reparations settlements were made with Southeast Asian countries, and the Japanese began to play a major economic role in the whole region. Japan became the dominant trading partner of many Asian countries and an important provider of economic aid through reparations, small supplementary grants, and commercial investments, which of course were largely for trade expansion from the Japanese point of view. She joined the other advanced nations in setting 1 percent of gross national product as the target for aid to the less-developed countries, and in the latter part of the sixties came close to meeting this target, according to the generous international standards which count commercial and industrial investments as aid. When the Asian Development Bank was founded in 1965, Japan equaled America's contribution of $200 million to its capital, the first time since the war that any country had matched the United States in a major undertaking of this sort. Subsequently, when a large-scale consortium was formed to save Indonesia from financial ruin, the United States and Japan each assumed a third of the total burden, leaving only a third for the other advanced nations to divide among themselves. Trainees in Japan from other Asian countries passed the 1,000 mark annually, and Japan started a small "peace corps" type of operation, with over 300 volunteers in certain South Asian and African countries. In 1966 she joined ASPAC (the Asian and Pacific Council), originally sponsored by South Korea, but she insisted that this and the other regional groupings in which Japan participated should not be either military or anti-Communist organizations.

Sato, after being elected party president for a second two-year term late in 1966, held a general election on January 29, 1967. For the first time since its founding, the Liberal Democratic party fell below the halfway mark in popular votes. The old sociological erosion of its vote was continuing, but there were also other factors at work. Dissident conservatives who had failed to obtain the party label won more votes than usual as independents, but upon election, most of them joined the party. The Komeito also had drawn away some voters. And there was a tremendous popular furor about the "black mist" of corruption in the Sato government, though the specific cases cited turned out to involve only a few individuals and often bad judgment on their part rather than actual corruption. If one includes the independents with the Liberal Democrats, however, the conservative vote still was 54.35 percent of the total, and the division of the opposition among four parties gave the Liberal Democrats a solid majority in the lower house of 277 seats out of a total of 486, with 9 more won by independents.

Sato was reelected party president for a third term late in 1968, and on the strength of successful negotiations with the United States over Okinawa in November 1969, he called for general elections the next month. The results were very heartening for the Liberal Democrats. The combined votes of the three Leftist parties declined sharply from 40 to 36 percent of the total. Even the erosion of the Liberal Democratic vote seemed to be slowing up, for the party's popular support had declined only from 48.8 to 47.6 percent over a three-year period. The division of the opposition into four more evenly balanced parties also permitted the Liberal Democrats to increase their seats from 277 to 288. Independents, who were largely younger Liberal Democrats who had failed to win the party label but were seeking to replace aging or fading conservative incumbents, did remarkably well, picking up 16 seats; and since 12 of them immediately joined the Liberal Democratic party, it ended up with 300 seats out of 486, the largest majority any party had enjoyed since the war. The Liberal Democrats obviously could stay in power until the next general elections, which could be as long as four years off. More important, they seemed to be starting to stem the ebb tide in votes flowing against them. If they could redirect their energies toward the problems of urban Japan, as their more forward-looking members advocated, and thus win a larger share of the urban vote, it appeared possible for them to maintain their hold on the Japanese government well into the future.

Almost unbelievable economic success, unsurpassed cultural vigor, and a relaxation of political tensions made it clear in the sixties that Japan was approaching a time of fulfillment—fulfillment far beyond the desperate yearnings of the early postwar years and even beyond the grandest dreams of the Meiji leaders. But a nagging question remained—fulfillment of what?

Once again, the Japanese, having achieved their immediate goals, were not clear where they should be heading beyond these. The postwar aim had been to build an economically viable and secure society. This the Japanese had done far better than anyone could have predicted. But was it enough to be prosperous, or to be the third largest economy in the world? Was this the ultimate goal? The sleek, vibrant Japan that had emerged was hardly the socialist utopia the Left had always sought. Nor was it the "old" Japan some conservatives yearned for. Even to the products of the new age, it sometimes appeared spiritually empty.

What did it mean to be Japanese? What were the national goals? A better quality of life—but if so, what quality and how was it to be achieved? Leadership toward international understanding and world peace? These were objectives that had tremendous appeal, but if these were the goals, then what was Japan doing to achieve them? She had remained extremely timid and tongue-tied in world affairs, like the big boy who prefers to sit in the back row of the classroom in the hope that no one will notice him. People abroad seemed to regard Japan as a cipher in world affairs. Europeans scornfully referred to her as only an "economic animal," and De Gaulle was said to have called the Japanese foreign minister "a transistor salesman." Japan's foreign policy, in fact, had been little more than to maximize trade and minimize other involvements—a businessman's foreign policy. China and even India, at least while Nehru was alive, seemed to be regarded abroad as more important nations than Japan, and yet Japanese felt sure that their country was far greater; many of them held China in patronizing disdain and India in not very well concealed contempt.

Thus, for all Japan's economic success and cultural brilliance, there was a lingering sense of malaise in the sixties, and this was still directed primarily toward the relationship with the United States. In fact, as Japan's economic triumphs at home became obvious, foreign relations became even more the area of major debate. Not that many domestic issues did not remain to determine in large part the grass-roots vote—rising prices, inadequate housing, political corruption, traffic problems, pollution, university unrest, and the like. By the late sixties there was also general agreement among Japanese that they must concentrate less on industrial expansion and foreign trade and more on solving their own internal social problems and improving the quality of life in Japan. Still, what continued to worry Japanese most and divide them in political debate was the threatening external environment that seemed to prevent Japan from taking her rightful place in the world—and this they continued to blame largely on the United States.

Many people in Japan felt that she still stood entirely

in America's shadow, denied a foreign policy of her own, and forced reluctantly and fearfully to cooperate with America's hazardous Far Eastern strategy because of Japanese dependence on trade with the United States. America's perilous nuclear rivalry with the Soviet Union, her confrontation with Communist China, and the growing war in Vietnam loomed, in Japanese eyes, as the major threats to world peace. In a now more nationalistic and self-confident Japan, American military bases were a growing irritant, as was also the continued American rule over close to a million Japanese in Okinawa and the other Ryukyu Islands. Insofar as Japan still had economic fears, these were focused mainly on American protectionism against Japanese exports and threatened penetration by American industry and capital into Japan.

There was a pronounced sharpening of these critical attitudes toward the United States in the second half of the sixties. A significant turning point came with the great escalation of American involvement in the Vietnam War in 1965. Some Japanese had for long looked with disapproval on what was going on there, but now most of the public became concerned, and demonstrations against the American role in the Vietnam War proliferated. To many Japanese, it seemed that the old Marxist theory was proving true after all: the great "capitalist" power was indeed showing itself to be an imperialistic menace and was mindlessly pressing forward a constantly growing war. The war could easily spread to China and possibly even to the Soviet Union, and then Japan, because of the American bases and defense alliance, would be drawn into the holocaust too. Thus, the security treaty, just as the Leftists had said, instead of giving Japan protection, seemed to threaten her safety.

Japanese also tended to equate the American entrapment in the quagmire of Vietnam with the fate of their own armies in China in the thirties. Battles might be won with superior weapons, but Asian nationalism would triumph in the long run. American bombing also reminded them of what they had suffered in World War II, and while they were on the whole closer to Americans in thinking and in ways of life than to Vietnamese, there was also an element of racial identification. The enterprising Japanese press and television networks provided the Japanese public with the same visual and verbal fare that shocked the American public, and they reacted with even greater revulsion. The image of the United States, which had been so favorable just a few years earlier when Kennedy was President, became steadily worse.

Many other factors entered in, such as race relations and urban disorders in the United States, but the Japanese reactions to these problems were less intense than in many other parts of the world. Accustomed to their own extremely homogeneous country, the Japanese were appalled by the problems of a multiracial society made up of many ethnic groups, and they often viewed America's domestic difficulties more with sympathy or condescension than with condemnation.

Older tensions with the United States, however, became exacerbated during these years, in part because of the worsening image of America, but probably more because of a rising sense of national pride within Japan. The unsatisfactory relationship with Communist China had always been a matter of great uneasiness to Japanese, and was almost universally blamed on the United States. To Japanese, it seemed that Americans, safely across the Pacific from China and possessing their own great natural resources, could ignore trade with China and maintain an attitude of unrelenting hostility, but that Japan could not take the same attitude toward this fifth of humanity, living, as it were, right next door. China through most of history had been Japan's chief source of new technology and knowledge, and before the war she had seemed a vital economic area for Japan. There naturally were strong pressures throughout Japanese society for improved relations with Peking and deep resentment against the United States for seeming to stand in the way.

Japan's recognition of the Nationalist government on Taiwan in 1952 and her steadfast stand with the United States against Peking's admission to the United Nations had undoubtedly been influenced originally by American attitudes, but by the mid-sixties inhibitions on relations between Tokyo and Peking were for the most part not of America's making. Actually, under the formula of "the separation of politics and economics," Japan had again built up her trade with continental China, and by 1966 she had become China's largest trading partner, with a two-way trade of $621 million. Part of this was carried out under a semi-official agreement between the two governments, the rest through so-called friendly traders in Japan, some of which were dummy firms set up by big companies that did not wish to risk endangering their relations with their American associates by trading directly with China. Japan had also developed more cultural contacts of all sorts with China than had any other country, including even the Communist nations.

The United States did not stand in the way of these developments or of further advances in Tokyo-Peking relations. What did stand in the way was the Nationalist government on Taiwan and, to a lesser extent, other anti-Communist trading partners of Japan in East Asia, such as South Korea. Japan had rapidly growing investments in Taiwan, and her trade with the island was beginning to almost equal the trade with continental China. The Nationalist government repeatedly threatened reprisals if Japan extended generous credit terms to Peking, to say nothing of recognizing it formally, and the Japanese usually backed off from taking new steps toward a rapprochement with China.

Political disorders and economic decline in continental China reduced Japanese-Chinese trade somewhat after its high point in 1966. Even in that year it had constituted only a little over 3 percent of Japan's foreign trade, and the limiting factors had been the poverty of the Chinese economy and its lack of attractive exports, rather than artificial bars to trade. By the end of the decade trade with China had dropped to 2 percent or less of Japan's foreign commerce, showing that, until China made much faster economic progress, she could not constitute an important trading partner for Japan.

Relations with the Soviet Union, on the other hand, improved steadily during the sixties and became a lessening source of tension in Japanese-American relations. The Japanese looked on with approval at the steps toward détente between the United States and the Soviet Union, however hesitant and uncertain they might be. But what changed the situation most was a shift in Soviet attitudes toward Japan as an outgrowth of the Sino-Soviet split. Recognizing that Japanese emotionally leaned more toward the Chinese, even if intellectually they were more sympathetic with the Russians, Moscow embarked on what the Japanese called a "smiling diplomacy" toward Japan to help ensure that she would not side with Peking.

The continued Japanese demand for the return of the southern Kuriles and Russian obstinacy on this point still prevented the conclusion of a full peace treaty, but relations otherwise became almost warm, trade expanded, and there was much talk of a massive Japanese development of the natural resources of eastern Siberia. This made excellent sense from the point of view of the Japanese, for whom Siberia could provide a relatively close source for some of the natural resources they needed. It also made sense from the point of view of the Russians, who were eager to have underpopulated Siberia developed to withstand a possible threat from the Chinese masses on its southern borders. Soviet political rigidities and the differences between the two economic systems, however, made actual economic deals extremely slow to materialize.

The most persistent and severe strain in Japanese-American relations remained the question of the defense alliance and American bases in Japan. The stronger the economy became and the more self-confident the Japanese grew, the less tolerable became a situation in which Japan seemed forced to follow American foreign policies against her will and was required to suffer the inconveniences and indignity of the presence of American troops, presumably for American interests rather than Japan's.

Actually, the conservative leaders among the politicians, bureaucrats, and big businessmen had always supported the relationship with the United States and had helped shape it. From Yoshida on, they had strongly believed that the defense alliance was strategically necessary for Japan and that the resulting saving in Japanese defense expenditures was a great economic boon. The ambiguous and unsatisfactory Chinese relationship was largely of their own creation, and resulted from their desire to trade with both Taiwan and the mainland. The Japanese government was even fearful that the United States might suddenly soften her stand on Peking, leaving Tokyo out on a political limb. Some of the conservative leaders were outright hawks on Vietnam, wishing that the United States would try to end the war by prosecuting it more vigorously. Most of them, far from opposing the security treaty, feared that if it were broken or even seriously reduced in efficacy, the result might be an American military pullback from the whole area that would leave Japan militarily exposed in a highly unstable part of the world.

The Japanese public, however, continued to regard the defense alliance more as a favor unwisely granted to the United States than as an arrangement of benefit to Japan. The opposition parties clung to their old goals: a Communist Japan, or, in the case of the Socialists, an unarmed neutralist country, or, in the case of the Democratic Socialists and the Komeito, a rapid scaling down of the American alliance and military presence until these were eliminated. The man in the street too was fundamentally hostile to American bases and dubious about the benefits of the defense relationship.

Here was a dangerous gap between the perceptions of the government and those of the general public, and the leaders moved too slowly in trying to close it by educating their people. The conservative political leaders had all along found it convenient to dodge troublesome foreign policy issues by giving the impression that a weak and therefore necessarily subservient Japan was forced, somewhat against her better judgment, to cooperate with American foreign policies. They could in this way hide behind the American skirts on foreign policy, on which their popular appeal was weak, and concentrate on domestic issues, on which their appeal was strong. In the relatively harmonious days of the early sixties, Ikeda had taken steps to correct this situation by talking of an "autonomous" foreign policy for Japan. But not enough had been done, and now the tides were again running against the relationship with the United States. It was perhaps too late to convince the public that it was not just Japan which cooperated with America's foreign policy, but the United States which cooperated with Japan's.

The Vietnam War created a growing sense of crisis, and this was greatly increased by rising concern in Japan over Okinawa. It is surprising that the separation of Japan's 47th prefecture from the rest of the country in 1945 and its continued rule by Americans as a great military base did not stir up a quicker reaction, but in the early postwar years the Japanese in the main islands were too demoralized and too occupied with their own economic recovery to worry much about Okinawa. The Okinawans themselves were at first somewhat ambivalent in their attitudes. They spoke a decided variant of Japanese, closer to the ancient language; they had had a distinct history before the late nineteenth century and had had their own kings; they resented the second-class status the mainland Japanese had accorded them before the war and the fact that they suffered so heavily during the war. But American military rule gradually made them the most patriotic of all Japanese, and they began clamoring for eventual return to Japan long before other Japanese became much exercised over the issue.

In the peace treaty of 1952 Japan had promised to

support American proposals that Okinawa be made a strategic trusteeship of the United States, but it had soon become evident that the United Nations would not grant this. Secretary of State Dulles then began to speak of Japan's "residual sovereignty" in the islands. This term came to be understood as a promise that Okinawa would be returned to Japan some day, when strategic considerations in East Asia permitted. But this remained a distant goal, and most of the attention of the Okinawans was focused on winning in the meantime better economic treatment and more political autonomy.

In 1965, however, parallel with the increase in concern over the Vietnam War, there was a decided rise of interest in Japan in the Okinawa *irridenta*, and within two years the clamor for "reversion" had become intense. The return to Japan in June 1968 of the small and lightly populated Bonin Islands, strung far out in the Pacific south of Japan, did nothing to alleviate the situation. It seemed intolerable to many Japanese that close to a million Japanese in Okinawa should be ruled by Americans in what amounted to the only colony in the world created since World War II. A comparable situation between the United States and its European allies was unthinkable, illustrating how unusual the Japanese psychology had been after the war, and also perhaps the lingering racist attitudes Americans brought with them to Asia. It became increasingly clear that an early solution of the Okinawa problem was necessary. The year 1970, when the original term of the 1960 security treaty would end, was sure to be a time of crisis in Japanese-American relations in any case, and it was imperative to keep the mounting excitement over Okinawa from adding to the turmoil over the treaty.

"Reversion," however, was no simple matter. American bases and the Okinawan population were both heavily concentrated in the southern half of the island of Okinawa, and the transfer of this area from American to Japanese rule involved many complex problems. Much more difficult was the question of the status of the bases themselves. With the possible exception of the naval port of Yokosuka near Yokohama, these were the most vital bases the United States had in East Asia, and while the Vietnam War lasted, there was great reluctance on the part of the American military to see any limitations put on their use. But political sentiment was such in Japan that, once Okinawa had "reverted," it would of course be necessary to have the limitations of the 1960 security treaty apply to these bases too. The Japanese called this the "mainland level" (*hondo-nami*) formula, and it meant no nuclear weapons and no "free use" of the bases for direct military action elsewhere without "prior consultation" with Japan, which was generally understood to mean consent.

The problem was finally solved by an agreement, announced by Prime Minister Sato and President Nixon on November 21, 1969, that Okinawa would be restored to Japan some time in 1972 and the limitations of the security treaty would thenceforth apply to the American bases there. This promise of early reversion was expected to meet the nationalistic demands of Okinawans and other Japanese. The delay until 1972 was believed necessary not only to permit time to work out the many technical problems involved, but also to allay American fears that the reversion of Okinawa would have an adverse effect on their still-continuing involvement in the war in Vietnam. The delay was also probably necessary in order to give time for both Americans and Japanese to adjust to a situation in which the use of the bulk of America's most important bases in East Asia would be, in effect, under a Japanese veto, and the Japanese, therefore, would have to take a clear stand on the military role they wished the United States to play in the area.

Sato indicated his attitude on the problem by asserting the importance to Japan of peace and security in Korea, the Taiwan area, and the Far East in general and the vital role of the security treaty in maintaining this peace and security. There was more question whether the public, long accustomed to regarding the security treaty with the United States as an unwelcome association forced on Japan for the benefit of Americans, would follow him in these judgments and permit the Japanese government to support the use of American bases on Japanese soil to maintain American commitments to South Korea and the protection of the freedom of the seas in the region. Sato obviously judged that the public would. Reversing the usual Liberal Democratic electoral approach of seeking to dodge foreign policy issues and run only on its domestic economic record, he centered his campaign in the election of December 1969 on his recent achievement in the Okinawa settlement and the continuing relationship with the United States. The extent of the Liberal Democratic success in this election may show that Sato judged correctly.

However great the excitement over Vietnam and Okinawa, the most severe tension in American-Japanese relations was caused by the approaching end on June 23, 1970, of the first ten-year period of the 1960 security treaty, after which either side could give one year's notice of its termination. The prospective inclusion of the bases on Okinawa under the treaty provisions further concentrated attention on the future of the treaty. All opponents of the defense relationship with the United States, ever since their failure to block the treaty in 1960, had aimed at 1970 as the time to break the relationship and throw the conservatives out of power. As the date drew nearer, political tensions mounted steadily, and many groups consciously began preparing and practicing for the crisis of 1970.

This was particularly true of the organized student movement. The Zengakuren had splintered after 1960 in a way typical of radical ideological movements. By the late sixties, there were three main radical factions, each controlling the student movement in some universities or in certain schools of universities, and all battling desperately with one another for supremacy. They had by this time come to wear construction-worker helmets of different colors for purposes of protection and identification, and they used square-cut poles as their chief weapons and, on occasion, Molotov cocktails. A larger and better-disciplined movement was under Communist control, though it remained somewhat quiescent, presumably saving its strength for 1970. There was also a Socialist-dominated group of lesser significance.

Student outbreaks mounted steadily in frequency and violence in the second half of the sixties, until by 1969 a large number of Japanese universities were in serious trouble. Buildings were seized and wrecked, university officials and professors were held prisoner and tried by kangaroo courts, and pitched battles were fought between rival student groups or with the police. Prestigious Tokyo University was knocked out of operation in whole or in part for more than a year, and many other universities were forced to suspend operations for many months at a time. The public's fear of "thought control" and "police suppression," engendered by Japan's earlier experiences, made Japanese professors extremely reluctant and slow to resort to the courts or the police to attempt to quell the rising chaos, even though the Japanese police forces, at least as compared with those of the United States, were superbly trained and equipped to contain and damp down public violence. Strong traditions of university autonomy, even for government schools, and of faculty control within universities also militated against the use of police power or external governmental authority. Finally the government, alarmed at the situation, forced through a bill on August 17, 1969, providing for the reduction of professorial salaries in disrupted universities and for the eventual dissolution of institutions that could not put their house in order. The bill was aimed at forcing faculties to handle student violence more effectively, and in this it had some success. There was a marked drop in the number of universities that were seriously disrupted, but the new law did nothing to cure the underlying causes for student unrest.

Many of the fomenters of violence in the universities clearly had political goals, and they stirred up their cohorts for any plausible anti-American cause, such as the many old base problems; visits of nuclear-powered vessels of the American navy to Japanese ports, which started in the sixties; the transportation of fuel oil for American planes; an American military hospital in Tokyo, where it was alleged sick soldiers from Vietnam would spread dangerous tropical diseases; the departure of Sato for visits to Southeast Asia and the United States; and even the building of a big new civil airport east of Tokyo, which it was argued, would be used by American military planes.

Student unrest, however, drew also from other, deeper sources. Japanese students, like young people elsewhere, were becoming increasingly concerned over the quality of life in an urban, industrial society. In many ways, they were under even greater pressures than their contemporaries in the West. Japan had become a socially egalitarian country, but one of strict educational hierarchies. Everything depended on education, and the pressure to get into the best universities, through extremely mechanical examinations, extended downward until Japanese children felt compelled to compete and excel in examinations at the primary level. People called this the "examination hell." Those who failed to win entry to the university of their choice on their first try commonly tried again and again, becoming what were called *ronin*, the "masterless samurai" of the Tokugawa period. Once accepted into a university, students found classes boring and graduation almost automatic, in a very lax, large-scale, and impersonal system. Many devoted themselves more to political agitation or other sports than to study. But another crisis loomed at the end of university life— admittance, again commonly through examinations and presumably for the rest of one's active career, into some big business firm or a branch of the government bureaucracy. College was a momentary escape between the rat race of competition to excel in school and the rut of an unchangeable career. It did not take the advent of computers to convince many young Japanese that modern life was being dehumanized.

Japanese students also had more specific reasons for dissatisfaction with their universities. Enrollments had increased enormously, to more than 20 percent of the age group which either went to regular four-year universities or to junior colleges, the latter being especially popular with girls. This increase had not been met by a corresponding investment on the part of society in higher education. Many of the new government schools were inadequately equipped and staffed, and the private universities were simply overwhelmed. The war had wiped out what endowments the private universities might have had, and the lack of tax benefits to donors and of a tradition of this sort of giving meant that private universities were almost entirely dependent on tuition and fees for entrance examinations. On this entirely inadequate financial base, they tried to accommodate about 75 percent of the student population. (By way of contrast, only about 40 percent of students are in private universities in the United States, and virtually none in Europe.) The quality of Japanese university education was further impaired by the Germanic tradition of putting research above teaching and by faculty control, which meant that entrenched faculty interests made innovation in teaching methods or in the development of new fields extremely difficult. Japanese students were understandably dissatisfied with the impersonal mass techniques of education, the antiquated organization and curriculum, and facilities that often would have been considered inadequate in a less-developed country. All in all, university education was one of the areas where Japanese society was clearly in serious trouble.

One other aspect of the looming crisis with the United States was growing friction over economic relations. Japanese-American trade relations had been tense ever since the early fifties—but also extremely successful. Trade had grown rapidly to around $7 billion, the largest transoceanic trade in world history and far greater than America's trade with any other country except her large Canadian neighbor. The Japanese, however, had always resented and fretted over American restrictions of one sort or another on Japanese imports. Lower Japanese wages at one time had meant that, without limitations, the Japanese might win the whole American market in certain labor-intensive light industries and thus cause economic disruption in some areas in the United States and serious political repercussions and demands for higher tariffs in Washington. To guard against this happening, the Japanese, under strong pressure from the United States, had set "voluntary controls" on their exports of textiles and many other goods. While textiles in the early sixties were put under a more formal agreement applying to other countries as well as Japan, "voluntary controls," or "orderly marketing" as they came to be called as a euphemism, still applied in many fields, and as the Japanese began in the late sixties to invade the American market in steel, automobiles, and other products of heavy industry, they began to be applied in these fields too.

The shoe, however, was by now really on the other foot. Japan in her desperate fight to restore her economy had built far higher walls against foreign industrial imports than had any other industrialized country. As a consequence, American cars and a host of other American manufactures had for all practical purposes been excluded from Japan. Almost everything the Japanese exported to the United States was in competition with American products, but America for the most part was limited in exports to Japan to noncompetitive goods, such as raw materials (coal, scrap iron, cotton, tobacco, and wood), food (soybeans, wheat, and feed grains), and some highly complex machinery not produced adequately in Japan. Detroit was restive at the influx of Japanese cars to the United States when its own products could not enter Japan. Such a situation was understandable in the fifties, when Japan's economic future was still in doubt, but not in the late sixties, when she had become one of the world's great economic powers. Somewhat the same situation applied to American investments in Japan. Earlier, when Japanese industrial and financial resources were no match for those of the United States and when the Japanese feared they might never be able to stand on their own feet, they had perhaps been wise in constructing a system to regulate the inflow of foreign investments and limit them to a minority status in Japanese firms. But it was now no longer reasonable for Japan to expect free economic access to the rest of the world, but to deny access to Japan to others.

American discontent with the inequalities of the economic relationship mounted steadily, and there were growing demands for Japanese "liberalization" of both import and investment policies. A billion-dollar deficit in America's trade with Japan and serious gold-flow problems caused by this and by military expenditures in Japan made Americans all the more bitter. Intellectually, Japanese businessmen tended to agree with the criticism that came not just from the United States, but from all the Western countries. However, emotionally it was hard for Japanese to open up their country. Perhaps because of their old tradition of isolation, they had an instinctive fear of foreign ownership of anything in Japan, and a powerful bureaucracy continued to guard the gates jealously. There was much talk of "liberalization," but little actual motion.

Many Americans, agonized by the disaster in Vietnam, also became critical of Japan's "free ride" in military defense at the expense of the American taxpayer. Few expected aid from Japan in Vietnam or even a greatly expanded Japanese military effort, but they were irritated that Japanese were so critical of the defense they felt the United States provided them free, and they wondered why Japan did not do more for the economic development of other East Asian countries and why she did not take a leadership role befitting her great economic power. But despite increasing grumblings about Japan, there was little realization among Americans that relations with Japan faced a grave crisis. In fact, one of the dangers in the situation was that 100 million Japanese felt 1970 was a crisis year in the all-important relationship with the United States, while 200 million Americans seemed quite unaware of this.

Of course, beneath the excitement in Japan over the impending 1970 crisis, there was the same strong, steady flow that had carried her so far in the two decades since the occupation. Most Japanese were reasonably affluent, satisfied, and happy. Life was exciting and culturally rich. No one could doubt Japan's continued economic success, unless there were some world catastrophe, in which case all countries would be in trouble. Except for the university debacle, she seemed to be meeting the problems of modern industrialized society as well as the countries of the West and in many ways better. Most Japanese looked forward eagerly to the great International Fair to be held in Osaka in the summer of 1970.

Although the rising crescendo of disputes over foreign policy was threatening, domestic politics remained essentially steady. Emotional commitments to democracy might still be weaker than in some Western countries, but few Japanese could imagine a tolerable alternative to the type of parliamentary democracy they had evolved.

Support for the constitution, whatever its origin, remained overwhelming, and there was still strong abhor-
rence of past policies of imperialistic conquest abroad
and authoritarianism at home. Rightists of the prewar
variety constituted no more than a tiny, disreputable
fringe on the political scene. The far more numerous
Leftists used the vocabulary of Marxism and revolution,
but few Japanese believed that any other economic system could do better than Japan's own mixed economy of
private enterprise and government controls. Economic
debate focused not on fundamentals, but on the details
of prices, wages, and the nature of controls.

It seemed possible that, in the course of the seventies,
the Liberal Democrats would lose their Diet majority,
but few expected this to bring a Socialist triumph or any
great change in Japanese politics. A more likely outcome
seemed to be a coalition of the Liberal Democrats with
the Democratic Socialists or the Komeito, or both, in a
government a little more toward the center of the political spectrum. Another possibility might be a kaleido-
scopic realignment of the parties. If the Socialists split,
as increasingly seemed possible, the moderate factions
from this party might join with the two Center parties
and the more Centrist factions of the Liberal Democrats,
which were becoming increasingly restive, to form a new
Center party that might then dominate Japanese politics
for a long period, just as the Liberal Democrats had.
The more conservative Liberal Democrats would then
become the major opposition party, and the Communists
and more radical Socialists, a smaller minority at the
other end of the spectrum. Neither prospective change
would bring a great shift in Japanese politics or policies.
The parliamentary ice had thickened a great deal since

the twenties, and was now able to bear a much heavier load of problems and crises than it had been then.

The area of doubt remained, as always, Japan's position in the world. The 1970 crisis, together with pressures from the Vietnam War, threatened trouble in the vital relationship with the United States. It was conceivable that civil disorder, like that in 1960, could become so severe that the Japanese government, in order to calm the situation, would be forced to ask the United States for a major change in the defense relationship. On top of serious American frustrations over Vietnam and mounting concern over domestic problems, this could conceivably produce an isolationist reaction in the United States and a military withdrawal to mid-Pacific. Such a turn of events would leave vital Japanese interests in serious jeopardy. Without the Japanese defense alliance and bases in Japan, the United States would probably find it too costly and hazardous to continue a military commitment to South Korea in her perilous balance with an aggressive North Korea. A resurgence of the Korean War would then become more of a possibility, and this would threaten Japan. Because of Korea's strategic location between three of the largest countries in the world—China, the Soviet Union, and Japan—a Korean War could even escalate into a worldwide catastrophe. The removal of the American Seventh Fleet from the Western Pacific might also endanger the freedom of the seas in that area and Japan's economic lifeline of oil from the Middle East, which passes through the narrow straits of Southeast Asia.

Faced with these hazards, many Japanese would undoubtedly wish to see Japan more strongly armed. The postwar generation of Japanese had already showed itself much less sensitive to military matters than its elders. Japan might rush to massive rearmament, but not without serious internal turmoil. Rearmament would also cause dangerous new problems. It would cut down on economic growth and would worsen Japan's relations with her neighbors, who remember her all too well as a military conqueror. Japan's economic aid to her neighbors would also probably be reduced, and this, together with the reduction or elimination of American aid resulting from a United States withdrawal into isolationism toward Asia, would undoubtedly heighten tensions and slow economic advance throughout East Asia.

A large-scale rearmament effort in Japan would also probably not stop short of nuclear weapons. In the sixties there was increasing talk in some circles that a great nation like Japan could not be without her own nuclear arms. There had already been considerable development of industrial nuclear power, and in June 1969 Japan launched an experimental nuclear-powered ship. A well-financed space program had also developed skills in rocketry, thus keeping Japan's options open for a quick entry into the field of nuclear weapons if this seemed desirable. But, as the third richest country in the world, Japan's development of nuclear weapons might well prove the most dangerous of all possible steps in nuclear proliferation.

These were all gloomy possibilities, but they did not seem like probabilities in the late sixties. It appeared more likely that the crisis, together with the reversion of Okinawa to Japan in 1972, would precipitate motion toward a healthier relationship between Japan and the United States and a more desirable, as well as important, role for Japan in the world. It seemed possible that the very severity of the crisis might help Americans and Japanese come to realize the overlapping of their basic interests and their dependence on each other.

Both countries were global traders, deeply committed to a system of relatively free worldwide trade. For this, what was needed was not military and economic blocs, such as Japan and Germany had tried to create three decades earlier and the Soviet Union still maintained to some extent, but an international community of independent nations living at peace with one another under some accepted system of international rules. For both nations, world peace was of the greatest importance, and a world war the ultimate catastrophe. Thus their fundamental interests coincided closely, and they were further aided in their relationship with each other by the fact that both believed in and had democratic political systems, an open society, and the mixed economy of private enterprise and government controls that, contrary to Marx, had turned out to be the evolutionary product of nineteenth-century capitalism.

More specifically, a friendly United States was clearly more important to Japan than anything else, just as for the United States, a friendly Japan was of supreme importance in Asia. Both had deep interests in the economic and institutional development of the less-developed countries of East Asia, though Japan's interests, as a neighbor and major trading partner of these countries, were larger. Both hoped for friendly relations with China, though again Japanese desires were naturally stronger than American, and Japanese abilities to make progress toward the achievement of this goal were probably greater. At the same time, both countries faced the same stumbling block in their relations with China, which was that they both had intimate and important relations with Taiwan. A war in Korea or elsewhere in

East Asia would clearly be a threat to the interests of both countries, though the danger to Japan, of course, would be much greater. While neither country could contribute much to the internal stability of the less-developed countries, as the Americans had discovered at great cost in Vietnam, both desired international stability in East Asia, and Japan was particularly concerned with the safety of the seas in that area and free passage through the straits of Southeast Asia.

In all these matters, Japanese and American interests not only coincided closely, but each found the other the most important potential partner in facing them. Co-operation and the sharing of responsibilities therefore seemed to be obvious common sense for both. Other nations, of course, were also involved, particularly the other advanced nations of the Pacific area. It would make good sense to form, as some Japanese advocated, a "Pacific community" of the donor countries of the area, which had special interests in the stability and development of East Asia and could with advantage coordinate their respective efforts and thus maximize their effect. The proposal was that Canada, Australia, and New Zealand should join Japan and the United States in a program of this sort.

The United States and Japan, however, would remain the two giants in any such grouping, and in many ways Japan was beginning to loom as the more important of the two. Her faster rate of growth, her location in East Asia, her greater concentration on the affairs of that area, and her non-Western background, which perhaps gave her a special role to play, all suggested that what she did in East Asia might prove more important in the long run than what the United States might do. In any case, Japan would obviously be more benefited or more threatened by whatever developed in East Asia than would the United States. Obviously, Japan had to have an equal voice with the United States, and perhaps a greater one, in deciding what should be the joint aims and policies of the defense alliance and of the other forms of co-operation between the two. Decisions on how best to share responsibilities in the economic, technological, political, and military fields were clearly as much up to Japan as to the United States.

While Japan faced a foreign policy crisis, her achievements in the sixties appeared to have set the stage for what promised to be a somewhat clearer "fulfillment" in the seventies. What this would be depended in no small measure on the outcome of the crisis, and there were of course many other imponderables, some far removed from Japan itself. Without world peace and world prosperity, Japan's future would be seriously threatened. But her potential for influencing the rest of the world was also great. It seemed possible that she might become the most significant country in the world before the end of the century, not just as a global economic power, but in other more basic ways. As the one great modernized nation of non-Western origin, she was somewhat distinctive from the rest. She might well possess traits and skills the others lacked for meeting the manifold problems of an industrialized society. She might conceivably do better in this than any of the others, and thus help point the way to the solution of problems they all faced.

Japan also had a very special potential role in what loomed as the greatest problem of the age. This was the widening gap in wealth and skills between the less-developed countries and the industrialized nations, and as a consequence the growing tension between them. This gap coincided for the most part with two other major fault lines in humanity—that between the countries of Western cultural background and all the rest, and that between the white race and the other races. Only Japan among important countries straddled this triple chasm, being the third largest unit on the side of the industrialized nations, but at the same time the fifth largest population grouping on the non-Western, non-white side. This unique position, together with her special experience in modernizing herself, which seemed likely to prove more relevant for the non-Western world than the experiences of North Americans, Russians, or Western Europeans, gave her a special chance to lead in the solution of this most threatening of all world problems. The question was whether Japan would rise to the challenge.

BIBLIOGRAPHICAL NOTE

Those for whom this volume is their introduction to Japanese history may wish some guidance in further reading. I have limited myself below to a few readable books of general interest, which in turn can serve as guides to the more detailed studies. I have made a special effort to include in this listing books available in paperback editions, which I have marked by asterisks.

A relatively brief presentation of the whole of Japanese history can be found in John Whitney Hall, *Japan From Prehistory to Modern Times* (New York: Delacorte Press, 1970), which is close to twice as long as this book and unlike it devotes more than two-thirds of its pages to the premodern period. A more detailed account, particularly of modern history, is provided by the chapters on Japan in a large two-volume set: Edwin O. Reischauer and John K. Fairbank, *East Asia: The Great Tradition* and Fairbank, Reischauer, and Albert M. Craig, *East Asia: The Modern Transformation* (Boston: Houghton Mifflin, 1960, 1965). The chapters on China and Korea in the first of these volumes afford a useful background for Japanese history for those who wish to go more deeply into the subject.

On premodern Japanese history, G. B. Sansom, *Japan: A*

341

Short Cultural History (revised edition, New York: Appleton-Century-Crofts, 1944) is a classic, full of illuminating insights delightfully presented. The same author, this time signing himself George Sansom, has also provided the most detailed, scholarly coverage of the subject in his three-volume set: *A History of Japan to 1334; A History of Japan 1334–1615; A History of Japan 1615–1687* (Stanford *). Another outstanding general work is John Whitney Hall, *Government and Local Power in Japan 500–1700: A Study Based on Hizen Province* (Princeton, N.J.: Princeton University Press, 1966). A more specialized but very readable book, which was a best seller when first published, is Oliver Statler, *Japanese Inn* (Pyramid *). Peter Duus, *Feudalism in Japan* (Random House*) gives a brief overview of Japanese feudalism.

An excellent series of original readings (with helpful commentary) drawn from premodern and modern Japanese writings is provided by the two-volume set: Wm. Theodore de Barry, Donald Keene, and Ryusaku Tsunoda, *Sources of the Japanese Tradition* (Columbia*). For literature, there is Donald Keene, *Japanese Literature: An Introduction for Western Readers* (Evergreen*), and the same author's two fine anthologies, *Anthology of Japanese Literature From the Earliest Era to the Mid-nineteenth Century* (Evergreen*) and *Modern Japanese Literature From 1868 to the Present Day* (Evergreen*). Among more specialized books are Faubion Bowers, *Japanese Theatre* (Dramabooks*), and Howard Hibbett, *The Floating World in Japanese Fiction: Tales of Ukiyo and Their Background* (Evergreen*). There are many good translations of both premodern and modern literary works, but special note might be taken of certain classics introduced to the West by the great English translator Arthur Waley: *The Tale of Genji* (Doubleday*), *The Tale of Genji: Part II: The Sacred Tree* (Doubleday*), *The Pillow Book of Sei Shonagon* (Evergreen*), and *The No Plays of Japan* (Evergreen*).

The field of religion is less satisfactorily covered by general surveys, but the work of the distinguished prewar Japanese scholar Masaharu Anesaki is available in paperback under the title of *Religious Life of the Japanese People* (East-West Center, Hawaii*), and there is a more recent survey, William K. Bunce, *Religions in Japan* (Tuttle, Tokyo*). Among the better books on Zen available in paperback editions are Alan W. Watts, *The Way of Zen* (Mentor*) and several of the works of the great Japanese Zen scholar D. T. Suzuki, including *Essays in Zen Buddhism* (Evergreen*) and *An Introduction to Zen Buddhism* (Evergreen*).

In the field of art, a standard survey is Robert Treat Paine and Alexander Soper, *The Art and Architecture of Japan* (Penguin Books, 1955). Another survey in paperback edition is Hugo Munsterberg, *The Art of Japan: An Illustrated History* (Tuttle, Tokyo*), and an older classic in paperback edition is Langdon Warner, *The Enduring Art of Japan* (Evergreen*).

Among the general histories of modern Japan, there are two brief accounts, Richard Storry, *A History of Modern Japan* (Penguin*), and W. G. Beasley, *The Modern History of Japan* (Praeger*), and two more detailed works, Hugh Borton, *Japan's Modern Century* (New York: Ronald Press, 1955), and Chitoshi Yanaga, *Japan Since Perry* (New York: McGraw-Hill, 1949), as well as a fine general economic survey, William W. Lockwood, *The Economic Development of Japan: Growth and Structural Change, 1868–1938* (Princeton*). My own book, *The United States and Japan* (Compass*) discusses in some detail the modern Japanese character as well as American-Japanese relations, particularly since World War II. A classic on the Japanese personality is Ruth Benedict, *The Chrysanthemum and the Sword* (Meridian World*). Donald Keene, *Living Japan* (New York: Doubleday, 1959) provides a helpful introduction to Japanese culture through pictures and essays. *Twelve Doors to Japan* (New York: McGraw-Hill, 1965), which was edited by John Whitney Hall and Richard K. Beardsley, offers solid essays on twelve historical as well as contemporary aspects of Japanese civilization.

There is a host of more specialized books on modern Japan. A multivolume series of collected essays dealing with the modernization of Japan, which resulted from a carefully planned series of conferences, has been published by the Princeton University Press under the titles: *Changing Japanese Attitudes Toward Modernization* (ed. Marius B. Jansen*), *The State and Economic Enterprise in Japan* (ed. William W. Lockwood*), *Aspects of Social Change in Modern Japan* (ed. R. P. Dore, 1967), *Political Development in Modern Japan* (ed. Robert E. Ward, 1968). Two final volumes of this series, *Tradition and Modernization in Japanese Culture*, edited by Donald H. Shively, and *Dilemmas of Growth in Prewar Japan*, edited by James Morley, will be published soon.

Among the volumes on specific aspects of Japan's modern history which are sound, significant, and readable are the following, listed in the chronological sequence of the periods they treat:

Oliver Statler, *Shimoda Story* (New York: Random House, 1969), on aspects of early American relations with Japan.
Albert M. Craig, *Choshu in the Meiji Restoration* (Cambridge, Mass: Harvard University Press, 1961).
Marius B. Jansen, *Sakamoto Ryoma and the Meiji Restoration* (Princeton, N.J.: Princeton University Press, 1961).
Robert A. Scalapino, *The Beginnings of Political Democracy in Japan* (Berkeley, Calif.: University of California Press, 1955).
Tetsuo Najita, *Hara Kei and the Politics of Compromise 1905–1915* (Cambridge, Mass.: Harvard University Press, 1967).
Peter Duus, *Party Rivalry and Political Change in Taisho Japan* (Cambridge, Mass.: Harvard University Press, 1968).
James B. Crowley, *Japan's Quest for Autonomy: National Security and Foreign Policy 1930–1938* (Princeton, N.J.: Princeton University Press, 1966).
Herbert Feis, *The Road to Pearl Harbor* (Atheneum*).

Robert J. Butow, *Japan's Decision to Surrender* (Stanford*).

John Hersey, *Hiroshima* (Bantam*).

Kazuo Kawai, *Japan's American Interlude* (Chicago: Chicago University Press, 1960), on the American occupation of Japan from 1945 to 1952.

R. P. Dore, *Land Reform in Japan* (Berkeley, Calif.: University of California Press, 1958).

R. P. Dore, *City Life in Japan* (California*).

Ezra F. Vogel, *Japan's New Middle Class: The Salary Man and His Family in a Tokyo Suburb* (California*).

Robert E. Ward, *Japan's Political System* (Prentice-Hall *).

George R. Packard, II, *Protest in Tokyo: The Security Treaty Crisis of 1960* (Princeton, N.J.: Princeton University Press, 1966).

Nathaniel B. Thayer, *How the Conservatives Rule Japan* (Princeton, N.J.: Princeton University Press, 1969).

Index

Transportation, 131, 154, 247, 289, 293, 305
Treaties, 115, 118, 146–8, 150, 176, 207
Treaty of Mutual Security and Cooperation, 281
Tribalism, 12–14, 19, 23, 53
Tri-Partite Alliance, 207
True Pure Land sect, 58, 68, 73, 79, 89
Trusteeship, 240, 324
Tsingtao, 150, 177, 178
Tumuli, 12–13, 15
Twenty-one Demands, 150–151, 176
Two-party system, 165, 167, 308

Uji, 14–15, 45, 53
United Nations, 240, 277, 319, 324
United States, see America
United States Initial Post-Surrender Policy for Japan, 222
Universal manhood suffrage, 167–8, 171, 174–5
Universities, 38, 136, 156, 172–3, 199, 232–3, 250, 255, 257, 264, 274, 283, 297, 316; imperial, 136–7; private, 136, 139–40, 330
University disruption, 327–330
Urbanization, see Cities

Versailles treaty, 150–1, 183
Vietnam, 6, 206, 276; War, 317–18, 322–5, 328, 332, 335, 338

Violence, 263, 268–9, 327–8
Voluntary controls, 331
Voting trends, 305–8, 310, 313–15

Wages, 102, 152–3, 246, 249, 256, 270, 290, 292, 295, 331
Wakadoshiyori, 87
Wakayama, 83
Waley, 35
Wang Ching-wei, 206
War, 46–8, 55, 60, 66–7, 70, 79–80, 92, 120, 129, 146–148, 150, 160, 190, 197–8, 204–17; casualties, 214–16, 218; criminals, 224–6; psychology, 160, 191, 197; tales, 55
Warrior, 12, 15, 45–6, 54, 61–2, 66, 91, 102, 185, 220; class, 67–9, 89–90, 125, 127; cliques, 46–8, 50–1, 63, 67
Waseda, 140, 173
Washington Conference, 177–8, 190
Water resources, 4–6, 151, 252, 293
Way of the warrior, 91, 200
Weihaiwei, 147
Western experts, 129, 132, 135–6
Western Japan, 65–6, 75, 92–93, 119, 121, 129, 181
Westerners, 113, 124–5, 200; see also Europeans
Westernization, 123, 141, 157–8, 297–8

About the Author

Edwin O. Reischauer returned to Harvard University as a University Professor in September 1966 after serving with distinction as United States Ambassador to Japan from 1961 to 1966. His mission there was the culmination of long experience and study in East Asia. He was born in Tokyo in 1910 and lived in Japan until 1927, and he has returned many times since then for study and visits to Japan as well as to China, Korea and other areas in the Far East. He received his A.B. degree from Oberlin College in 1931 and his Ph.D. from Harvard in 1939. In the interval he studied at the Universities of Paris, Tokyo, and Kyoto and in Korea and China. He became an instructor at Harvard in 1939, an associate professor in 1945, and professor of Japanese history in 1950. During World War II he served in the Military Intelligence Service of the War Department General Staff. He was director of the Harvard-Yenching Institute from 1956 to 1961 and president of the Association for Asian Studies from 1955 to 1956. Among his books are *The United States and Japan*; *Wanted: An Asian Policy*; *Ennin's Travels in T'ang China*; *East Asia: The Great Tradition* (with J. K. Fairbank); *East Asia: The Modern Transformation* (with J. K. Fairbank and A. M. Craig); and *Beyond Vietnam: The United States and Asia*.

A Note on the Type

This book was set on the Linotype in Electra, designed by W. A. Dwiggins. The Electra face is a simple and readable type suitable for printing books by present-day processes. It is not based on any historical model, and hence does not echo any particular time or fashion.

The book was composed, printed, and bound by
THE COLONIAL PRESS INC., CLINTON, MASS.

Typography and Binding design by
CYNTHIA KRUPAT